A History of

This is a book about prejudice and democracy, and the prejudice *of* democracy. In comparing the historical struggles of two geographically disparate populations – Indian Dalits (once known as Untouchables) and African Americans – Gyanendra Pandey, the leading subaltern historian, examines the multiple dimensions of prejudice in two of the world's leading democracies. The juxtaposition of two very different locations and histories, and within each of them of varying public and private narratives of struggle, allows for an uncommon analysis of the limits of citizenship in modern societies and states. Pandey, with his characteristic delicacy, probes the histories of his protagonists to uncover a shadowy world where intolerance and discrimination are part of both public and private lives. This unusual and sobering book is revelatory in its exploration of the contradictory history of promise and denial that is common to the official narratives of nations such as India and the United States and the ideologies of many opposition movements.

Gyanendra Pandey is Arts and Sciences Distinguished Professor of History and Director of the Interdisciplinary Workshop in Colonial and Postcolonial Studies at Emory University. His books include *Remembering Partition: Violence, Nationalism and History in India* (2001) and *Routine Violence: Nations, Fragments, Histories* (2006).

A History of Prejudice

Race, Caste, and Difference in India and the United States

GYANENDRA PANDEY
Emory University

*For David & Ruth —
native speakers, world
citizens & dear friends —
Gyan.
Aug. 2013*

CAMBRIDGE UNIVERSITY PRESS
Cambridge, New York, Melbourne, Madrid, Cape Town,
Singapore, São Paulo, Delhi, Mexico City

Cambridge University Press
32 Avenue of the Americas, New York, NY 10013-2473, USA

www.cambridge.org
Information on this title: www.cambridge.org/9781107609389

© Gyanendra Pandey 2013

This publication is in copyright. Subject to statutory exception
and to the provisions of relevant collective licensing agreements,
no reproduction of any part may take place without the written
permission of Cambridge University Press.

First published 2013

Printed in the United States of America

A catalog record for this publication is available from the British Library.

Library of Congress Cataloging in Publication Data

Pandey, Gyanendra, 1950–
A history of prejudice : race, caste, and difference in India and the
United States / Gyanendra Pandey.
p.   cm.
Includes bibliographical references and index.
ISBN 978-1-107-02900-2 (hbk.) – ISBN 978-1-107-60938-9 (pbk.)
1. Racism – United States – History – 20th century.   2. Caste-based discrimination –
India – History – 20th century.   3. African Americans – Social conditions – 20th
century.   4. Dalits – Social conditions – 20th century.   5. Discrimination.
6. Prejudices.   I. Title.
E185.61.P22   2013
305.800973–dc23   2012016724

ISBN 978-1-107-02900-2 Hardback
ISBN 978-1-107-60938-9 Paperback

Cambridge University Press has no responsibility for the persistence or accuracy of
URLs for external or third-party Internet Web sites referred to in this publication and
does not guarantee that any content on such Web sites is, or will remain, accurate or
appropriate.

for Ruby
&
for Nishad

mere hamnafas, mere hamnawā

Contents

List of Figures	*page* viii
Preface and Acknowledgments	ix
1. Introduction	1
2. Prejudice as Difference	34
3. Dalit Conversion: The Assertion of Sameness	61
4. "Double V": The Everyday of Race Relations	97
5. An African American Autobiography: Relocating Difference	131
6. Dalit Memoirs: Rescripting the Body	162
7. The Persistence of Prejudice	194
Select Bibliography	221
Index	233

List of Figures

1 Dr. B. R. Ambedkar and the Buddha *page* 93
2 (a) Lynching of John William (Willie) Clark, Cartersville, Georgia, September 1930; (b) Funeral of George Dorsey, Monroe, Georgia, July 1946   126
3 Viola Andrews, Atlanta, Georgia, 1975; George Andrews, Madison, Georgia, 1975; and George's parents, Jessie Andrews and James Orr (Mr. Jim) in the 1940s   154
4 Babytai Kamble, Phaltan, Maharashtra, January 2012   173
5 Narendra Jadhav with his wife, Vasundhara, and parents, Damu (Dada) and Sonu, Mumbai, December 1979   184

Preface and Acknowledgments

Not many people have the opportunity of writing a second "first book." My move to the USA has afforded me this unusual privilege and pleasure by enabling me to embark on a series of inquiries into what is for me an entirely new field. The list of institutions and individuals who have supported and guided me through this unfamiliar field is long, and my debt to them impossible to acknowledge adequately.

Among institutions, foremost is Emory University, which has provided me a home and an extraordinarily supportive and collegial intellectual environment for the last six years. I owe special thanks to Earl Lewis, provost and professor of history; to Bobby Paul and Cris Levenduski, respectively dean and associate dean of the College of Arts and Sciences until 2011; the current deans of the College, Robin Forman and Michael Elliott; and Lisa Tedesco, dean of the Graduate School of Arts and Sciences, for their unfailing support and their personal interest in my work. I also thank the Department of History (my primary home on campus), the Department of Middle Eastern and South Asian Studies, and the erstwhile Institute of Critical International Studies and its energetic director, Bruce Knauft, for their continuous generosity.

I owe a great debt of gratitude to the librarians and staff of Emory Library, especially Randall Burkett, Elizabeth Chase, and Randy Gue, and their colleagues in the Manuscripts and Rare Books Library – that wonderful resource and research establishment on the tenth floor, with its marvelously efficient, well-informed, and welcoming staff and services. Warm thanks too to librarians, archivists, and staff in the following places: the Library of Congress, Washington, D.C.; the University of Chicago; Johns Hopkins University, Baltimore; the University of Amsterdam; the British Library, London; the National Archives of India, New Delhi; Nehru Memorial Museum and Library, New Delhi; Institute of Dalit Studies, Delhi; Indian Social Science Institute, Delhi; Babasaheb Ambedkar University, Aurangabad; Nagpur University; the Vasant Moon library in Nagpur; and the English and Foreign Languages University, Hyderabad.

Some of the ideas and material contained in this work were presented at seminars and workshops in a number of different places: the Centre for Studies in Social Sciences, Calcutta; Pune University; the English and Foreign Languages University, Hyderabad; the Banaras Hindu University; Jawaharlal Nehru University and Jamia Millia Islamia, New Delhi; the Centre for Study of Developing Societies, Delhi; the Institute of Asian Studies, University of Amsterdam; the Social Science Research Institute, Berlin; the National University of Singapore; the University of Tokyo and Ryūkoku University in Japan; and the Sydney University of Technology, Australia. I presented parts of the work at the following universities in the United States apart from Emory: University of Minnesota; University of Texas, Austin; University of Washington, Seattle; University of Michigan, Ann Arbor; University of Colorado, Boulder; University of California at Santa Barbara and at Berkeley; Oberlin College, Oberlin, Ohio; City University of New York; and Columbia University, New York; as well as at the annual South Asian Studies Conference in Madison, Wisconsin, in 2007 and the annual meeting of the American Historical Association in Boston in 2010. Shortly before the manuscript went to press, Mahesh Rangarajan, Crispin Bates, and Sumathy Ramaswamy invited me to present its arguments in a seminar at the Nehru Memorial Museum and Library, New Delhi; a series of lectures at the University of Edinburgh; and a half-day workshop at Duke University, Durham, North Carolina, respectively. I am deeply grateful to the organizers and participants in all these meetings for their encouraging and critical responses.

One last set of "institutional" acknowledgments. Marigold Acland has, once more, been a wonderful editor to work with: quietly enthusiastic, efficient, and judicious. Heartfelt appreciation and gratitude to her and her colleagues at Cambridge University Press. I owe thanks to two anonymous readers for the Press whose thoughtful responses

Preface and Acknowledgments

have helped tighten my arguments and fill out the context for readers less familiar with one or the other locus of my investigation; Shirley Andrews and Veronica Villa for permission to use four photographs of the Andrews family from the family collection; Narendra Jadhav and Maya Pandit for permission to use the photographs that appear in Chapter 6; and the Manuscript, Archives, and Rare Books Library at Emory University and Corbis Images, New York, respectively, for permission to use the photographs that appear in Chapter 4; to Nene Humphrey, wife of the late Benny Andrews, and VAGA, New York, for permission to use Benny's painting "Evening Prayer" on the cover; Sue and Neil Williams, the owners, for allowing us to photograph the painting; Myron McGhee for the photograph; and Juana McGhee and Julie Delliquanti for facilitating the photography. Kelly Basner, Pankhuree Dube, and Marcy Alexander helped most generously in the final preparation of the manuscript; Kelly took on the additional burden of preparing the index. My sincere thanks to all of them.

Other individuals who guided and helped me in the course of the research and reflection that went into the making of this book are far too numerous to name. My awareness of their incredible generosity, and my deep sense of gratitude for their help, are not reduced by my failure to list all of them. First among these are the many people who taught me about African American and Dalit lives by inviting me into their homes and social circles and telling me about their life and work. In India, I owe huge thanks to Narendra Jadhav and his extended family in Mumbai, Pune, and Ozer; Gopal Guru in Pune (and in Delhi); Sukhdeo and Vimal Thorat in Delhi; Chandrabhan Prasad and his extended family in Delhi and Lucknow (especially Mr. Dhanai Ram); S. R. Darapuri, K. M. Sant, Chedi Lal, Mata Prasadji, Rita Chaudhuri, and Suraj Bahadur Thapa in Lucknow; Kumud Pawde and Puran Meshram and their families in Nagpur; Meenakshi Moon (and her daughter and son-in-law, Bharti and P. T. Wakode), in Nagpur; Urmila Pawar and Laxman Gaikwad in Mumbai; Yashwant Manohar, Datta Bhagat, Gangadhar Pantawane, R. K. Kshirsagar, P. E. Sonkamble, Avinash Dholas, S. L. Gaikwad, and Desarda in Aurangabad; Raja Shekhar Yundru and Neerja Shekhar in Chandigarh; and Balwant Singh and his extended family in Saharanpur.

In addition to these well-wishers, Ram Bapat, Sharmila Rege, Vilas and Usha Wagh, Milind Wakankar, and Shrikant in Pune; Sailesh

xii   *Preface and Acknowledgments*

Darokar and Anuradha and Ajay Kumar in Mumbai; Subhashini Ali in Kanpur; Salim and Sufia Kidwai and Akhilesh in Lucknow; Paramjit Singh, Gurpreet Kaur, and Harish Puri in Amritsar; Bhola and Pramodini Varma in Delhi; and Maya Pandit in Hyderabad provided guidance and support, the comfort of their homes, and transport, without which much of this research would have been impossible. David Page and Ruth Kirkwilson have made us part of the family and welcomed us into their home in London many times over. Bruce and Sally Cleghorn have provided warm welcome and friendship in places as far apart as Cambridge and Kuala Lumpur, as have Anish and Susan Mathai in New York. Evean and Kashmir Chand and their families in Bedford and Milton Keynes have extended great hospitality and support throughout this research. Shashank Sinha in Delhi has been unbelievable with his generosity, interest, and assistance. Warm gratitude for their friendship and support.

In the United States, members of the extended Andrews family in and around Atlanta have welcomed Ruby and me most warmly, and (almost!) made us honorary members of the family. I am especially grateful to Shirley Lowrie, her late husband Richard, and their daughter Ramona, and to Shirley's sisters, Veronica Villa and Deloris White, for their generosity with time, information, and free-wheeling conversation. Thee Smith and his family have invited us into their home and church, as have Minnie Peek and Jesse Freeman and their families in Madison, Wis., and Tony Grooms and Pamela Jackson in Atlanta. I am humbled by, and deeply appreciative of, their warmth and hospitality.

The colleagues, students, friends, and interlocutors I have leaned on and learned from are spread across the continents. Several leading Americanists have acted as tutors and guides as I have entered the new area of American history, suggesting further readings, sources, and perspectives and saving me from many errors of fact and judgment, among them Randall Burkett, Joseph Crespino, Leslie Harris, Earl Lewis, Mary Odem, and Jonathan Prude at Emory; Steve Hahn at the University of Pennsylvania; Nell Painter at Princeton; Colin Johnson at Indiana University; and Donald Carter, Ron Walters, and William Connolly at Johns Hopkins in Baltimore. I am most grateful for their stewardship.

Apart from those already mentioned, numerous colleagues in the departments of History, Middle Eastern and South Asian Studies,

Preface and Acknowledgments xiii

African American Studies, Women's Studies, Anthropology, and Religion, and the Institute for Liberal Arts, at Emory University have been generous with their time, interest, and suggestions, among them Angelika Bammer, Kathleen Cleaver, Clifton Crais, Vince Cornell, David Eltis, Martha Fineman, Joyce Fleuckeger, Shalom Goldman, Lynne Huffer, Bruce Knauft, Chris Krupa, Ruby Lal, V. Narayana Rao, Gordon Newby, Laurie Patton, Jim Roark, and the late Elizabeth Fox-Genovese. My graduate students – Kelly Basner, Debjani Bhattacharya, Moyukh Chatterjee, Aditya Pratap Deo, Pankhuree Dube, Navyug Gill, Emma Meyer, and Durba Mitra – have been equally forthcoming with constructive ideas and criticism. Durba, Debjani, and Pankhuree also served as invaluable research assistants, nosing out unexpected sources and information, chasing small leads, and helping greatly to fill out my knowledge of American history and the African American struggle.

In India, in addition to Narendra Jadhav, Sukhdeo Thorat, Gopal Guru, Kumud Pawde, Ram Bapat, Sharmila Rege, and other colleagues mentioned earlier, I need to thank Anand Teltumbde, Bhalchandra Mungekar, P. G. Jogdand, Arjun Dangle, S. Krishna, Padma Velaskar, and Rammanohar Reddy in Mumbai; Surinder Jodhka, Valerian Rodrigues, Vivek Kumar, Mushir and Zoya Hasan, Gulam Sheikh, Sudhir Chandra, Geetanjali Shree, and Suresh Sharma in Delhi; Maya Pandit, Abhai Maurya, Alok Bhalla, and Javeed Alam in Hyderabad; and Mohandas Naimisharay and Meera Kumar in Delhi for extended conversations and helpful suggestions. To Maya Pandit I owe great gratitude for her extraordinary help with translations from a number of difficult Marathi manuscripts and texts that I have used extensively in Chapter 6.

Among colleagues in Europe, special thanks go to Peter Geschiere and Willem van Schendel in Amsterdam; David Hardiman, David Arnold, and Carolyn Steedman in Warwick; Christopher Bayly and Francis Robinson in Cambridge and London; Crispin Bates in Edinburgh; Monica Juneja in Hanover; and Margrit Pernau in Berlin for reading and commenting on various parts of this work. Similarly warm thanks go to colleagues in Eastern Asia and Australia: Peter Reeves and Tan Tai Yong in Singapore; Nariaki Nakazato in Tokyo; Naoko Nagasaki in Kyoto; and Devleena Ghosh and Jim Masselos in Sydney.

xiv *Preface and Acknowledgments*

Among my older Subaltern Studies colleagues, I need to thank Gyan Prakash for an astute comment at a seminar in Delhi; Partha Chatterjee and Susie Tharu for solidarity even at a distance; M. S. S. Pandian for his comments on the chapters dealing primarily with Dalits; Gayatri Spivak for her deeply engaged and insightful comments on the chapter on difference; and Ajay Skaria for his wonderfully engaged, insightful, and encouraging comments on the entire manuscript. Among newer subalternist colleagues, I owe special thanks for extended conversations, suggestions, and shared enthusiasms to Eleanor Zelliot, doyen of Dalit studies in the United States (and India); Kamala Vishweshwaran, historian and anthropologist of race, caste, and gender; Swati Chattopadhyay, indefatigable warrior for the subaltern and the popular; and Michael Fisher, Anuradha Needham, Anand Yang, Priti Ramamurthy, and Paul Brass, chroniclers of subaltern travels and travails on land, sea, and beyond.

My greatest intellectual debt is to a group of scholars in the United States, Europe, and India who have lived with this investigation almost from its beginnings. Apart from guiding me to many different sources, texts, and arguments, my Americanist colleagues, Leslie Harris, Jonathan Prude, Mary Odem, Nell Painter, Steve Hahn, Colin Johnson, Joe Crespino, and Randall Burkett, and my non-Americanist world historian friends, Peter Geschiere, Rita Costa-Gomes, and V. Narayana Rao, have also commented most helpfully on various parts of the manuscript. Jonathan Prude, Leslie Harris, and Colin Johnson took on the additional task of reading and commenting on the entire manuscript in a small one-day workshop in February 2011, where they were joined by three other seasoned interlocutors: Rashmi Bhatnagar, Milind Wakankar, and Ruby Lal. Further, Ruby Lal and Lynne Huffer have welcomed me into a small writers' group that has given me unparalleled sustenance and pleasure in the course of the writing: they have read every part of this book, some of it many times over, and provided gentle but incisive criticism, unfailing encouragement and cheer, and the kind of intellectual camaraderie one can only dream of.

An equally great debt is owed to loved ones who take on the burdens of one's research through thick and thin, in their waking hours and sometimes even when they are trying to sleep! Among these special people are my mother, Shree Kumari Pandey, and my son, Nishad, who

Preface and Acknowledgments   xv

have wanted so much to see this book in finished form; my sisters, Jayanti, Geetanjali, and Gayatri, who have been supportive and, by turns, admiring and amused; and Ruby's sister and brother-in-law, Beena and Prabhakar, and her parents, Prabha and Manmohan Lal, who have given us a home in Noida and in Dehradun.

Ruby has provided, and continues to provide, intellectual sustenance, unequaled companionship, home, love, and joy – from before the inception of this book until (I have no doubt) long after its completion. A dedication is meager recognition of her place in my life.

Gyanendra Pandey
Atlanta, March 2012

I

Introduction

How does one begin to write a history of prejudice, something that by definition resists historicization – and even acknowledgment? I attempt to do so in this book by examining the process of otherization (an inelegant word to describe an inelegant practice), of social and political distancing that is a central part of the history of African Americans and Dalits (ex-Untouchables, or Scheduled Castes as they are called in the Indian constitution of 1950), two long subordinated and stigmatized groups in the United States and India, respectively. It is my view that the juxtaposition of two very different locations and histories (the African American and the Dalit) and, within each of them, of very different kinds of public and private narratives of struggle allows for an uncommon analysis of the workings of prejudice in an intriguing complex of forms and places.

In order to deepen and extend the inquiry that follows, I make another move that is perhaps not entirely predictable. I start with a rough-and-ready distinction between what one might call "vernacular" and "universal" prejudices. The former is, in simple terms, local, localizable, relatively visible, and sometimes acknowledged: say, the prejudice against blacks, "Untouchables," gays, Muslims, Jews, conquered indigenous populations, recent immigrants, women, and other "minorities." It refers to calculated behavior that we sometimes condemn – when we notice it, or when it is forced on our attention: racism, casteism, patriarchy, heteronormativity, reductive monoculturalism, prejudice thus as bias, malice, or inherited structures of discrimination, which the state believes it can measure or contain. I have called such prejudice "vernacular" in order to distinguish it from another kind, which is largely invisible because it is widespread ("universal") and hence seen as "natural." This "universal" is the language of law and state, and it passes for the common sense of modern society, rarely acknowledged as prejudice. At this level, the history of prejudice becomes even more intractable for it is, simultaneously, everywhere and nowhere.

Prejudice – the "already known" – of course always appears in the guise of common sense. It hardly requires explanation and is seldom archived. The difficulty of archiving its history is evident. The common sense of race, caste, class, or gender relations, even when made visible, as it sometimes is in sharply polarized societies and contexts, is articulated in historically unpretty, and therefore generally unacknowledged, actions and statements: derogatory names and forms of address, verbal and physical abuse, and sexual exploitation (justified by the alleged "immorality" of subordinated and marginalized castes and classes), to name a few of the most obvious. Moreover, given the fact of disproportionately skewed access to resources and power in historical societies of the past and the present, such abuse and dismissiveness has not always needed to be fully articulated. It has often been reserved for the spat-out, half-suppressed, word-of-mouth and, one might add, for the gesture of disdain, contempt and disgust, the pause and the recoil, the refusal to touch, what in India is called Untouchability.[1] How, out of what archive, are we to write a history of these gestures?

The question will surface repeatedly in the following pages since it lies at the heart of the specificities and challenges of writing a history of prejudice. At this point, however, and as part of the difficulty of pursuing such a history, I need to say one word more about the claims of the modern as the quintessentially normal, rational, "unprejudiced."

---

[1] On the question of "touch" and its significance for political/historical analysis, see Gopal Guru, "Power of Touch," *Frontline*, 23, no. 25 (December 16–29, 2006), http://www.frontlineonnet.com/fl2325/stories/20061229002903000.htm; Gopal Guru, "Archaeology of Untouchability," *Economic and Political Weekly*, 44, no. 37 (September 12, 2009), 49–56. For discussion of this piece, see Sundar Sarukkai, "Phenomenology of Untouchability," *Economic and Political Weekly*, 44, no. 37 (September 12, 2009); and Balmurli Natrajan, "Place and Pathology in Caste," *Economic and Political Weekly*, 44, no. 51 (December 19, 2009). See also Yoginder Sikand's interview with Kancha Ilaiah, *Mukta Mona*, February 13, 2007.

Introduction 3

The Prejudice of the Modern

Modern, Raymond Williams tells us, was through the nineteenth century and very markedly in the twentieth "virtually equivalent to IMPROVED or satisfactory or efficient... something unquestionably favourable or desirable." *Modernity*, in Peter Brooker's words, "names the processes of increasing rationalization in social and political life, along with the associated technological development and accumulation [concentration] of people in cities that combined to produce the... new society of the late nineteenth and twentieth centuries." It also describes

the processes of industrialization associated with capitalist development... [as well as] the "philosophy" of modernity: namely, a belief in scientific and social progress, human rights, justice and democracy, which inspired the American and French Revolutions as well as much later social, economic and political theory, including Marxism [and, we might add, many of the great anticolonial struggles of the eighteenth to the twenty-first centuries].[2]

Other characteristics might be noted. It is a ruling, if generally unstated, prejudice of the modern world that it has produced an ideal grammar (the *correct* form of speaking and writing), a rational order (the rule of reason), and an unmarked citizen (*man*, in the broader sense of humans as well as the narrower sense of the male of the species) entirely competent to implement this rule and this grammar.[3] This prejudice is closely linked to ideas of what it is to be modern, liberal, and democratic; in a word, to use a term that has been carried over from a "medieval" discourse into the modern, *civilized*.

Let me be clear. In highlighting the invisible, unacknowledged, yet global prejudice of the modern, I refer to preconceptions generalized not by a claim of being eternal but as a historically situated "universal," located in the era of the modern, itself overdetermined by the tenets of Western imperialism and worldwide nationalisms. More specifically, I allude to the common sense of mid-twentieth-century (post–World War II) political discourse, which is the focus of inquiry

---

[2] Raymond Williams, *Keywords: A Vocabulary of Culture and Society* (Oxford: Oxford University Press, 1976), 208–9 (capitalization in original); and Peter Brooker, *Glossary of Cultural Theory* (London: Arnold, 2003), 166–7.

[3] For a fine articulation and elaboration of the proposition, see Paul Gilroy, *The Black Atlantic: Modernity and Double Consciousness* (Cambridge, MA: Harvard University Press, 1993).

in this book. The era of the establishment of the nation-state as the exclusively legitimate form for the political existence of peoples; of modernization and development, and the much vaunted equality of nations (and individuals) across the globe; of the universal declaration of human rights; and of the "universal" condemnation of continuing European imperialism, apartheid in South Africa, segregation in the United States, and Untouchability in India.

Through the media, and through wider political and intellectual commentary, contemporary common sense propagates a belief in the modern as enlightened, rational (or scientific), secular (or "modern," "enlightened" Christian, which is often equated with the "secular"), liberal (although that has become a derogatory term in contemporary American politics), and democratic. Masculinity is not commonly mentioned, but it is implicit, for the male of the species is taken as the standard – the assumed, deliberative, decisive, self-made, self-making, and self-same subject of the modern. Importantly, this narrative provides an overwhelmingly economic/institutional account of modernity: it omits any significant analysis of the philosophy of modernity and makes it appear natural and normal.

In spite of that economic/institutional bias, however, the discourse of the enlightened modern, with its emphasis on rationality, deliberation, order, and equal opportunity, conspicuously understates the calculus of capitalism in its account of modern society. It also shies away from naming violence as a significant factor in organizing and upholding existing social and political arrangements. Like violence, religion and religious belief become part of the great unsaid in the modern. What we hear about instead is the nonmodernity or premodernity of other (non-"European") religions, themselves brought into view with the modern claim to be secular.[4] Again, the variations are interesting, for if a Christian secular is what reigns in the West, a Hindu secular is clearly dominant in India. Through all of this, the discourse of the modern overlooks, undervalues, and cultivates a deep-seated anxiety about the rich variety and contradictoriness of human life and history.

---

[4] See Talal Asad's proposition about the simultaneous birth of the categories of religion and secularism in Talal Asad, *Formations of the Secular: Christianity, Islam, Modernity* (Stanford, CA: Stanford University Press, 2003).

Introduction 5

A final trait to be noted in the modernist account of itself is that it deals with uncomfortable facets of modern existence – slavery, untouchability, drug-trafficking, genocide – by declaring them an aberration or exception, the work of deviants or criminals, or of people who are simply not modern enough: not *our* history, or at least not the most significant part of our history. It is here, in the tortuous construction of the nonmodern, the backward, and the deviant, that we move into the realm of what I have called vernacular, visible, prejudice.

Modernity brings with it a fable of freedom, prosperity, and peace, available to all. A rider is quickly added. Freedom can be extended only to those who are ready for it: not to children, for example, nor (for the longest time) women, or the colonized, the "backward," the illiterate, the propertyless, and so on. The pledge of "life, liberty, and the pursuit of happiness" regularly announced has also been regularly deferred. The point may be illustrated by reference to the experience of groups who have not been easily assimilated into the narrative of homogenous modernity and nationhood in the nineteenth and twentieth centuries, among them African Americans and Dalits. Before moving on to the latter, however, I want to address one other issue, concerning the advantages and risks involved in juxtaposing the histories of these disparate "communities" from two different continents.

Juxtaposing African American and Dalit Histories

Much of my research and writing over the past three decades has focused on the conditions and histories of marginalized and disenfranchised groups in colonial and postcolonial South Asia. Why, then, the present shift to an investigation of the histories of Americans of African descent and Dalits (Indians of "Untouchable" descent) in tandem? The answer is by no means straightforward. It has much to do with the political struggles and debates of the last half century and more, the internationalization of those struggles in fascinating ways from the early and middle decades of the twentieth century, and the new perspectives on human society and history that have followed in the wake of these conflicts. However, some proximate "causes" are more easily identified.

The first is personal. After several years of living and teaching in the United States, from 1998 onward, I woke up to the realization

6   *A History of Prejudice*

that I actually *lived* in this country and was not just a visitor as I had been for various lengths of time earlier. I recognized at the same time the importance, for me, of a robust and ongoing engagement with the politics and history of the society in which I lived. My current work on the history of African Americans and Dalits has grown out of that recognition.

The Dalit and the African American struggles (if we may as shorthand reduce them for the moment to two) have shared common ground in several respects, and the connections and parallels between them have often been noted. The nonviolent campaigns of civil disobedience against British colonial rule in India led by M. K. Gandhi were an important inspiration for Martin Luther King, Jr., and many of his followers. And Gandhi himself developed many of his ideas about nonviolence and civil disobedience from reading authors like Henry David Thoreau. Similarly, though this is less commonly remarked, Frederick Douglass, William Lloyd Garrison, Horace Greeley, Harriet Beecher Stowe, and other black and white abolitionists used the idiom of caste extensively in mounting their critique of race relations in the USA. W. E. B. Du Bois, perhaps the leading intellectual spokesperson of the African American struggle in the first half of the twentieth century, deeply invested in the internationalist and anti-imperialist dimensions of the movement, declared "color-caste" to be the ideology of imperialism, and noted that the "caste of color" was so pervasive in his own country "as to correspond with the caste of work and enslave not only slaves but black men who were not slaves."[5]

On the other side, the foremost Dalit intellectuals repeatedly invoked the black experience in their articulation of the Dalit struggle. Jyotirao Phule in the late nineteenth century and B. R. Ambedkar in the twentieth, to take two of the most prominent examples, translated key terms from the Anglo-American abolitionists' idiom. Phule described the Dalits' condition as one of *"Ghulamgiri"* ("slavery"), affiliating the historical degradation of "Untouchables" with trans-Atlantic slavery. Ambedkar transcoded racial segregation in the United States as the Dalits' *"bahishkrut samaj"* ("outcaste community"). And in the 1970s a militant group of ex-Untouchable writers and activists in

---

[5] Kamala Visweswaran, *Un/common Cultures: Racism and the Rearticulation of Cultural Difference* (Durham, NC: Duke University Press, 2010), 112, 114, and passim.

Introduction

western India invoked the Black Panthers in naming themselves "Dalit Panthers," thus serving to popularize the name "Dalit" for groups earlier described as Untouchables, Depressed Castes, Scheduled Castes, or (in Gandhi's favored term) Harijans.[6] It is almost as if exigent history writing in these instances cannot be done in narrowly regionalist or nationalist terms but requires a wider, universal frame.

Dalit – meaning (literally) "crushed," "ground down"; (metaphorically) the wretched of the earth; (historically) those who labor so that society and "civilization" may advance; and (politically today) low-caste and low-class groups who demand fair compensation for their labor and equal opportunities for their talents – is not an inappropriate term to describe the condition of subordination and marginalization of the more impoverished and disadvantaged of these groups. *Dalit* as the laboring body – the body on whose back, on whose labor, the whole edifice of the economy and society, the privilege of culture and civilization, and leisure and power has been built, and as the female body that appears center stage in the later chapters of this book, as inordinately ground down and subjected to a sometimes literally unbearable combination of sexual and social labor – doubly subalternized: *dalit* twice over. Intimations of this wider history may be readily seen in the experience of people of African descent in the USA as well as in that of ex-Untouchable castes and subcastes in India.

In a sense, my own reflection on Dalit and African American histories simply acknowledges and pays tribute to the universalist impulse, and the search for new kinds of politics and new locations for them, found in the histories of so many subaltern constituencies. It may thus be seen as a contribution to the ongoing reexamination and rewriting of history that has gone on actively from the middle of the twentieth century. This reassessment includes the fundamental feminist challenge to the male universal that has until now ruled in the realms of philosophy, history, and democratic politics, and the widespread interrogation of the past and the present by anticolonial and postcolonial scholarship. It includes as well the wide-ranging African American analysis of the

---

[6] Harijans means "children of god," and Dalits have understandably expressed displeasure at the patronizing quality of the name. Ironically, Gandhi, who is a hero for many African Americans, has been seen as the "enemy" by activist Dalits. The reasons for this will become clearer below.

race and caste underpinnings of European imperialism and the Dalit reinterpretation of the strategies through which abolitionists seized on liberal discourses to make political claims for black freedom and equality.

In spite of this long history of transnational and transcontinental inquiries, I am aware of the dangers of juxtaposing the examples of subaltern struggles in the very different societies and historical contexts of India and the United States – or what one might call the pitfalls of comparative history. I share the skepticism and misgivings of many scholars about the value of a dominant tendency in comparative history or sociology, which relies, as one leading historian puts it, "on the most slender trace of an analogy here, a touch of resemblance there, and a suggestion of parallelism in yet another respect." "Comparison is not a neutral analytic method but a highly pointed claims-making device," observes another.[7]

Like them, I am uncomfortable about practices of comparison that assume the givenness of the units to be compared and deal in universals, against which particular societies, communities, or histories are either found wanting or declared commendable. For any comparative history that consciously or unconsciously proposes a supposedly "neutral" standard – commonly that of the Western European and North American experience as understood by the ruling elites – whereby one may assess success or failure in modern world conditions, and proceed to make judgments and hand out prizes on that basis ("mature democracy," "increasingly enlightened community," "incipient secular consciousness"), is liable to be reductionist, if not deceptive or indeed disingenuous.

My hope is that my investigation of African American and Dalit histories side by side will not detract from the specificity, complexity, and integrity – that is, the very *history* and *politics* – of the building of these diverse struggles. The unlikely juxtaposition of bodies of scholarship and debate taken from two different continents – scholarship and debate that is intensely local and impressively transnational at the

---

[7] Ranajit Guha, "Subaltern Studies: Projects for Our Time and Their Convergence," in Ileana Rodriguez, ed., *The Latin American Subaltern Studies Reader* (Durham, NC: Duke University Press, 2001), 37; and Micol Seigel, *Uneven Encounters: Making Race and Nation in Brazil and the United States* (Durham, NC: Duke University Press, 2009), 225.

Introduction

same time – should extend our awareness not only of shared histories and shared struggles in the making of the modern world but of the particularities and features of different histories and societal conditions that experts have assumed to be well understood and hence taken for granted. By that means, I hope it may also make for a new kind of comparative history, one in which we deal not in universals already understood but in the assumptions that underlie our individual histories and our particular universals – thereby challenging the very claim to a single overriding and ahistorical universalism (or prejudice!).

To begin with, the juxtaposition of processes of minoritization responsible for the production of multiple "minorities" at the very time that nations and "majorities" come into being should underscore the coexistence of very different kinds of thinking on matters like race and caste, racism and casteism – an understanding of these in terms of parallel but incongruent histories of class and power on the one hand, as against those that stress a more primordial sense of identity and inheritance on the other. I have written elsewhere of how the concept of "communalism" in India – the notion of religious communities perennially ranged against each other – was derived from "communal conflict" and the "communal riot" (the marking of violence as the true, if not the only, relation between people belonging to different religious denominations) and not from "community" or collective modes of being and thinking self and history.[8] So, too, I submit, notions of race and caste derive from the attempted perpetuation, or recuperation, of particular structures of power and privilege through a politics of racism and caste discrimination, not the other way around.

In spite of such beginnings, race and caste (like the politicized religious community in India) are represented as the ground or foundation of a series of repetitive actions that regularly breach the walls of social organization (i.e., as a societal phenomenon outside the domain of political practice, including the political practice of the state). My juxtaposition of different histories of racism and casteism should show once more how incoherent and messy the parameters and logic of caste, race, and other categories of social and political exclusion have been

---

[8] Gyanendra Pandey, *The Construction of Communalism in Colonial North India* (Delhi: Oxford University Press, 1990; Perennial edition, Delhi: Oxford University Press, 2012).

10 *A History of Prejudice*

and at the same time invalidate any attempt to root these constructions purely in a sociological domain, excluding their political charge.

Racism and the African American question have been central to the political debate in the United States for a very long time; hence Du Bois's declaration in 1903 that the problem of the twentieth century was the problem of the color line and the Nobel Prize–winning Swedish social scientist Gunnar Myrdal's Carnegie-sponsored (and state-supported) 1944 analysis of the "Negro problem" as the "American Dilemma."[9] There has been less open engagement with the stigma and humiliation attending caste practices, and the underlying question of Untouchability, in India. In part, this was because the "Muslim problem," as it was called, and the struggle for and ultimate establishment of a separate Muslim nation called Pakistan, had long been seen as *the* national question in India. In part, it followed from a widespread belief that class struggle, the emergence of new economic and social forces (and, with them, of modern reason) – what the country's first prime minister, Jawaharlal Nehru, called the forces of world history – would carry all before them and relegate caste and religion, and other such "relics" of the past, to the periphery of public life. The history of India (and the world) has not quite lived up to that expectation. Yet, questions of caste and Untouchability, and the liberation of the lowest (and often poorest) castes, have not attracted urgent attention outside Dalit circles, at least until quite recently. A small piece of anecdotal evidence will serve to illustrate the point.

Over several years at the Johns Hopkins University in Baltimore and at Emory University in Atlanta, I offered four semester-long courses, two on "A Black Bourgeosie? The Making of the African-American and (South Asian) Dalit Middle Classes" and two on "Autobiographies/Histories: the African American and Dalit Struggles." Both universities have numerous undergraduates of South Asian background, described as "heritage" students, as well as a number who come directly from South Asia. A good number of African American students, a few students of Caribbean background, a few who have come from Africa more recently, and some Caucasian Americans opted to

---

[9] See W. E. B. Du Bois, *The Souls of Black Folk* (1901; reprint New York: Signet Classic, 1969), 54; and Gunnar Myrdal, *An American Dilemma*, Volume 1: *The Negro in a White Nation*, 2 vols. (1944; reprint New York, McGraw-Hill, 1964).

Introduction 11

take these courses – both men and women, though in every instance more women than men. Strikingly, however, only on one occasion did a student of South Asian background sign up for any one of these courses. He was Sri Lankan.

That would seem to suggest, at first glance, that the Dalit question, the rise of the Dalit middle classes, and the matter of Dalit autobiographies and histories, not to mention African American history and politics, are of little interest to students of Indian background, whether second- (or third-) generation, American-born, "heritage" students as they are called in the United States, more recent immigrants, or students coming directly from the subcontinent, the vast majority of whom, at Hopkins and Emory as in other U.S. colleges and universities, come from well-to-do, upper- (and less often, middle-) caste backgrounds. Indeed, I think something of the same prejudice – this is not "our" history, or not the most significant part of our history, and in any case a thing of the past – would apply to the majority of university students in India from relatively well-off, upper-caste backgrounds. It is no surprise to find that the issue of the invisibility of Dalits, or of women, in undergraduate and graduate courses on the subcontinent is addressed chiefly by adding on modules or topics on, say, notable women, Dalit literature, or B. R. Ambedkar, the outstanding leader of the Dalits in the twentieth century.[10]

To complicate matters, when I offered a similar course at Emory University in 2011, under the amended title "A History of Prejudice: Race and Caste in the USA and India," it yielded a very different composition of students: roughly 60% of South Asian (Indian) background and 40% black, Caucasian, or East Asian Americans. Perhaps this confirms the point that Untouchability (like slavery) is thought of as an aberration – a matter of the past, with unfortunate echoes (if indeed any such echoes are acknowledged) in the present – whereas caste and race, removed from the stigma and violence of deep-seated racism and casteism, and watered down to resemble other kinds of social division and difference, are recognized as matters of vernacular, localizable prejudice, to be dealt with, appropriately, by reform, education, and (perhaps) political struggle. It is in this context that we need to consider

---

[10] Cf. Sharmila Rege, *Writing Caste/Writing Gender: Reading Dalit Women's Testimonios* (New Delhi: Zubaan, 2006), 5 and passim.

the more nuanced conception I have offered of what constitutes prejudice in the contemporary world and of what the "prejudice of the modern" accounts as "history," as opposed to "dross," "relics," issues and attitudes left over from the past and on the way to oblivion in the forward march of history.

That said, we may proceed to a closer examination of Dalit and African American struggles and the account of them that is found in the received histories of India and the USA.

Internal Colonialism and Local Prejudice

Both Dalits in India and African Americans in the United States have been visibly stigmatized groups, long marginalized and disenfranchised (in both the narrow and broad senses of that term) because of that very stigmatization. Both have had to organize and fight against the consequences of what could be described as a disguised form of internal colonialism. I need hardly note that there are other groups who have been as, if not more, seriously affected by the fact of such colonialism in these lands, most notably the indigenous communities of the two countries. Like Native Americans and the Scheduled Tribes (depressed castes and classes who make up the bulk of the *adivasi*, or putatively aboriginal, population of India), neither Dalits nor African Americans have inherited geopolitical conditions that would allow them to carve out a place for themselves as "mainstream." However, given an ascendant discourse of democracy, and the establishment of many formal democratic structures and practices in the nineteenth and twentieth centuries, these two political groups mounted powerful and important challenges to existing structures of power and claims of democratic practice in India and the United States as they advanced the quest for full citizenship, more equal political and cultural opportunities, greater social justice, and recognition of human worth.

In both the US and India, claims to the exceptional character of the local state and society are tied to questions of modernity and nationhood, and to debates about democracy and justice, pluralism and secularism, and with them to particular languages of representation and of morality. Official discourse and popular history alike have long emphasized the idea of tolerance and openness in both countries – the idea of the melting-pot, of syncretism and assimilation: *not* the

Introduction 13

exceptionalism of slavery or the obliteration of indigenous nations in a modern, "democratic" country called the USA; or Untouchability, which, in colonial and postcolonial India, has marked relations not only among people supposedly belonging to the "Hindu," "Sikh," or "Christian" communities but between the bulk of the Hindus on the one hand and the bulk of the Muslims and Christians on the other as well.

A large proportion of India's population has long been treated as Untouchable, in the context of the dominant Hindu tradition and the inherited concern with practices that are thought to be polluting. While there is no easy way of making an accurate estimate, given the fuzziness of the category and of the boundaries between castes and subcastes in general, the population of castes qualifying as Scheduled Castes (or ex-Untouchables), going by the list drawn up in the Indian constitution of 1950, was 57.5 million, or 14.67% of the total population in 1961. Scheduled Tribes, also listed for affirmative action in the Indian constitution and also *dalit* in social, economic, and cultural terms, but differentiated from the ex-Untouchable castes in being inhabitants of hilly and forested tracts that were "Hinduized" (and colonized by the modern state and capitalism) at a relatively recent date, made up another 29.1 million, or 6.87% of the population. In the 2001 Indian census, the population of Scheduled Castes is given as 166,635,700, or 16.2% of the population, and that of Scheduled Tribes as 84,326,240, or 8.2% of the population.[11]

In Hindu society, some people are born into "purer" upper castes: their men wear a sacred thread after an initiation ceremony that makes them "twice-born" (women are of course excluded from this), do not traditionally work with their hands, and have privileged access to sacred texts, "learning," and other valued cultural and economic assets. Alongside the upper castes is the larger body of lowly peasants, service communities, artisans, and workers (none of whom wear the sacred thread or shun physical labor), and further, on the margins of the community, groups of menial workers, laborers, and servants, who

---

[11] For the 1961 figures, see Brij Raj Chauhan, "Scheduled Castes and Scheduled Tribes," *Economic and Political Weekly*, 4, no. 4 (January 25, 1969), 257, 259, 261–3. For 2001, see Government of India, Ministry of Home Affairs, "Scheduled Castes and Scheduled Tribes Populations," http://www.censusindia.gov.in/Census_Data_2001/India_at_Glance/scst.aspx [accessed March 16, 2011].

are decidedly "unclean." The distinction between the lowest "touchable" castes and the untouchable is not always very marked. In the reigning social system, as one scholar observes, "everyone is to some extent impure, and ... impurity is a relative concept."[12] The Untouchables, too, even after they have come to be a socially or politically recognized category, remain divided into hundreds of castes and subcastes, most of which do not intermarry and many of which refuse to dine together or recognize one another as social groups of equivalent status.

Nevertheless, Dalit deprivation has had several dimensions historically. It was once located, and is still to be seen, in the Untouchables' (or ex-Untouchables') extremely low ritual status, frequently wretched economic conditions, and (until quite recently) denial of access to common cultural and political resources. It was also to be seen in the sexual exploitation of their women, which the Dalits' alleged impurity and untouchability did nothing to prevent.[13]

An analogous statement might be made about the conditions and politics of blacks in the United States, again a population group that is not easily tallied. According to the 1950 U.S. census, "Negros" comprised about 10% of the total population, a little over 15 million people out of a total of over 152 million. For the purposes of this calculation, as a special report attached to the census noted,

The concept of race ... [was] derived from that which is commonly accepted by the general public. It does not ... reflect clear-cut definitions of biological stock, and several categories obviously refer to nationalities. The information on race is ordinarily not based on a reply to questions asked by the enumerator but rather obtained by observation. Enumerators were instructed to ask a question when they were in doubt.

By 2000, according to the census, approximately 12.9% of the population was classified as being black. In this instance, the data were

---

[12] Robert Deliege, *The Untouchables of India* (Oxford: Berg Publishers, 2001), 50.

[13] As an old Dalit of the Satnami (or Chamar) caste from Chattisgarh said bitterly to a senior anthropologist in 1985, "The upper castes would not touch us. They would never eat with us. But they were always ready to fornicate. For 'doing it' our women were not untouchable.... Even after licking the privates of Satnami women, they would not lose their purity." See Saurabh Dube, *Untouchable Pasts: Religion, Identity, and Power among a Central Indian Community, 1780–1950* (New Delhi: Vistaar Publications, 2001), 171.

Introduction 15

calculated by reference to "the answers provided by the respondents, as well as responses assigned during the editing and imputation processes." The 12.9% included Afro-Caribbeans and recent immigrants from Africa, which underscores the point that "African American" is only a political/cultural construct. It included as well those who reported themselves as belonging to the black *and* another race. The report seems to suggest that, in cases where individuals identified themselves as black as well as some other race, they were counted as blacks to prevent double-counting.[14]

During the period of slavery and for a century afterward, people of African descent were commonly barred from access to a common water supply, places in restaurants, schools, desirable residential localities, public transport, and other public spaces. In addition, they were denied access to a huge array of jobs and political opportunities, especially in the southern states, where these denials were legally enforced and where the overwhelming poverty of the majority of the black population had also been accompanied by the sexual exploitation of poor black women. Following a short period of "reconstruction" and democratization after the abolition of slavery in the 1860s, Jim Crow laws were passed to regularize and perpetuate segregation, and the distinctly subordinate status of blacks, throughout the southern United States. As Langston Hughes observed in 1952, "I saw [FOR WHITES ONLY] signs when I first went South in the 1920's. I see them still there today.... A dog can sit on a WHITE bench in a WHITE park and, if his legs are long enough, lick water out of a WHITE fountain. I cannot. I will be put in jail. My color makes me less than a dog to those who run the South."[15]

---

[14] U.S. Bureau of the Census, "Table A-9: Race for the United States, Regions, Divisions, and States: 1950 (100-Percent Data)," http://www.census.gov/population/www/documentation/twps0056/tabA-09.pdf [accessed March 16, 2011]; and Jesse McKinnon, "The Black Population: 2000," *Census 2000 Brief*, C2KBR/01-5, accessed online at www.census.gov/prod/2001pubs/c2kbr01-5.pdf. By the last decade of the twentieth century, a very large proportion of Americans came from categorically "mixed" families: 1 of 7 whites, 1 of 3 blacks, 4 of 5 Asians, and 19 of 20 Native Americans were closely related to someone outside their supposed racial group, and some 12% of young people called themselves multiracial. See Jennifer L. Hochschild, "Looking Ahead: Racial Trends in the United States," *Daedalus*, 134, no. 1 (Winter 2005), 76.

[15] *Chicago Defender*, April 26, 1952.

16   *A History of Prejudice*

Walter White, a distinguished leader of the National Association for the Advancement of Colored People (NAACP), had made the same point in his 1948 autobiography, recalling the Atlanta riots of 1906, when as a boy he gained a new awareness of the fact – and consequences – of his being black:

I was a Negro, a human being with an invisible pigmentation which marked me as a person to be hunted, hanged, abused, discriminated against, kept in poverty, and ignorance, in order that those whose skin was white would have readily at hand a proof of their superiority. No matter how low a white man fell, he could always hold fast to the smug conviction that he was superior to two-thirds of the world's population.[16]

There is a parallel between post–Second World War developments in India and the USA, in the formal abolition of Untouchability in India in the 1950s and the dismantling of the legal apparatus of racial segregation in the American South in the 1960s and '70s, although the consequences of the long history of stigmatization, discrimination, and exploitation against large segments of the population may still be observed in both cases. The differences between the framework and texture of U.S. and Indian, African American and Dalit, histories should not be understated. For example, it is clear that India's Dalits have remained trapped in a more intractable position than that of African Americans because of a poorer economy and slower economic growth in the nineteenth and twentieth centuries and because of the more restricted opportunities of escape from the stranglehold of caste, which is countrywide in its spread and has long been shored up by a claimed religious sanction in the prevailing (Hindu) tradition of social organization and interaction.

American democracy was established in the service of what is proclaimed as a new, young, expanding, frontier society, a land of opportunity (and of incredible, and expanding, resources and wealth) open to every enterprising individual, whatever his (and only much later, her) background. The country saw itself as being quintessentially modern, entirely comfortable with the spirit of bourgeois liberalism (the primacy of the individual, the sanctity of private property,

---

[16] Walter White, *A Man Called White: The Autobiography of Walter White* (New York: Viking Press, 1948), 11.

Introduction

faith in the justice of the free market, and a suspicion of government intervention). Indian democracy was established, by contrast, in an old, well-settled, densely populated land, struggling with some success, but slowly, to overcome the worst effects of feudal and colonial relations, long-established patriarchal and familial structures, and the extreme inequality – the entrenched hierarchies and skewed access to resources – that they perpetuated. Through all the dislocations and transformations of the last two centuries, people of the Indian subcontinent have lived in anguished relation to the discourse of a colonial and postcolonial modernity and have been locked in an ongoing debate on the appropriate structures and conditions of "the good society" in the modern age (individual versus communal rights; private versus public property and enterprise; state protection and welfare versus free market individualism and profit-seeking).

The passionate commitment to local and individual rights in American political discourse may well have flowed originally from the *ad hoc* character of the establishment of claims in the immigrant European expansion westward. The marked variation in social, political, and demographic conditions in the North, South, and West of the United States through the eighteenth and nineteenth centuries probably served to deepen this sense of local entitlement. The emphasis on individual rights is accentuated again by the differentiated character of the African American and other assemblages, the existence of "free men" and slaves, from the very beginning of the history of the North American colonies. Black families of wealth, a so-called black aristocracy, have long existed, and free black immigrants have continued to arrive throughout, to add to the large numbers of enslaved, ex-slave, and other black people already in North America, and to extend the differentiation among them. There has been no equivalent Dalit aristocracy or Dalit bourgeoisie in India, at least until very recently. Quite simply, a local community would not have remained Dalit – "Untouchable," or even very low in the caste order – if it had become aristocratic or particularly well-to-do, as various local groups did in past centuries, with the predictable result of finding a rather more exalted place in the caste hierarchy.

With all these differences, what marks both U.S. and Indian histories is an uphill and long, drawn-out struggle waged by a whole variety of subordinated and marginalized population groups for the establishment of common (and, often, long-promised) rights. In the African American and the Dalit instances, as in several others, the difficulty is accentuated by the overwhelming poverty of large sections of the subaltern groups in question: the condition of immiserization is especially noticeable in the Indian case. The continued economic and cultural power of the traditionally dominant classes, upper castes and whites, and the continued use of violence (psychological, physical, legal, and illegal) to maintain "society" and perpetuate "order," in both countries, makes the politics of this encounter all the more obscure. Long habits of stigmatization, degradation, and denial are not easily overturned in the minds of the oppressors, nor is the fear that accompanies them in the minds of the oppressed. Prejudicial structures rule, and set unacknowledged limits to democracy. Let us revisit in this light the modern promise of freedom and development for all.

"Rags to Riches" – or the Middle-Class Dream

Neither freedom nor prosperity and peace, the promises of the modern, have been readily or very substantively achieved for the majority of people even in advanced capitalist societies, let alone the bulk of countries around the globe. But the fable of freedom and opportunity lives on. It has found a particularly enduring form in the narrative of a largely self-made and independent middle class – a proposition of self-making, of lifting oneself up by one's bootstraps, as in the classic histories of the Western European and North American middle classes, that bears further reflection.

The privileging of the "middle class" idea flows at least in part from its claimed universality. At times, as in nineteenth-century England or in the first half of the twentieth century in India, the term middle class was used pejoratively to refer to the upstart bourgeois, the uncultured and frequently migrant *nouveaux riches*, who attempted to mimic upper-class practices and manners. In the longer run, however, middleclassness came to be seen as the wave of the future, and the middle classes as the makers of their own (as well as the wider modern society's) destiny – a destiny made through an individual's and a people's own unaided efforts. To be middle class could even be described as the common aspiration of all "modern" groups and individuals.

Introduction 19

The ideal society would be one in which no one had the benefit of aristocratic wealth or the afflictions of inherited poverty. The emergence and strength of the middle classes appeared to be the measure of human equality, of the possibility of self-fashioning, of individual achievement and capability – the very signs of the modern.

It is merit, not inherited wealth or privilege or sectional loyalty or networks, that counts in the making of the middle-class world, we are told. It is improvement, and self-improvement, through education and moral reform, individual effort, and sheer determination, that brings advancement for society, family, and individual. The rags to riches tale, great men building fortunes out of nothing, has been a staple of the middle-class fable not only in the United States but also in Victorian England and colonial India. *Anyone* can be middle class; and, in a sense, *everyone* should be. Those who do not make it are simply not determined or talented enough. The urge to "make it" and the promise of its possibility are the transparent, evident sign of the modern and the good society.[17]

At the same time, middleclassness – like the "modern" – has always been defined by a series of exclusions; in other words, by what it is not. On the one hand, the middle classes were distinguished from manual workers by the kinds of professions they entered (occupations in which they did not soil their hands through labor),[18] the houses they lived in, the language they spoke, and their supposedly temperate behavior. On the other, and as critically, they were distinguished by a notion of masculinity in which the man was the breadwinner and presided over a household with a clearly separated private domain inhabited by "nonworking" women and children. Middle-class men claimed political rights and the status of citizens; the exclusion of workers and women was long seen as being entirely natural. It was only in later discourses of citizenship and middleclassness – such as those

---

[17] "In democracies," as one sociologist puts it, "the middle class is the nation proper. The typical member of a national community is a member of the middle class." See Akos Rona-Tas, "Post Communist Transition and the Absent Middle Class in Central East Europe," quoted in Sam Vaknin, "Russia's Middle Class," http://samvak.tripod .com/brief-middleclass01.html.

[18] It is ironic, then, that in some countries, like today's United States, and more generally among groups I call the subaltern middle classes, anyone, working class or professional, who holds a steady job and even temporarily occupies a position of intellectual, civic, or political leadership can be thought of as "middle class."

represented in the women's movement – that this kind of exclusion came to be challenged.

The housewife as the linchpin of domesticity and the private sphere was largely a creation of this new middle-class world and thus integrated into it. Along with laboring peoples and the aristocracy, nonwhites and the "Third World" in general were, however, seen to lie outside the domain of the new middle-class life. Catholics, Jews, and the Irish would not be recognized as middle class in England for a long time; nor would Jews, Italians, or Irish in North America. Native Americans and African Americans in the USA and Dalits in India are not easily accommodated in the category to this day.

These exclusions are not explicable in terms of the "common sense" middle-class proposition that these latter groups – "immigrants," "negroes," "natives," "untouchables," "criminal castes," Native Americans, and *adivasis* (literally, the "original inhabitants" of India) – were inherently poor, disorganized, and lazy, culturally unsuited to middle-class modernity. To make sense of them, we need to recall not the middle-class fable of liberal advancement in lands of the free but the destruction and alienation that attended the establishment of modern industrial society and imperialism, along with the economic and technological advances and promises of unprecedented opportunity and wealth that came with them.[19]

The effects of this dislocation and alienation have been marked among the working classes and immigrant populations, themselves made up in the main of uprooted working people. They may be seen in the history of several immigrant groups in Western Europe and North America from the late nineteenth century to today. And they have of course had long-lasting consequences in Europe's Asian and African colonies and in the condition of the internally colonized (indigenous peoples in Australasia and the Americas, African Americans in the United States, Dalits in India, and so on); that is to say, among

---

[19] For a few important commentaries, see Karl Marx and Friedrich Engels, *On Colonialism* (Moscow: Foreign Languages Press, n.d.); Marshall Berman, *All That Is Solid Melts Into Air: The Experience of Modernity* (New York: Penguin Books, 1982); Frantz Fanon, *The Wretched of the Earth* (New York: Grove Press, 1963); Jean Suret-Canale, *French Colonialism in Tropical Africa, 1900–1945*, English trans. Till Gottheiner (New York: Pica Press, 1971); Mike Davis, *City of Quartz: Excavating the Future in Los Angeles* (London: Verso, 1990); and Gilroy, *Black Atlantic*.

Introduction

populations marked as subordinate on the basis of race, religion, or other inherited social condition and denied access for that reason to a whole range of public economic and cultural resources.[20]

In the postcolony as in the colony, in the United States and India, in the nineteenth century and today, notwithstanding all the political advances that have taken place, a violence – institutionalized in practices of racism, slavery, and Untouchability – still serves to maintain the existing social order and persistent boundaries between racially or socially segregated communities.[21] Numerous studies of the African American middle classes have shown how black middle-class areas in most large American cities still remain bound within segregated black communities. In some instances, where black middle-class groups have moved out of traditionally black neighborhoods, their relocation has been followed by the phenomenon of "white flight" from the areas they have moved into, leading to the establishment of separate white and black neighborhoods once again.[22] Even where this is not so obviously the case in physical terms, as might be claimed for Dalit professionals (smaller in number than their African American counterparts and less easily distinguished by skin color or physical appearance), segregation has long been the social-psychological condition under which the ex-slave, "subaltern" middle classes have to live and find their being.[23]

The violence I refer to is encountered not only in physical and sexual abuse, rape, and flogging of lower-caste and lower-class servants and workers, and not only in riots and police violence against blacks and Dalits. It is found, too, in the upper-caste desertion of neighborhoods,

---

[20] For more on these variations, see Gyanendra Pandey, "Can There Be a Subaltern Middle Class?" in *Subaltern Citizens and Their Histories: Investigations from India and the USA*, ed. Gyanendra Pandey (London: Routledge, 2010), 15–30. See also Chapter 7, this volume.

[21] This is a situation in which, as Gilroy points out, the lines between public and private violence have often been very hard to draw. See Gilroy, *Black Atlantic*, 175.

[22] The literature on this theme is considerable. For two important recent studies, see Mary Patillo-McCoy, *Black Picket Fences: Privilege and Peril among the Black Middle Class* (Chicago: University of Chicago Press, 1999); and Kevin Kruse, *White Flight: Atlanta and the Making of Modern Conservatism* (Princeton, NJ: Princeton University Press, 2005).

[23] Cf. Darryl Michael Scott, *Contempt and Pity: Social Policy and the Image of the Damaged Black Psyche, 1880–1996* (Chapel Hill: University of North Carolina Press, 1997).

clubs, schools, public transport, and sometimes even jobs into which the lower castes have been allowed entry. It is found in demonstrations against affirmative action, in the courts and the legislatures as well as on the streets, and in the continued abuse and punishment of Dalits, blacks, and other such subaltern groups for appearing where they are still not expected to be. The African American addition to the list of offenses related to drinking and driving in the USA (not only DUI, "driving under the influence," and DWI, "driving while intoxicated," but also DWB, "driving while black" – which is, obviously, not a legally cognizable offense!), and the Native American version of it (in which DWI becomes "driving while Indian"), is a profound comment on the necessity of being white, modern, and monolingual in a very particular way to access fully the resources and opportunities of modern civic existence in many parts of the world.

In spite of these inherited structures of prejudice and denial, which clearly contradict the simple modernist faith in the triumph of reason and science, important analysts, economic entrepreneurs, and political leaders have continued to believe in the narrative of freedom and development that democracy and rational government are poised to bring about all over the world. Two old but well-known studies by the Swedish economist Gunnar Myrdal serve to illustrate the intricacies of this argument as applied to the cases of the United States and India.

Quandaries of Development and Democracy

Myrdal was invited by leading corporations (supported by state authorities) to write about the major problems of America and "Asia" in the 1940s and 1960s. His central concern was the (statist) question of the management of "minorities," internal divisions, and obstacles to development and democracy in the various countries he investigated: and he presented with clarity and intriguing detail the "common sense," if elite, perception of the fundamental problems in these different lands.

In *An American Dilemma*, his detailed investigation of the "Negro problem" in America, which I referred to earlier, Myrdal declared that the average American (whatever he meant by "average") was "a practical idealist." Compared with members of other Western societies, "the ordinary American is a rationalistic being, and there are close

Introduction
23

relations between his moralism and his rationalism." "This moralism and rationalism are to many of us . . . the glory of the nation, its youthful strength, perhaps the salvation of mankind," he wrote, and "the inherited liberalistic trust that things will ultimately take care of themselves and get settled in one way or another, enable the ordinary American to live on happily, with recognized contradictions around him and within him, in a world of bright fatalism which is unmatched in the rest of the Western world." And further, in italics:

The American Negro problem is a problem in the heart of the American. . . . The 'American Dilemma', referred to in the title of this book, is the ever-raging conflict between, on the one hand, the valuations preserved on the general plane which we shall call the "American Creed", where the American thinks, talks, and acts under the influence of high national and Christian precepts, and, on the other hand, the valuations on specific planes of individual and group living, where personal and local interests; economic, social, and sexual jealousies; considerations of community prestige and conformity; [and] group prejudice against particular persons or types of people . . . dominate his outlook.[24]

This stirring commentary may be put in context by reference to a review of Myrdal's book written by the great African American writer Ralph Ellison. In Ellison's view, the chief virtue of the book, apart from the mass of information it had assembled, was that it drew attention to "the clash on the social level between the American Creed and anti-Negro practices." However, he went on, Myrdal's talk of the American Creed allowed him to circumvent the "American class struggle," which was the historical and material ground of the "American dilemma," and to deny the existence of "*two* American moralities" – money-making on the one hand and national and Christian brotherhood on the other.

He also challenged Myrdal's patronizing proposition that all of the African American's life and struggle in the United States had been but a "secondary reaction to more primary pressure from the side of the dominant white majority."[25] "Can a people (its faith in an idealized American Creed notwithstanding) live and develop for over three hundred years simply by *reacting*?" Ellison asked. "Are American

---

[24] Myrdal, *An American Dilemma*, vol. 1, lxx–lxxi (emphasis in original).
[25] Myrdal, *An American Dilemma*, vol. 1, lxxv.

Negroes simply the creation of white men, or have they at least helped to create themselves out of what they found around them?"[26]

Writing on India two decades later, Myrdal presented a rather different, but equally arresting, top-down view, which indicated the asymmetry of conditions and histories in India and the USA, and (consequently) the asymmetry of views about the two. The basic story he told about India was that of a relatively enlightened, modern nationalist political elite attempting – somewhat arbitrarily, and often without much support from other sections of the dominant classes – to uplift a passive population. It may be well to start by noting the title of his three-volume study of India and Indonesia (and some other newly independent countries of South and Southeast Asia), published in 1968: *Asian Drama: An Inquiry into the Poverty of Nations*. Not the "dilemma" or "dilemmas," the self-examination and rational deliberation, of a rich, young, and pluralist nation like the United States. The study of "Asia" has a very distinct problematic, produced by the very "backwardness" of these nations, with their faceless masses of poor, unenlightened people, entering into the modern world. Given that understanding, some of what Myrdal observed was surprising, to say the least.

At the dawn of national independence after the Second World War, he wrote, India (and other South Asian countries) "accepted the ideology of planning for development, and, more fundamentally . . . treated economic development as a concern of the state and thus a political issue." A "commitment to egalitarianism . . . [was] an integral part of their ideology of planning." The inequalities of the inherited social structures were recognized as serious obstacles to development. "Certainly the caste system in India is an obvious obstacle. It fortifies the contempt and disgust for manual work prevalent in all social strata. Since an orthodox Hindu regards not only those who perform this work but everyone else outside his own caste as beyond the pale, it also warps and stultifies ordinary human feelings of brotherhood and compassion."

---

[26] Review of *An American Dilemma* (written for *The Antioch Review* in 1944), in Ralph Ellison, *Shadow and Act* (New York: Quality Paperback Book Club, 1994), 304, 305, 313, 315 (emphasis in original). For a more recent critique of Myrdal's propositions, see Gary Gerstle, *American Crucible: Race and Nation in the Twentieth Century* (Princeton, NJ: Princeton University Press, 2001), 4–5, 193.

Introduction

From the beginning, too, India's leaders embraced the ideal of political democracy, with universal adult franchise, irrespective of caste, class, sex, religion, language, literacy, ownership of property, or place of birth. In the US, the majority of African Americans did not effectively have the right to vote until the civil rights revolution of the 1960s. By that time, as Myrdal noted, India had "a firmly established parliamentary government based on universal suffrage and a comparatively high turnout of the electorate." However, he added, in another display of a narrow Western (if not colonial) perspective, "in spite of this the masses are more the object of politics than its subject. They remain passive and inalert [inert?]."[27]

Jawaharlal Nehru, patrician, stalwart of the Indian struggle for independence from British rule, Gandhi's able lieutenant, self-styled socialist and modernist, and prime minister from Indian independence in 1947 until his death in 1964, in an odd way concurred. He had written in the 1930s of an unlikely relationship between the hopeful, sad, expectant masses and the educated, nationalist leadership: it was

as if we were...the guides who were to lead them to the promised land. Looking at them and their misery and overflowing gratitude, I was filled with shame and sorrow, shame at my own easy-going and comfortable life and our petty politics of the city which ignored this vast multitude of semi-naked sons and daughters of India, sorrow at the degradation and overwhelming poverty of India. A new picture of India seemed to rise before me, naked, starving, crushed, and utterly miserable.[28]

But the "spirit of the age" was with the enlightened leadership: that spirit was in favor of equality ("though practice denies it almost everywhere"), and it would triumph. In Nehru's view, religion was already dated, supplanted by nationalism, which in turn would give way to a new internationalism: "Everywhere religion recedes into the background and nationalism appears in aggressive garbs, and behind nationalism other isms which talk in social and economic terms."

---

[27] Gunnar Myrdal, *Asian Drama: An Inquiry into the Poverty of Nations*, abridged by Seth S. King (New York: Pantheon Books, 1971), 146, 147, 150, 152, and passim. For the more elaborate recension from which the statements I have quoted are drawn, see Gunnar Myrdal, *Asian Drama: An Inquiry into the Poverty of Nations*, vol. 2 (New York: Twentieth Century Fund, 1968), 745–6, 767, 774–6.

[28] Jawaharlal Nehru, *An Autobiography: With Musings on Recent Events in India* (London: John Lane The Bodley Head, 1936), 52.

26   *A History of Prejudice*

Further: "I wonder how people in India can worry about sectarian problems of civilization and culture when hunger and poverty are staring the nation in the face. It is an imperative necessity to relieve all this which vitally affect the country before people can apply themselves to any minor issues."[29] And so the Nehruvian regime moved toward "planning" and "development" to bring about "a classless society with equal economic justice and opportunity for all." Anything that came in the way would "have to be removed, gently if possible, forcibly if necessary."[30] In this scenario, the "people" indeed appeared like passive recipients; the rule of "experts" was at hand.

Many segments of the people, and many critical thinkers, have articulated other ideas, however, and challenged the assumptions underlying these elitist propositions, even if they subscribed to "developmentalist" views of their own. The Indian nationalist claim of an already existing unity – a mass of people living in a common territory under a single political system, automatically constituting a nation irrespective of what caste, class, and other privilege had done to them in the past and continued to do in the present – was widely questioned, by Muslim politicians as well as Dalits and others. B. R. Ambedkar, as the most prominent spokesperson of the Dalits in 1931, made the point to the man who would be hailed as the Father of the Indian Nation, "Gandhiji, I have no homeland."[31] And soon after Independence:

How can people divided into several thousands of castes be a nation? The sooner we realize that we are not as yet a nation in the social and psychological sense of the word, the better for us. For then only we shall realize the necessity of becoming a nation and seriously think of ways and means of realizing the goal.[32]

E. V. Ramaswamy Naicker, or "Periyar" ("the Great Leader"), founder of the Self-Respect Movement and militant leader of lower-caste assertion in South India, put it more strongly, declaring as early as 1925:

---

[29] Nehru, *Autobiography*, 472; and S. Gopal, ed., *Selected Works of Jawaharlal Nehru*, vol. 7 (New Delhi: Orient Longman, 1975), 401.

[30] Nehru, *Autobiography*, 551, 552.

[31] Dhananjay Keer, *Dr. Ambedkar: Life and Mission* (1954; reprint Mumbai: Popular Prakashan, 1990), 166.

[32] Vasant Moon, ed., *Dr. Babasaheb Ambedkar: Writings and Speeches*, vol. 13 (Mumbai: Education Dept., Government of Maharashtra Press, 1994), 1217.

Introduction   27

In our present situation many fear that Swaraj if granted will only usher in Brahmana Raj. If, in these days of British rule, it is possible for some to prevent others from walking down certain streets and . . . from having access to water from village wells and ponds . . . what would they [Brahmans and other upper castes] . . . do if they come to wield [the] authority [of Government]?

Or again, in an address to Dalit Christians in 1933: "If you desire true freedom you must have the courage to destroy that which validates and constitutes the basis of your abject and enslaved condition."[33]

What remains insufficiently acknowledged in much modern, nationalist discourse is that while certain sections of a population emerge as "natural," unmarked citizens of a land, others become hyphenated ("Native/African/Hispanic Americans," "Indian Muslims," "Dalit middle class"), second-class, and sometimes even suspect. The latter must measure up to declared national standards and can only then be "assimilated." "White but not quite," "white Negro," and "Dalit Brahman," and other such contradictions in terms, abound in political and intellectual discussions of such "minoritized" social groups. Such deferral and qualification has been a large part of the history of the African American and the Dalit communities in the period of open and intense political struggle for their rights over the last half century and more. These are subaltern citizens for whom the promise of freedom, of equal opportunity and an equal share in the fruits of modernity, has long been constantly renewed, and constantly deferred.[34]

In seeking to interrogate the "common sense" of the modern in the following pages, I examine some of the more specifically marked (more local and visible) vernacular prejudices that have gone into the making of the recent history of African Americans and Dalits in the United States and India. It is important to note that these vernacular prejudices are sustained by the universal, and by the very pretense that this universal is not itself a vernacular (the vernacular with the strongest army, air force, and navy?): "The tradition of the oppressed teaches us that the 'state of emergency' in which we live is not the

---

[33] Cited in V. Geetha and S. V. Rajadurai, *Towards a Non-Brahmin Millennium: From Iyothee Thass to Periyar* (Calcutta: Samya, 1998), 291, 364.

[34] For an elaboration of the idea of the "subaltern citizen," see Gyanendra Pandey, "The Subaltern as Subaltern Citizen," introduction to Pandey, *Subaltern Citizens and Their Histories.*

28 *A History of Prejudice*

exception but the rule."[35] Following Benjamin, I attend closely to the *normalcy of the exception*, to the violence of order and of inherited "common sense" – a sinister shadow in the life of the oppressed – in the following investigation of the history of the African American and Dalit struggles for equal rights in the United States and India, and of the place of caste, race, and patriarchal prejudice, Untouchability, segregation, and masculinism in holding them back.

Freedom's Dawn

The great Urdu writer Saadat Hasan Manto has a short story about a poor hackney-cab driver Ustad Mangoo's eager anticipation of the day on which a *"Naya Qanoon"* (New Law or New Constitution) is to come into being, his early-morning jaunt and anticipation of celebration on that day, and the consequences of his exercise of the liberty he imagines coming with that "new dawn." Mangoo is called "Ustad" (Master or Teacher) by fellow cabbies at his cab stand because of his incredible fund of information, garnered from the gossip of his passengers, regarding political developments the world over: the Civil War in Spain, workers' and peasants' rule in Russia, which has become mixed up in his mind with the "New Constitution," and so on. The denouement of Manto's story is reached in Mangoo's encounter with an Englishman he recognizes as the drunken passenger whose verbal abuse he'd had to suffer quietly following an altercation between them some months earlier, aware as he was of the consequences of standing up to a white *sahib*. Now, on the day of the promulgation of the New Law, Mangoo demands an increased fare for a short trip and refuses to alight from his seat when the sahib beckons him. When the latter advances, threatening Mangoo with a cane, the proud cab driver can contain himself no longer. He knocks the sahib over, proceeds to beat him, and continues to do so until two police constables manage, with difficulty, to drag him away and put him in jail, saying, "What 'New Law' – what are you talking about – the law is what it always was."[36]

---

[35] Walter Benjamin, "Theses on History," no. 8, in Walter Benjamin, *Illuminations* (London: Fontana, 1973), 259. Cf. Georgio Agamben, *Homo Sacer I: Sovereign Power and Bare Life* (Stanford, CA: Stanford University Press, 1998).

[36] Atahar Parvez, ed., *Manto ke Numaindah Afsane* (Aligarh: Educational Book House, 1981), 31–44.

Introduction 29

The point of citing Manto's nonlinear and noncontinuist satire on the subaltern Mangoo's first experience of "freedom" is not to indicate once more the violence of the white man and of British colonialism, for this has been amply documented, and ruling classes in postcolonial Asia and Africa (and in noncolonized countries like China) have been no less skillful, or brutal, in perpetuating their power. Nor is it to suggest that the law is, and always will be, what it has always been for cab drivers, working people, Dalits, and blacks. It is rather to say that there are histories beyond those written by sahibs and police officers, histories as perceived and lived and anticipated by the Mangoos of this world – and that a history of prejudice must reckon with these different perspectives.

It is precisely such a contested account of long-anticipated, and contradictory, moments of freedom that I present in the following pages. For India, the "New Dawn" that I examine is the time of independence from British rule (in 1947), the inauguration of the Indian republic and the extension of voting rights to all inhabitants of the territory (1950), and the abolition of Untouchability, regarded almost universally as the worst aspect of the inherited practice of caste discrimination, in a series of constitutional provisions and laws between 1950 and 1955. In the United States, a set of events that is often seen as a parallel departure is the civil rights movement and legislation of the 1960s, which, following the abolition of slavery a hundred years earlier, established more securely the conditions for something like equal citizenship and political participation for the African American population of the land. In what follows, however, I shall consider a longer struggle for civil rights and citizenship in both cases.

How does one write a history of unacknowledged prejudice, of simultaneous belief in the promise of freedom and the necessity of continued deferral, to repeat the question I began with? How does one reckon with the vexations and challenges of thinking the "subaltern citizen," with the history of long-subordinated groups claiming citizenship, and of those who willy-nilly inhabit the double bind of the internally colonized? I have chosen to do so by focusing for a start on the politics of prejudice as a politics of difference, for prejudice often appears in the pronouncement of difference, as a marker of natural, obvious talents and hierarchy: man versus woman, white versus black, Hindu versus Muslim, Christian versus Jew, heterosexual versus homosexual, rational versus irrational, modern versus primitive, civilized versus barbarian.

The proclamation of difference, I submit, forms the core of the majority of judgments on the question of enfranchisement and disenfranchisement, the privilege of unmarked citizenship on the one hand and the handicap of marginality on the other. Through a tracing of these conscious and unconscious markers of hierarchy, and some of the consequences that flow from them, one might begin to chart a history of prejudice in specific times and places, as I do in Chapter 2. I analyze the matter in some detail in that chapter, as a technique of organizing social order and yet as a discourse that provides a range of resources to Dalits and African Americans, and other disenfranchised communities, for struggles against marginalization and subordination.

In Chapter 3, I consider the question of Dalit conversion, which might also be described as the struggle for Dalit liberation, in several of its aspects. As an entry into the history of the civil rights movement in the USA, I devote Chapter 4 to the campaign for Double Victory (or "Double V") against the opponents of American democracy and freedom at home and abroad during the Second World War. Through an analysis of the call for Dalit conversion to citizenship in India and the "Double V" campaign in the USA, I seek to interrogate the received history of liberation and democracy in the two countries. I go on in Chapters 5 and 6 to investigate other aspects of the yearning for dignity, opportunity, and equal access – the struggle for control of the body as well as for access to mobility, schools, and other resources of modern society – within these communities and outside, within the confines of the home as well as in the public arena. I conclude in Chapter 7 by pointing to the persistence of narrow-mindedness, bigotry, and intolerance in many forms, very much at odds with the promise of democracy and claims of exceptional tolerance, justice, and enlightenment that are central to the official U.S. and Indian narratives of themselves.

A word of explanation about the variety of sources I have drawn on in the following pages. As I have indicated, the archive that a historian of prejudice must use is likely to be unconventional, and even "illicit." Prejudice is not always set out openly in political manifestos, media commentary, or individual articulations and pronouncements. The evidence of prejudice surfaces in improbable forms and unexpected

Introduction 31

places, and often appears as impressionistic and anecdotal; not quite the stuff of disciplinary history. Given the particular challenges confronting anyone who would write a history of prejudice, and given the shadowy character of its archive, I make no apology for my use of fragmentary, "trivial," unarchived (and perhaps unarchivable) evidence, along with records and documents emanating from the state and recognized intellectual and political movements. I have therefore turned to an array of autobiographical and fictional writings, folksongs and poetry, letters to the press, and blogs on the Internet, as well as published and unpublished public documents and correspondence related to the history of African Americans and Dalits, to construct my account of their struggles.

The question of how we may write a history of prejudice is, however, even more recalcitrant than this comment on sources might suggest. How does one begin to write a history of a notion that has itself undergone a sea change since the Enlightenment? Until the Renaissance, as Gadamer reminds us, prejudice referred to the assumptions we work with, which were clearly subject to challenge and rewriting by evidence that contradicted them. Following the Enlightenment's "prejudice against prejudice," however, the term came to refer only to the assumptions (of others) of which we disapprove.[37] How, one might ask, do we write a history of prejudice, the common-sense assumptions of others, from which we do not exclude ourselves?

What I do in this study is to inhabit the realm of prejudice – the common sense of the modern – even as I write about it. What I undertake is, to a large extent, a work of translation between vernacular and universal prejudices. In attending to narratives of the modern and stories of democracy, as these are found (heard and invoked, appropriated, translated, and recast) in the lives and histories of America's blacks and India's Dalits, I pay close attention to arguments about why the resources of modernity and democracy are (sometimes) kept from such groups because of their "difference," their need still to catch up and to become worthy of participating fully in the fruits of modern democracy. I seek to examine the record of the articulation of difference

[37] Cf. "Hans-Georg Gadamer," sect. 3.1, "The Positivity of 'Prejudice,'" *Stanford Encyclopedia of Philosophy* (Stanford, CA: Stanford University Press, first published March 3, 2003; substantive revision June 8, 2009).

32 *A History of Prejudice*

both by "outsiders" viewing America's blacks and India's Dalits as unified objects of inquiry or commentary and by African Americans and Dalits themselves. I take both African Americans and Dalits, therefore, as important subjects, as well as objects, of prejudice.

Thus, to anticipate an argument I will elaborate in the following chapters, the Dalit leader Dr. B. R. Ambedkar presented himself, and continues to be presented, as a consummately modern figure. Nevertheless, he harbored and expressed many of the signature contradictions of liberalism when it came to the governance and rights of "tribes," or dalit groups of hill and forest tracts in India now classified as Scheduled Tribes. In the course of the Indian Constituent Assembly debate on the Fifth and Sixth Schedules for "tribal-areas," for instance, Ambedkar declared: "The Aboriginal Tribes have not as yet developed any political sense to make the best use of their political opportunities and they may easily become mere instruments in the hands either of a majority or a minority and thereby disturb the balance without doing any good to themselves." The "tribes" for him fell below what Uday Mehta has called the anthropological minimum of inclusion into the space-time of the modern.[38] The proposition epitomizes my argument about universal prejudice – all the more so because it is the most important leader of the Dalits in the twentieth century who here articulates the narrow-mindedness of the modern.

One may point to other, very different kinds of examples. "How can we be prejudiced against our own selves; we are all of one race," a group of older black women teachers said to Alice Walker when she asked them to write about color prejudice within their own families at a workshop in 1969.[39] "Historically," writes Audre Lorde, "difference had been used so cruelly against us that as a people we were

---

[38] Babasaheb Ambedkar, "Communal Deadlock and a Way to Solve It" (1945), in Moon, *Dr. Babasaheb Ambedkar*, vol. 1 (1979), 375. I am grateful to Townsend Middleton for drawing my attention to this statement. See Townsend Middleton, "Beyond Recognition: Ethnology, Belonging, and the Refashioning of the Ethnic Subject in Darjeeling, India," (PhD dissertation, Department of Anthropology, Cornell University, 2010), 228–339, for his analysis of Ambedkar's views on Scheduled Tribes. See also Uday Singh Mehta, *Liberalism and Empire: A Study in Nineteenth-Century British Liberal Thought* (Chicago: University of Chicago Press, 1999).

[39] Alice Walker, *In Search of Our Mothers' Gardens* (Orlando, FL: Harvest Books, 1983), 29.

Introduction

reluctant to tolerate any diversion from what was externally defined as Blackness.... [W]e could not bear the face of each other's differences because of what we feared those differences might say about ourselves."[40] Following Walker and Lorde, I believe we have to ask how questions of power and privilege, subalternity and difference, are navigated within subalternized constituencies and assemblages themselves.

What happens within the African American and Dalit communities to issues of class and gender, not to mention color? When and how have these internal contradictions been resolved, or shelved, in the interests of the larger struggle? How do "unpoliticized" women write about the struggles of the poor and the disadvantaged in comparison with "politicized" men, writing of a more visible, public struggle? What happens when we set these public and private narratives side by side (as I do in Chapters 4 and 5), narratives that appear at first sight simply to talk past each other, speaking in rather different voices about what would appear to be rather different worlds, unable (or unwilling) to engage one another? What does this dissonance tell us about the prejudices of modern society and history as encountered in the ghettoes and other neighborhoods that are home to people of African descent in the United States and those belonging to formerly Untouchable castes in India? And what does it tell us about ourselves, the readers and writers of books like this one, university and college students and teachers, educated professionals and other well-to-do middle-class folk, the "unmarked" citizens of modern fantasy?

---

[40] Audre Lorde, *Sister Outsider* (Berkeley, CA: Crossing Press, 2007), 136.

2

Prejudice as Difference

Prejudice, I have suggested, often parades as difference. The positing of difference works as a means of othering – or otherization. Let me spell out the argument in terms of dominant discourses of social and cultural difference (that is, the common sense of the modern) before turning to an investigation of how subaltern assemblages and constituencies like African Americans and Dalits have, in their turn, deployed ideas of difference (and sameness) in their own political struggles.

A prominent theme in the history of the world since the eighteenth century has been the promise of emancipation, including the emancipation of societies and groups marked out as "backward," disadvantaged, or simply adrift from the "mainstream" of human history and progress as it has been conceived since the Enlightenment. It is against this background that differences of gender, sexuality, caste, race, and so on were foregrounded by the state (colonial and noncolonial), and by dominant groups and classes, in different parts of the world through most of the nineteenth and twentieth centuries. It is important to note the terms of this differentiation. Men are not described as *different*; it is women who are. Foreign colonizers are not *different*; the colonized are. Caste Hindus are not *different* in India; it is Muslims, "tribals," and Dalits (or ex-Untouchables) who are. White Anglo-Saxon Protestant heterosexual males are not *different* in the United States; at one time or another, everybody else is. White Australians are not *different*; Vietnamese boat people, Fijian migrants to Australia, and, astonishingly, Australian Aboriginals are.

Prejudice as Difference

Difference becomes a mark of the subordinated and the marginalized, measured as it is against the purported mainstream, the "standard" or the "normal." What we are presented with are two terms in binary opposition, "hierarchically structured so that the dominant term is accorded both temporal and logical priority."[1] As Simone de Beauvoir pointed out long ago, the binary of man and woman, for example, is hardly symmetrical, for the former is not only one pole in the pair but also the "sole essential" against which the other will be evaluated.[2] It is in the attribution of difference, then, that the logic of dominance and subordination commonly finds expression. And the proclamation of difference becomes a way of legitimating and reinforcing existing relations of power.

In the context of new discourses of nationhood in nineteenth-century Europe, the problematic of difference takes the political form of the "Jewish Question," and Marx's essay on that question becomes a lasting comment on the impossibility of the political emancipation of the Jew as Jew: that is, of political emancipation in a liberal mode – tolerating difference but demanding uniformity. The supposedly enlightened, tolerant, civil society of modern Europe, and with it the idea of the abstract citizen subject in the rational, universal order of the nation-state, is challenged by the very existence – and individuality – of the Jew, who is seen as being too particularistic and yet too global, too rooted, and yet too dislocated at one and the same time.[3] This is of course a very specific, nationalist contextualization of the question of difference, but it informs a more pervasive discourse of the political in modern times.

It is necessary to note that the Jewish Question is a metaphor for far more than the Jews. We may notice, if we care to do so, that it is Muslims who are the Jews of the late twentieth and early twenty-first

---

[1] Elizabeth Grosz, "Derrida, Irigaray, and Deconstruction," *Intervention: Revolutionary Marxist Journal*, 20 (1986): 72.

[2] Simone de Beauvoir, *The Second Sex* (1949; reprint London: Vintage, 1997), 17 and passim.

[3] There is extensive writing on this theme. For one important example, see Hannah Arendt, *The Jewish Writings*, ed. Jerome Kohn and Ron Feldman (New York: Schocken Books, 2007). For a postcolonial elaboration, focused on the question of Muslims in South Asia, see Aamir Mufti, *Enlightenment in the Colony: The Jewish Question and the Crisis of Postcolonial Culture* (Princeton, NJ: Princeton University Press, 2007), 51 and passim.

36 *A History of Prejudice*

centuries – once again, too narrowly community-centered and too worldwide, too parochial and too deracinated, to fit in as responsible (read: unmarked and naturally belonging) members of the nation-state. This is not to deny the critical differences between the history of the Jews – a consistently tiny minority in Europe, perceived as radically Other, as killers of Jesus, as the only religious minority until the post-Reformation era (given that European Muslims were so largely rendered invisible), a people without a state until the formation of modern Israel – and that of the world's Muslim communities, substantial populations that have controlled large territories and held state power in many places from the inception of Islam until today. In that respect, the oft-noted parallel between Jews and homosexuals may be somewhat more tenable, given their similar histories of being small minorities that were persecuted in Christian Europe (the experience elsewhere was perhaps more mixed) until late modernity, culminating in the Nazi Holocaust.[4] My point, however, is about *metaphor* in contemporary political discourse. The Jew and now the Muslim is a metaphor for a minority that never quite fits and is seen as dangerous to the nation-state; hence, the Jewish Question in nineteenth-century Europe and the *problem* of Muslims today.

Yet, there is another dimension to the question of difference and marginalization in the modern nation-state. If the Muslims are the Jews of recent decades, the unrecognized Other of the era from the eighteenth century onward have been slaves and Untouchables, women, and other "invisible" groups whose existence and particularity mount an equally important challenge to the existing discourses of civil society, uniform civil rights, and the abstract citizen subject of the new national and democratic order. Whereas the Jew/Muslim is viewed very quickly as a fully formed, alternative culture, the "eternal outsider" and dangerous Other, the precise status of women or slaves or Untouchables as Other (or as minority) is itself in doubt, for they are insider/outsiders, essential to the maintenance and survival of a given social order and yet not recognized as key to it.

---

[4] Cf. Hannah Arendt, *The Origins of Totalitarianism* (1951; reprint New York: Houghton Mifflin Harcourt, 1994); and Matti Bunzl, *Symptoms of Modernity: Jews and Queers in Late-Twentieth-Century Vienna* (Berkeley: University of California Press, 1999).

Prejudice as Difference 37

In rethinking the diverse uses of the idea of difference and the beliefs underlying them, then, the example of what have in different contexts been seen as classically subaltern communities – Dalits, blacks, conquered indigenous populations, women – may have something unusual to tell us. These are uncertain and fluid assemblages that have at particular junctures been accorded collective yet secondary status and come to be described as "different," "backward," "not quite ready" for full citizenship.[5] The politics of their pronouncement as different is likely to repay closer examination.

The specific character of the Dalit or black and, stretching the point a little, also the women's case is that it is seen as being marked above all by conditions of subordination and deprivation, as opposed to the Jewish/Muslim case, which is reckoned primarily in terms of what would be described as "cultural deviance." What are the distinguishing features of the history of this classically "subaltern" difference and consequent marginalization? In turning to this question, we need to attend first to the *making* of difference or otherness, or, in other words, of a minority (or minorities) not already established in their difference from the start. Moreover, if we take seriously the proposition that the production of difference, and minority, is a process, not a given demographic or sociological condition,[6] it is necessary to examine the kind of minoritization we encounter in the history of particular states and societies as well as the implications of distinct forms of minority existence.

A postcolonial critic, Aamir Mufti, has written of his interest in "how liberalism historically has talked about the modes of apartness of the Jews and the history of their persecution in Western society, and the kinds of solution it has offered."[7] Is the same kind of statement even conceivable for Dalits, or blacks, or women? Is the

---

[5] I should explain why the laboring poor do not appear as a central instance here. Although they were long categorized as *different* – in being "dangerous classes," physically and mentally wanting or even deformed, almost a different species of being – laboring people have emphatically (more so than women, for example) claimed sameness, rather than difference, as the grounds of their politics, except insofar as they present themselves as ethnic, caste, or racial communities (Irish, Italians, Hispanics, Dalits, blacks, Protestants, Hindus, etc.). They have therefore not been described as an identifiable minority, except in the latter sense.

[6] Mufti, *Enlightenment in the Colony*, 209.

[7] Ibid., 11.

Dalit/black/women's question ever so precisely formulated? What would be the "modes of apartness" of Dalits, blacks, or women? Can the Dalit/black/women's question be posed as a question of emancipation/assimilation by a dominant discourse that already claims to accommodate or include them? To say nothing of the question, how can women – or for that matter assemblages like Dalits or African Americans – lay claim to the rights of separate nationhood (although, as we know, both Dalits and African Americans have done so at certain stages)?

Or again consider the argument that nationalism necessarily "unsettles" large numbers of people, rendering the minoritized populations potentially movable and leading in many cases to the uprooting of entire populations.[8] One might point out that the minoritization of Dalits, blacks, or women does *not* automatically render them movable. On the contrary, given the nervousness about losing their labor in many instances (in the American South in the early decades of the twentieth century, or in the sphere of domestic work much more pervasively), subordination and minoritization is often a way of *keeping them in their place* – in both senses of the term. On the other hand, the uprooting of populations (in the sense of settled social structures) may be precisely what a subaltern minority calls for in many circumstances.

I have made the point that the deployment of difference by the state and the dominant classes of the modern era becomes a way of legitimizing established prejudices and existing relations of power. What the disadvantaged, the marginalized, and the subordinated – women, blacks, Dalits, sexual minorities, conquered indigenous peoples, migrants, and dislocated populations – have done in more recent times is to utilize the very category of difference to demand a re-arrangement if not an overturning of prevailing structures of access and privilege. Thus they have challenged anew the hierarchical arrangements and underlying structures of belief that, for two hundred years and more, from at least the late eighteenth century, disadvantaged groups had struggled to overturn largely through striving for recognition as equals – the *same*.

In the nineteenth and twentieth centuries, many colonized peoples, organized women's groups, and others stressed their distinctiveness

---

[8] Ibid., 13.

Prejudice as Difference

and special circumstances as grounds for a demand for changes in social and political regulation and order. However, it was the rhetorical power of the discourse of equality that undergirded their claims. The history of such struggles in different parts of the world appeared as a history of sameness and the right to sameness: "one man, one vote," equal pay for equal work, the need to end inherited structures of discrimination and denial, and gain an "equal" share in public resources and state power. By the late twentieth century, however, the battle of many such opposition forces had been self-consciously extended to encompass another rhetoric and another demand: the demand for an acknowledgment of the vitality and productiveness of difference.

The force of the revised argument on difference grows out of an awareness not only that differences of gender, of communal practices and ways of being, even of incommensurable languages and beliefs have provided the grounds for the diversity, density, and richness of human experience. The altered stance follows from a recognition that difference, and the very deployment of ideas of difference, has been the grounds for claims of identity, unitariness, priority, and privilege. A great deal of feminist work has refused to accept any simple dichotomy between claims to equality and claims to difference and has argued instead that equality requires the recognition and inclusion of differences. "It is not our differences which separate women," as Audre Lorde put it, "but our reluctance to recognize those differences and to deal effectively with the distortions which have resulted from the ignoring and misnaming of those differences."[9]

Such oppositional scholarship calls for an interrogation of the ways in which the idea of difference is deployed and of the operations of categorical difference – an operation that of course marks out only particular differences as relevant to the making of our broader social and political arrangements.[10] It mounts a critique of a politics that insidiously privileges certain kinds of difference – as *not* different. It leads us to ask how discourses of dominance and subordination, normalcy and marginality, come to be constructed, and by that means to investigate the play of prejudice in these constructions.

---

[9] Audre Lorde, *Sister Outsider*, 122; see also 112 and passim.

[10] Joan W. Scott, "Deconstructing Equality-versus-Difference," *Feminist Studies*, 14, no. 1 (1988), passim.

40   *A History of Prejudice*

It may help at this point to underline the central proposition I have
been advancing so far. Social or cultural *difference* is not a given,
flowing from manifest deviance, a disordered or medicalized condition, or genetic inheritance. What the pronouncement of difference
signals, rather, is political position and political maneuver. By definition, one might say, the idea of difference is manifold and fluid, and
it is always strategically invoked and mobilized. Like the notion of
dominance and subordination, only perhaps more obviously so, the
idea of difference cannot be thought of, or organized, along a single
(say, cultural or biological) axis. Distributed along multiple grids, it
comes in innumerable forms, appearing differently in different places:
malleable, evolving elements and tendencies that come into view and
disappear, change, coalesce, and reappear, in other forms, amid other
networks, in other contexts.

The deployment of the idea by the subordinated and the marginalized in modern national societies is marked, in turn, by its own contradictoriness, its own presumptions, and its own blindnesses, as I hope to
show in the next two sections of this chapter, dealing with the politics
of identity and difference as these are elaborated in the Dalit struggle in India and the African American and women's movements in
the USA.

India's Dalits

The Dalits, or ex-Untouchable castes, of India – known at different stages as Untouchables, Outcastes, Depressed Castes, Harijans,
or Scheduled Castes (referring to the list or "schedule" of Untouchable castes drawn up for the Government of India Act of 1935 and
included, with modifications, in the Indian constitution of 1950) –
have been haunted by deep internal divisions, even as important sections among them have sought to fashion new community and solidarity in the context of the anticolonial and postcolonial struggles
for democracy and social justice. In the decades preceding the end of
British rule, as is well known, a number of Dalit leaders laid claim
to being a "statutory minority," a "separate element in the national
life," a "necessary party" to political negotiations regarding the country's future, a separate community, even a "nation," like the Muslims

Prejudice as Difference

and the Sikhs.[11] There were many different grounds on which such spokespersons advanced the claim for the identification of the Dalits as a significant minority or community, among them the shared experience or history of labor and exploitation, propositions about shared sentiment and suffering, and at the other extreme the very fact of statutory recognition.

The particular difficulty faced by Dr. B. R. Ambedkar, the preeminent Dalit leader of the twentieth century, and by other Dalit spokespersons, in making the claim that Dalits were a minority no different from Muslims, Sikhs, Christians, Anglo-Indians, and other such minorities was plain. The Shudras, Atishudras, Untouchables, Depressed Classes, Scheduled Castes, whatever the term used for the assemblage, gained their distinctiveness – at least until they became a legally recognized minority – precisely from the fact of their untouchability, that is, the discrimination they suffered at the hands of Hindu society. Gandhi was quick to point out the paradox inherent in the Dalit claim to existence as a separate minority. "We do not want on our register and on our census Untouchables classified as a separate class," he declared at the Round Table Conference in London in 1931. "Sikhs may remain as such in perpetuity, so may Muhammadans, so may Europeans. Will Untouchables remain Untouchables in perpetuity?"[12]

In this respect, the Dalits were caught in an extraordinary bind, being defined by Hindu society and at the same time part and not part of it. Although one might argue that, with all the particularities of its diverse manifestations, this is in fact the general condition of subalternity: that of *the insider/outsider* – refined in some cases (Jews, Muslims, Dalits, blacks?) to *the outsider within*.[13] Consider the ambivalence that appears in Ambedkar's presentation, as independent India's first law

---

[11] See, for example, Moon, *Ambedkar: Writings and Speeches*, vol. 9 (1991), 181, 190; vol. 17, pt. 3 (2003), 418; and vol. 1 (1982), 368; Eleanor Zelliot, *From Untouchable to Dalit: Essays on the Ambedkar Movement* (Delhi: Manohar Publications, 1996), 97; and Sekhar Bandhopadhyay, "Transfer of Power and the Crisis of Dalit Politics in India, 1945–47," *Modern Asian Studies*, 34, no. 4 (2000), 903, 906.

[12] Moon, *Ambedkar: Writings and Speeches*, vol. 9, 68.

[13] For one articulation of the argument in the African American case, see Patricia Hill Collins, *Black Feminist Thought: Knowledge, Consciousness, and the Politics of Empowerment* (New York: Routledge, 1991), 11 and passim.

42   *A History of Prejudice*

minister, of the case for the reform of the personal law of the Hindus. At one stage in the debate on the Hindu Code Bill, he referred to the Hindu shastras as "your shastras." To a member's interjection ("Your shastras?"), he responded by saying, "Yes, because I belong to the other caste"; and, a little later, "I am an unusual member of the Hindu community." At another point in the same debate, he spoke of "our ancient ideals which are to my judgement, most archaic and impossible for anybody to practice."[14]

There was clearly no easy escape from the aggrandizing character of "Hinduism," even for a leader who had declared fifteen years earlier: "I had the misfortune of being born with the stigma of [being] an Untouchable.... It is not my fault; but I will not die a Hindu, for this is in my power."[15] It is in this context that Ambedkar opens up the question of the meaning of so-called Hindu society or community, with a radical reinterpretation of the Indian past – and therefore of the needs of the Indian future. Ambedkar's recasting of Indian history as an extended and unfinished struggle between Brahmanism and Buddhism was a move of far-reaching implication. He was able to propose it, I submit, precisely because he spoke for a constituency very different from that claimed by the leaders of other "preexisting" (that is to say, on the face of it, already given and recognized) religious or racial minorities (or majorities).

Whereas the Congress's distribution of the divide between the nation/people's friends and enemies was into something called "India" and its "development," on the one side, and anyone who would partition the country or detract from its development, on the other, and the best known "minority" version of the recent history and current predicament of the subcontinent was the Muslim League's proposition of a federation of communities threatened by an arrogant and unduly fixed "majority," Ambedkar went further in his reexamination of how these putative communities and their claims on the land and the people came to be. "India is the land which has experienced class-consciousness, class struggle [in its most extreme form]," he wrote, "... the land where there has been fought a class war between Brahmans and Kshatriyas which lasted for several generations and

---

[14] Moon, *Ambedkar: Writings and Speeches*, vol. 14 (1995), 270–1 and 1162.
[15] Zelliot, *From Untouchable to Dalit*, 206.

Prejudice as Difference

which was fought so hard and with such virulence that it turned out to be a war of extermination."[16]

Ambedkar saw caste formation as a group or class formation. "The history of India before the Muslim invasions is the history of a mortal conflict between Brahmanism and Buddhism."[17] Inequality was the "official doctrine" of Brahmanism; Buddhism opposed it root and branch: witness the very different opportunities it offered to Shudras and to women.[18] India's Untouchable communities were originally Buddhist, Ambedkar wrote in his 1948 book entitled *The Untouchables*. They were thrust into the demeaning position of untouchability when they clung to Buddhism in the midst of a warrior and court-inspired resurgence of Brahmanical Hinduism: "broken men," who declined with Buddhism. "We can . . . say with some confidence that Untouchability was born some time about 400 A.D. It is born out of the struggle for supremacy between Buddhism and Brahmanism which has so completely molded the history of India."[19]

And yet the claim on a Buddhist past, and the 1956 conversion to Buddhism, were not primarily aimed at recovering some lost "original" history of the Dalits and providing "memory to a memoryless people," to use D. R. Nagaraj's evocative phrase, although that was certainly part of the object. Rather, the presentation of Indian history as the history of struggle between Brahmanism and Buddhism was, to restate an argument I have made elsewhere in characterizing the South Asian Subaltern Studies intervention in historiographical debate, to rethink the pattern of historical development as a whole, grasp the contradictions that lie at its heart, and outline political possibilities that have been suppressed or that remain to be elaborated.[20]

---

[16] Babsaheb Ambedkar, "India and the Pre-requisites of Communism," in *Dr. Babsaheb Ambedkar: Writings, Debates, Interviews, Handwriting, Photos, Voice, Video*, edited and compiled by Anand Teltumbde (Mumbai, 2004), 8.

[17] Babsaheb Ambedkar, "Revolution and Counter-revolution in Ancient India," in Teltumbde, *Ambedkar: Writings, Debates*, pt. II, 32.

[18] Babsaheb Ambedkar, "What Is Saddhamma?" in Moon, *Ambedkar: Writings and Speeches*, vol. 11 (1992), 302; and Ambedkar, "Revolution and Counter-revolution in Ancient India," pt. II, 57.

[19] B. R. Ambedkar, *The Untouchables: Who They Were and Why They Became Untouchables* (1948; reprint Shravasti: Bharatiya Bauddha Shiksha Parishad, 1977), 204.

[20] Introduction to Pandey, *Subaltern Citizens and Their Histories*, 3.

44   *A History of Prejudice*

The Dalit conversion, as Ambedkar's restatement of Buddhism showed very clearly, was to be a conversion for the future. Ambedkar's reinterpretation of Buddhism cast it as a "religion" for our times, an ethic that promoted rationality and scientific thinking, refused all superstition, and recognized the need for the state to promote social justice and human dignity, or in more familiar political terms, Liberty, Equality, and Fraternity – tenets derived not from the French Revolution, as he said repeatedly, but from the ancient moral insights contained in the teachings of "my Master, the Buddha."[21]

Investigators from the 1960s onward found that the most common argument given by Dalit converts in western India in favor of the Buddhist *dhamma* was an argument about universal human dignity, the opportunity to "live like a man," the restoration of self-respect, and an end to feelings of inferiority, all of which followed from the rejection of Hinduism and its caste hierarchy: with conversion "we became human beings."[22] "Gautama's *dhamma* is like no other," as an anonymous Dalit woman's song has it, "A man finds humanity there."[23]

Let me cite one recollection of a conversion ceremony to illustrate the point. This account of the embracing of the Buddhist *dhamma* in a remote Konkan village, a few months after Ambedkar's death in December 1956, comes from Urmila Pawar's recently published autobiography, *Aaydaan* (items made of bamboo, the weaving of which was the traditional occupation of the Mahar community in her

---

[21] For some important discussions of Ambedkar's reinterpretation of Buddhism, see Valerian Rodrigues, "Buddhism, Marxism and the Concept of Emancipation in Ambedkar," in *Dalit Movements and the Meaning of Labour in India*, ed. Peter Robb (Delhi: Oxford University Press, 1993), 299–338; Surendra Jondhale and Johannes Beltz, eds., *Reconstructing the World: B. R. Ambedkar and Buddhism in India* (Delhi: Oxford University Press, 2004); A. K. Narain and D. C. Ahir, eds., *Dr. Ambedkar, Buddhism and Social Change* (Delhi: B. R. Publishing Corporation, 1994); Debjani Ganguly, *Caste and Dalit Lifeworlds: Postcolonial Perspectives* (Delhi: Orient Longman, 2005), chap. 7; and Anupama Rao, *The Caste Question: Dalits and the Politics of Modern India* (Berkeley: University of California Press, 2009), especially chap. 3.

[22] E.g., studies by Eleanor Zelliot, Adele Fiske, and Surendra Jondhale, cited in John C. B. Webster, *Religion and Dalit Liberation: An Examination of Perspectives* (Delhi: Manohar Publications, 1999), 84, 88.

[23] Cited in Eleanor Zelliot, "New Voices of the Buddhists of India," in Narain and Ahir, *Ambedkar, Buddhism and Social Change*, 196. See also the poems by Daya Pawar and Namdeo Dhasal, and Zelliot's commentary on them, at 203.

region).[24] "Actually none of us understood very well what exactly conversion meant," writes Pawar, "nor did we know much about this man Ambedkar who advised us to convert." Yet the day of Babasaheb Ambedkar's passing came to be "indelibly printed" on her memory.

Pawar, who was 12 at the time, returned from school to discover family elders and neighbors weeping. One of them, who worked in another town, decided to take the overnight train to Mumbai to catch a last glimpse of Babasaheb's body. The atmosphere of mourning lasted for months, while information about Ambedkar's death, his struggle, and his wishes trickled in through Dalits working in various places outside the village. Sometime during this period, preparations for *dharmaantar* (conversion) began. The "conversion" itself was a dramatic moment. Something changed, Pawar recalls. Faith in evil spirits, possession, and "incidents of 'actual' experiences of ghosts" ended with conversion, and people like Urmila's mother, who had strongly believed in such things, seemed to take on a new life.

The *dharmaantar* ceremony took place on the grounds of Gogaté College in Ratnagiri, the nearest large town. Urmila and her siblings went with their mother and other people of the village. "People... poured in from everywhere," she writes. In the midst of various announcements, the mantra of "*Buddham sharanam gacchami*" ("I enter into the Buddha's protection") "floated down to us and we joined our voices with the chanting crowd."

After the ceremony, the villagers were told to discard the gods they worshipped and throw the idols into the water. Urmila half expected that her mother would refuse, given that theirs was a priest's family and that many of the family idols were rather valuable. Instead, her mother "picked up some idols and threw them... [away] herself." A Dalit elder placed a small statue of the Buddha and a photograph of Ambedkar in Urmila's mother's prayer room. People went from house to house every evening venerating the Buddha, recalls Pawar. "Their faces glowed. *You would think there was no longer any need to ask for happiness... as... [it] had automatically come to us*" (emphasis mine).

---

[24] Urmila Pawar, *Aaydaan* (Mumbai: Granthali, 2003), 90–3. I have relied on Maya Pandit's translation of these passages in Rege, *Writing Caste/Writing Gender*, 285–8, with minor additions and emendations in the light of the original Marathi.

46   *A History of Prejudice*

Other recollections of Dalit conversions to Buddhism in different villages and towns following Ambedkar's embracing of the *dhamma* in 1956 provide a similar sense of anticipation and of a political difference already at hand. In account after account, "conversion" appears as a magical time. "The diksha ceremony was carried out in a joyful atmosphere," writes Shantabai Krishnaji Kamble of the ceremony in her husband's village of Kargani in 1957. "The struggle yielded us three jewels –," writes another Dalit memoirist, Baby Kamble, "humanity, education and the religion of the Buddha.... The flame of Bhim started burning in our hearts. We began to walk and talk. We became conscious that we too are human beings."[25]

Without wishing to understate the power of the continuing divisions among the hundreds, if not thousands, of Dalit castes and subcastes, differentially arranged as they are in an unyielding caste hierarchy, or the force of gender, age, and class divisions even among the lowest castes in India, I am suggesting that the Dalit conversion is ideally aimed at inaugurating a new difference, signaled by a new body, a new community, and a new politics and culture. This is a point to which I shall return later in this chapter.

African Americans and African American Women

By contrast with the history of the Dalit struggle to forge a unified and recognizable Dalit community to establish its difference, the separate identity of the African American people and culture appears to have been in place from their arrival on American shores – or so the legend has it. The experience of slavery, the legal and social barriers against access to basic resources for people of African descent in much of the USA for much of its history, the visibility of skin color, and the discourse of nineteenth-century "science," "civilization," and "race", have served to establish this as common sense. Hence the force of Du Bois's moving statement of how the African American

ever feels his twoness – an American, a Negro, two souls...in one dark body, whose dogged strength alone keeps it from being torn asunder. The

---

[25] Rege, *Writing Caste/Writing Gender*, 187, for Shantabai quotation; and Baby Kamble, *The Prisons We Broke*, trans. from the Marathi by Maya Pandit (Chennai: Orient Longman, 2008), 122.

Prejudice as Difference

history of the American Negro is the history of this strife – this longing to attain self-conscious manhood, to merge his double self into a better and truer self.

The American Negro does not seek to "Africanize America," Du Bois goes on to say, "for America has too much to teach the world and Africa. He would not bleach his Negro soul in a flood of white Americanism, for he knows that Negro blood has a message for the world. He simply wishes to make it possible for a man to be both a Negro and an American."[26]

And yet, as we know, an African American character, culture, and politics has never been present so simply or in such an accessible form. The point is well illustrated by the uncertainty, ambiguity, and contradiction that attends the claim of African American identity and culture, given the diverse origins, multidirectional migrations, miscegenation, and geographical and social dispersal of the peoples involved[27] and again by the debate among black feminists in the United States over black women's primary political identity or commitment and the "community" they would (or could) speak for.

Important activists and writers engaged with the issue of how the struggles against racism and sexism in American society might be brought into alliance have adopted divergent positions on the question. For bell hooks, "racial imperialism," as she calls it, trumps "sexual imperialism" in U.S. history. "Racism took precedence over sexual alliances in both the white world's interaction with Native Americans and African Americans, just as racism overshadowed any bonding between black women and white women on the basis of sex."[28] Theoretically and in the law, white women may also have been the "property" of their men, she notes, yet they were not systematically subjected to the brutal oppression and dehumanization of the black slave. The attempt of some white feminists to suggest a similarity in

---

[26] Du Bois, *Souls of Black Folk*, 45.

[27] For the wider context, and a powerful critique of the common sense of black/white relations in America, see Jack D. Forbes, *Africans and Native Americans: The Language of Race and the Evolution of Red-Black Peoples* (Urbana: University of Illinois Press, 1993).

[28] bell hooks, *Ain't I a Woman: Black Women and Feminism* (Boston: South End Press, 1981), 122.

48 *A History of Prejudice*

the day-to-day experiences of white and black women only reveals a shocking insensitivity to the plight of the latter.

Other commentators have reiterated the argument. "In their poverty and vulnerability," writes Jacqueline Jones,

black people experienced...historical economic transformations in fundamentally different ways compared to whites regardless of class, and black women, while not removed from the larger history of the American working class, shouldered unique burdens at home and endured unique forms of discrimination in the workplace.[29]

Consequently, black women have remained single more often, borne more children, had the burden of heading single-parent families more frequently, remained in the labor market longer and in greater numbers, had less education, earned less, and been widowed earlier than their white counterparts.

In addition, as several scholars have noted, white women have widely served as agents of racism in the USA. As one middle-aged black woman domestic worker cited by Jones put it, "Black men will make a fool out of me if I let them, but it was a white woman who had me crawling around her apartment before I was thirteen years old, cleaning places she would never think of cleaning with a toothbrush and toothpick!"[30] hooks recalls that in the mid-nineteenth century Sojourner Truth had to bare her breasts to prove that she was a woman before she was allowed to speak at a political meeting, and this happened at an antislavery rally of white women and men. For whom, and on whose behalf, could the black woman (or man) speak when blacks were recognized only as "female" and "male," chattel and property by most of white America?[31]

Audre Lorde writes about differences among women that American feminists must reckon with: "Poor women and women of Color know there is a difference between the daily manifestations of marital slavery [on the one hand] and prostitution [on the other] because it is our daughters who line 42nd Street [shorthand for New York City's major

---

[29] Jacqueline Jones, *Labor of Love, Labor of Sorrow: Black Women, Work and the Family, from Slavery to the Present* (New York: Vintage Books, 1985), 9.

[30] Ibid., 316.

[31] hooks, *Ain't I a Woman*, 159.

Prejudice as Difference 49

theater and red-light district]." Lorraine Bethel states the position more polemically: "WHAT CHOU MEAN WE, WHITE GIRL?"[32]

The point is simple. Although the importance of the women's movement is self-evident, the category of "women" and "women's rights," in the United States as elsewhere, is constituted only by suspending other differences – between women of different races, for example.[33] Likewise, the category of "blacks" or "African Americans" works to a large extent by covering over a number of important differences within the black "community" – differences of color, and the advantages that pale skin and straight hair might bring, in addition to differences of gender, sexuality, age, class, and so on.

In the reconstruction of the history of the Black Freedom Struggle, Darlene Clark Hine observes, "Black women were conspicuous by their absence." She notes that, for some time even after she became a professor of history, she herself had not thought of black women "as historical subjects with their own relations to a state's history." It was an unwelcome invitation from a local schoolteacher and head of the Indiana unit of the National Council for Negro Women, Shirley Herd, which shamed Hine – as the only tenured black woman historian in the local university – into turning her attention to the history of black women in Indiana.[34]

As she began reading late nineteenth- and early twentieth-century autobiographies of "migrating, or fleeing, black women," it became clear, says Hine, that these women were sexual hostages and victims

---

[32] Lorde, *Sister Outsider*, 112; Bethel cited in hooks, *Ain't I a Woman*, 152. We should note of course that after the early work of hooks and Lorde, intersectionality has opened up another lens on these questions; see Kimberlé Crenshaw, "Mapping the Margins: Intersectionality, Identity Politics, and Violence against Women of Color," *Stanford Law Review* 43 (1991), 1241–99; Kimberlé Crenshaw, "Combahee River Collective Statement," in *The Second Wave: A Reader in Feminist Theory*, ed. Linda Nicholson (New York: Routledge, 1997), 63–70; and Elsa Barkeley Brown, "'What Has Happened Here': The Politics of Difference in Women's History and Feminist Politics," in Nicholson, *Second Wave*, 272–87.

[33] hooks observes that the common comparison of "women" and "blacks" in white feminist critiques of American history serves to exclude black women from consideration. Even feminists like Helen Hacker and Catherine Stimpson use "women" to refer to white women and "black" to refer to black men, she argues, and others ("including even some black people") make the same assumption; see hooks, *Ain't I a Woman*, 140.

[34] Darlene Clark Hine, *Hine Sight: Black Women and the Re-construction of American History* (New York: Carlson Publishing, 1994), xxiii.

of domestic violence throughout the United States. The relationship between black women and the larger society – white men and women and, to a lesser extent, black men – "has always been, and continues to be, adversarial," involving as it does a "multifaceted struggle to determine who would control black women's productive and reproductive capacities and their sexuality."[35]

Interestingly, Hine now began to divide her survey courses on modern African American history into four broad themes: the Civil War and Emancipation, the Great Migrations, the Civil Rights Movement, and the Changing Status of Black Women. The lack of fit between the first three and the last tells its own story.[36] In any event, investigations of the history of black women underscored for Hine the need for intersectional analysis, for "this particular group of Americans has always occupied the bottom rung of any racial, sexual, and class hierarchy." Three issues have been central in the history of the protest and migration of black women, she argues: the fact (and fear) of rape, domestic violence, and the desire to escape severe economic exploitation and deprivation. Among other oversights, historians and other social scientists have paid too little attention to the working-class status and economic condition of black women: "The fact is that the vast majority of black women have lived in overwhelming poverty, and a lack of attention to that fact has helped to foster erroneous impressions in the larger society of the mythical, heroic, transcendent black woman able to do the impossible, to make a way out of no way."[37]

With those cautionary observations in mind, let us mark the specific conjuncture, and the specific constructions of history and social relations, that produce Du Bois's "problem of the color line" as the central problem of the age and his articulation of the "striving in the souls of black folk" toward the "ideal of human brotherhood, gained through the unifying ideal of Race." Recall that this is at the very beginning of the twentieth century.[38] Du Bois follows the preceding statement with the stirring lines:

---

[35] Ibid., 41.

[36] "The fourth theme has been problematic," writes Hine somewhat problematically; ibid., 51.

[37] Ibid., 38, 51, 52.

[38] Italy and Germany had been unified, Japanese nationalism was on the rise, a regime of Poor Laws (to protect all the nation's people) was well established in Britain and

Prejudice as Difference 51

[T]here are today no truer exponents of the pure spirit of the Declaration of Independence than the American Negroes; there is no true American music but the wild sweet melodies of the Negro slave; the American fairy tales and folklore are Indian and African; and, all in all, we black men seem the sole oasis of simple faith and reverence in a dusty desert of dollars and smartness.[39]

Here, race and culture emerge in a somewhat essentialist form as the unifying principles in the history of African Americans and their struggle for human dignity, attributes almost inherent in the genes – and in "the souls" of black folk. At a later stage in his career, when he was strongly influenced by Marxism, Du Bois would have shrunk from many aspects of the preceding formulation. The claims vary. Yet the subaltern assertion of difference – a claim to difference and sameness (a *different* sameness?) at one and the same time – has also commonly been a claim to an already existing subaltern unity and solidarity, although a great deal of the historical evidence points to the need to forge this unity and solidarity in the very course of struggle.

The Struggle for Identity

I want to return at this point to the history of the Dalit "conversion" to Buddhism, for Ambedkar's reflections on this long, drawn-out event help to clarify something about the manner of the establishment of political (or for that matter religious) community and difference. Increasingly from the 1930s, Ambedkar and a number of other Dalit leaders had begun to advocate the renouncement of Hinduism as a means of solving "the problem of the Untouchables." Gandhi, dedicated in his own way to the abolition of Untouchability, differed. What was needed, he argued, was the reform of Hinduism, or "self-purification." Conversion was not the answer. One cannot change one's religion as if it were a house or a cloak, Gandhi wrote. For him, the threat of Dalit conversion flowed from a political rather than a religious impulse.[40]

---

elsewhere, and even as European (and American) imperialism extended its sway in Africa and Asia, the idea of the self-determination of nations was gaining ground.

[39] Du Bois, *Souls of Black Folk*, 52.

[40] D. G. Tendulkar, *Mahatma: Life of Mohandas Karamchand Gandhi*, vol. 4 (New Delhi: Publications Division, Ministry of Information and Broadcasting, Government of India, 1960), 41.

Ambedkar's rejoinder to this is important for my purposes. Apart from making a pointed comment on precisely the political character of much of the religious history of the world, and of much that counted as conversion, he met Gandhi's house-and-cloak metaphor with an equally polemical but telling response. Religion today was like a piece of ancestral property, he noted, passed on from parent to child and accepted unthinkingly. "What genuineness is there in such [religious belief]?"[41] "The conversion of the Untouchables if it did take place," he wrote, after a Dalit conference in Bombay that considered the question in May 1936, "would take [place] after full deliberation of the value of religion and the virtue of different religions.... It would be the first case in history of genuine conversion."[42]

The Dalit leader here points to the long process of thinking and deliberation, both social and individual, that must accompany a Dalit conversion. It is the *process*, the epistemic effort, that counts, he might have added, for Ambedkar's "first case... of genuine conversion" might also be seen as a *first step* in the making of a *difference* – which would be a *political* difference, whatever else it was.

The articulation of a similar political difference is evident in Du Bois's *Souls of Black Folk*, too. Du Bois writes of the "little community" in the hills of Tennessee where he taught school for two summers in the 1880s, a community built around figures like the 20-year-old Josie, who worked day and night – at service (in white people's homes), in her own home, in the fields and orchards – and her mother, who talked of the sewing machine Josie had bought to supplement the family income, of how Josie longed to go to school but they never had the savings to allow it, how the crops failed, and how "mean" some white folks were. "I have called my tiny community a world," writes Du Bois:

and so its isolation made it. *There was among us but a half-awakened common consciousness, sprung from common joy and grief...; from a common hardship in poverty...; and, above all, from the sight of the Veil that hung between us and Opportunity.* All this caused us to think some thoughts together; but these, when ripe for speech, were spoken in various languages.[43]

---

[41] Moon, *Ambedkar: Writings and Speeches*, vol. 5 (1989), 404.
[42] Ibid., 404–5.
[43] Du Bois, *Souls of Black Folk*, 102–3, repeated sixty years later in W. E. B. Du Bois, *The Autobiography of W. E. B. Du Bois* (New York: International Publishers, 1968), 120 (emphasis mine).

For the blacks and the Dalits, as for many other subalternized minorities – the internally colonized, who do not inhabit a geopolitical space that provides easy grounds for a politics of separatism or of independent nationhood (and I would include women here) – it has never been a straightforward task to mark out a sequestered domain of an autonomous "culture." The claim of a unified and alternative culture and tradition is established here, if it is established, only through long and hard struggle. Witness the strong arguments for and against claiming a distinct culture of "womankind" in the early stages of the women's movement.

It is at the level of the everyday that the larger structures of prejudice are challenged – and reproduced. At this level, and among subaltern groups generally, "culture" and "tradition" are more deliberately forged, and far more openly contested, than the cultural claims of more privileged assemblages with rather more secure cultural institutions (and funding) and greater access to political power. And the politics that accompany their construction are never quite so easily wished away.

There are unexpected sites of struggle. The socially and culturally marked body becomes the most common sign of the difference, the otherness and lowly position of the subaltern. The black man "cannot escape his body" – the "slow composition of my *self* as a body," as Fanon puts it. A small white boy expresses fear at the mere sight of that body: "Mama, see the Negro! I'm frightened!" In the train, notes Fanon, the black man is given "not one but two, three places." His body is returned to him "sprawled out, distorted, recolored, clad in mourning."[44] The body, and the embodied difference of the Dalit/black/woman, comes to stand in for the cultural difference of classic minorities like the Jews and the Muslims, although of course the supposed deviance of the latter has its bodily markers, too. Consequently, the struggle of the Dalit/black/woman against these arguments – of preordained, or long-established, humors, dispositions, and disabilities – must necessarily take on the task of rescripting the subaltern body.

In the event, the subaltern finds resources in her experience and her body, even the body as it is ground down. Du Bois's first encounter

---

[44] Frantz Fanon, *Black Skin, White Masks*, trans. Charles Lam Markmann (1952; reprint London: Pluto Press, 2008), 47, 83, 84, 86 (emphasis original).

54   *A History of Prejudice*

with prayer in the southern black church illustrates the proposition very well:

A sort of suppressed terror hung in the air and seemed to seize them. . . . The black and massive form of the preacher swayed and quivered as the words crowded to his lips and flew at us in singular eloquence. The people moaned and fluttered, and then the gaunt-cheeked woman beside me suddenly leapt straight into the air and shrieked like a lost soul, while round about came wail and groan and outcry, and a scene of human passion such as I had never conceived before.[45]

Viola Andrews, a poor black woman from rural Georgia about whom I write in a later chapter of this book, provides another indication of the power of traditional resources. "The white man could not loose [lose]," she says in her unpublished autobiographical writings, "The colored man could not win." Most blacks in the early twentieth-century American South lived on plantations, chopped and hoed cotton, and worked "from can't to can't" (cannot see before day to cannot see after dark). "They *never* had enough" (emphasis original).[46]

However, although southern blacks had no wealth or social privilege, they had music. "That's one thing the colored folks had: they had a song. There is something about Singing, one can survive if they have a Song." So, Viola tells us, barefoot, working in the fields, or walking to church, the black folk sang:

"*Go down Moses: way down in Egypt land: Tell old pharaoh: let my people go.*"

or "*I'm so glad: trouble don't last always.*"

or "*I got shoes, you got shoes, all God's Chillins [children] got shoes.*"

"Mentally," she observes, "they dipped into the far future – into eternity: . . . when God will vindicate his own."

Her "greatest Blessing," Viola writes, "was finding and knowing God when I was young." At Easter in 1961, she heard on the radio, "He arose, He arose and he arose from the Dead." And "I believed it. . . . Yes I believed in the God of the Bible and I trusted in him."[47] As a

---

[45] Du Bois, *Autobiography*, 120.
[46] Emory University Manuscripts and Rare Book Library, Viola Andrews collection, Mss 813, Box 17, FF 7 and 8; and Box 21, FF 8, for this and the next paragraph.
[47] Andrews collection, Box 18, FF 3.

child, she recalls, she sometimes thought that there were two Gods, two Heavens, one for the colored, one for the white. In general, however, she was skeptical about the white folks' religion. "The colored had no faith in thier [the white folks'] Christianity." Would blacks and whites be separated in heaven, someone in the African American community occasionally asked. The answer was "No." There would be no white people there since it says in the Bible, "Treat *every* man as a Brother" (Viola underscores "every" with a double line). On Sundays, passing by the white folks' church, where services began earlier than in the black churches, blacks sometimes heard them sing, "Will there be any stars in my crown?" The blacks often answered in song: "No not one, No not one."[48]

In the course of such struggles, subaltern groups have also appropriated weapons from the discourse of the dominant, from republican constitutions and universal declarations of human rights. Hence, we get the language of nationhood and of minority rights in much of the Dalit and African American politics of the twentieth century, as Dalit and African American thinkers explore and rewrite the history of labor and exploitation; the oppressions of caste and race, quite aside from the matter of economic production and distribution; the subordination and confinement of women; the challenges and prospects of different religious as well as political ideals and practices. This critical work underlines the process of the creation of specific historical confinements and oppressions, along with the accompanying ideologies and promises, identifications and ideals.

The body of the subaltern comes to be scripted in a new way in the articulation of a new "identity." Recall Baby Kamble's comment on how the Dalit struggle "yielded us three jewels – humanity, education and the religion of the Buddha. . . . The flame of Bhim started burning in our hearts. We began to walk and talk. We became conscious that we . . . are human beings."[49] "Yielded" is an important word, and it applies to the "us" in this statement, the Dalits, as well as to humanity, education, and religion. The struggle *yielded up* the Dalit community, a Dalit politics, and the outlines of a Dalit future, not in the sense of an already existing community coming to consciousness of itself but

---

[48] Andrews collection, Box 17, FF 7; also FF 8, 9, 10, 12.
[49] Baby Kamble, *Prisons We Broke*, 122.

of historical conditions and political practice producing new senses of community and difference. It is perhaps necessary to stress that the same kind of historical process is at work in the case of Jews/Muslims as well, even if that is not how it has been presented.

Difference – and Otherness

Let me sum up the argument I have been making in the preceding pages. The deployment of ideas of identity and difference, mainstream and minority, the nation and its Other, signals above all, and fundamentally, a claim to power. In the hands of dominant groups and classes, the move follows from a belief in enduring hierarchies based on natural or (in its most generous construction) historically very deep-rooted distinctions in the qualities and abilities attributed to discrete populations. In the rise of insurrectionary movements mounted by long-subordinated or marginalized sections of society, it more clearly indexes a history and politics of a becoming, and with that the search for an alternative ethics – of self in relation to others – a position from which to act without fear, to demand one's rights, to live.

In the case of dominant as well as oppositional discourses, the proclamation of difference (in the former case, usually also a declaration of otherness) flows from a certain political position and perspective. Plainly, the difference articulated in the Dalit, black, or women's movement is not that of an already available culture or identity – the culture or identity of women, ex-Untouchables, or people of African descent. What is involved rather is the *enunciation* of difference, as Homi Bhabha has it, "a process of signification through which statements of culture or on culture differentiate, discriminate and authorize the production of fields of force, reference, applicability and capacity."[50] The facet of resistance, the "foreign accent" and "respectful distance,"[51] found here is not the resistance of another culture. It is instead the resistance of a different politics, the call for a differently imagined future.

---

[50] Homi K. Bhabha, *The Location of Culture* (London: Routledge, 1994), 34.
[51] Cf. Doris Sommer, "Resisting the Heat: Menchu, Morrison, and Incompetent Readers," in *Cultures of United States Imperialism*, ed. Amy Kaplan and Donald E. Pease (Durham, NC: Duke University Press, 1993), 407–32.

Prejudice as Difference

The point is demonstrated again, if further demonstration is needed, in the very history of subordinated or marginalized groups naming a social assemblage as Dalit, black, African American, *adivasi*, aboriginal, First Nation, gay, lesbian (not to mention LGBTQ), and for that matter even women. The distance traveled in the quest for self-definition and self-respect by Dalits as well as African Americans is indicated in the changing names given to these assemblages or adopted by their spokespersons:

Negro → colored → black → Afro-American → African American → people of color → ___, in one case;

outcastes → pariahs → Untouchables → depressed classes → Harijans → Scheduled Castes → Dalits → ___, in the other.

In the latter case, Harijans, or "children of god," Gandhi's appellation for the untouchable castes, is now angrily rejected by Dalit militants as patronizing and vapid: "If we are children of god, whose children are you?" some of them have asked sarcastically. Scheduled Castes is still commonly used, even by Dalit professionals and political leaders. However, Dalit is the preferred term of self-description among Dalit activists today. Defined in the dictionary as crushed, broken, or downtrodden, it has since its use by the militant Dalit Panther movement in the 1970s become a term of self-assertion, reclaiming a millennial history of exploitation and humiliation and of resistance to it.

It is this ever-unfolding politics of becoming, this shifting, unpredictable struggle over inherited beliefs and practices and their underlying justifications, that makes the question of sameness and difference, self and Other, such a difficult and important one to track. Indeed, as I have suggested, the politics of becoming, the malleability of social networks and solidarities, and the internal contradictions of claimed community are downplayed by subaltern movements themselves.

While subaltern discourses on "conversion" (or liberation), such as that of the Dalits, regularly foreground the need for greater access and opportunity in the face of discrimination and oppression, and speak as well at times of the need to convert the oppressor in the course of converting the self, the "converted" self, the fullness of the new Dalit or black citizen, is often taken rather for granted – as if the self, the community, the Dalit or black already exists in her/his/its unity and integrity. The evidence to the contrary is of course substantial. For just one illustration, let me return to an autobiographical account I cited earlier in connection with the Mahar (Dalit) community's struggle for dignity and self-respect in central India in the mid-twentieth century, a memoir that graphically describes the village Others' (the Mahars') production of their own Others.

> The other world had bound us with chains of slavery. But we too were human beings. And we too desired to dominate, to wield power.... So we made our own arrangements to find slaves – our very own daughters-in-law!... Young girls, hardly eight or nine or ten years old, were brought home as daughters-in-law. Girls, even younger, were married off.... For the girl, marriage meant nothing but calamity.[52]

Baby Kamble's critique of the treatment meted out to daughters-in-law by community elders is detailed and insistent. The daughter-in-law of the better-off Mahar households "was kept busy all twenty-four hours of the day." The men sometimes brought in loads of meat, which had to be preserved. More often than not, this arduous task was assigned to the daughter-in-law, often no more than a child. Even at other times, she suggests, the child (bride) was continually harassed: wakened before dawn, set to grinding grains for flour, off to the river to fetch water once the grinding was done, returning to cook *bhakris* (local flattened bread). If any of this was done unsatisfactorily, the mother, sisters, and even brothers-in-law "slap[ped] the girl on the face..., pinch[ed] her cheeks, and shower[ed] a million abuses on her.... The poor girl had to endure the abuses of everybody in the household."[53]

The author notes that even when the influence of the Ambedkar movement spread strongly among the Mahars, and both her brother and her father could think of little else, her father forbade her mother from stepping outside their home. She writes of the "terrible thrashing" that her mother got as "almost a daily routine" because she protested against such confinement.[54] Husbands beat their wives severely on the slightest suspicion, she observes at several points in the memoir.

Notwithstanding such evidence of internal hierarchy and repression, propositions of a seamless unity, and of the need to maintain

---

[52] Kamble, *Prisons We Broke*, 87, 93.
[53] Ibid., 73–4, 94–5.
[54] Ibid., 107; cf. 97.

solidarity against all comers appear commonly in the militant discourse of insurrectionary subaltern movements. Sometimes the proposition is advanced by moving in an apparently reverse direction – and marking the oneness, and indivisibility, of the oppressive Other. Eric Goldstein cites an arresting example from Harlem, New York, in 1995 in his book on Jews, race, and American national identity.[55]

The violent attack and torching of a building in which eleven people were killed arose out of the attempt of a Jewish store owner, Fred Harari, to evict a black subtenant for business activities that he had presumably not permitted. Harari's employees included whites, blacks, Puerto Ricans, and Guyanese. In spite of knowledge of this complex racial mix, the African American attackers described the trader as "a white intruder" and "usurper" of black economic opportunities in the predominantly black business district. Even after the tragic fallout and the deaths of eleven employees and residents, their supporters continued to present the incident as an instance of black-white conflict, "a characterization that allowed them to view it with a certain moral clarity." For many blacks, concludes Goldstein, "the black-white divide is the inviolable boundary that separates the privileged from the oppressed."[56]

The upper-caste/lower-caste divide is presented in parallel black and white terms by many Dalits and Dalit spokespersons in India. A very good illustration is found in a well-known polemical treatise entitled *Why I Am Not a Hindu*, by the Dalitbahujan intellectual Kancha Ilaiah. Writing of his childhood, Ilaiah emphasizes the aspect of autonomous caste existence in his native Andhra Pradesh: "My parents had only one identity and that was their caste: they were Kurumaas.... My playmates, friends, and of course relatives, all belonged to the Kurumaa caste. Occasionally the friendship circle extended to Goudaa boys and Kaapu boys...friends because we were all part of the cattle-breeding youth." At the same time, however, he refers to the Dalits (or, more expansively, the Dalitbahujans, comprising

---

[55] Eric L. Goldstein, *The Price of Whiteness: Jews, Race, and American Identity* (Princeton, NJ: Princeton University Press, 2006), 221–2.

[56] Ibid., 222, 223. Compare the Nation of Islam's regular characterization of an undifferentiated white people as "devils" or "a devil race" of "bleached-out white people," neatly summarized in Nell Irvin Painter, *The History of White People* (New York: W. W. Norton and Co., 2010), 375.

60   *A History of Prejudice*

ex-Untouchable as well as other lower-caste laboring and artisanal groups) as a unit, as against that of the "Hindus":

> I, indeed not only I, but all of us, the Dalitbahujans of India, ha[d] never heard the word "Hindu" – not as a word, nor as the name of a culture, nor as the name of a religion in our early childhood days. We heard about *Turukoollu* [Turks, or Muslims], we heard about *Kirastaanapoollu* (Christians), we heard about *Bapanoollu* (Brahmins) and *Koomatoollu* (Baniyas) [or merchants] spoken of as people who were different from us.

With the Brahmans and the Baniyas, he writes, "we had no relations, whatsoever": no common religious or cultural festivals, no shared activities of labor or education.[57] Hence, implicitly, we have Dalits (Dalitbahujans) on the one hand, Brahmans and Baniyas (Hindus) on the other: a collective self against a collective Other. Recall again in this context the comment that the African American teachers made to Alice Walker, "How can we be prejudiced against ourselves; we are all of one race," or Du Bois's lament about the inescapable "twoness" of blacks in North America: "an American, a Negro, two souls... in one dark body."

Arguments of this kind go against the grain of what one might call a world-transforming vision, of the struggle to forge new communities and new social arrangements out of the multiplicity and contradictoriness of human interactions and inconsistencies, ambitions and foibles, in the past and the present. And they have held back such movements from squarely facing up to internal divisions within the constituencies invested in a new democratic future (Dalit, African American, or other) and confronting the problem of prejudice, discrimination, and lack of privilege *within* these putative communities. These are questions that I turn to directly in the second half of this study, but it is necessary to bear them in mind as we consider the Dalit and African American arguments for self-respect and citizenship at the "new dawn" of Indian independence and American civil rights, which I examine in Chapters 3 and 4.

---

[57] Kancha Ilaiah, *Why I Am Not a Hindu: A Sudra Critique of Hindutva Philosophy, Culture and Political Economy* (Calcutta: Samya, 1996), xi, 1, 2 and passim.

3

Dalit Conversion

The Assertion of Sameness

The term "Dalit conversion" refers at first glance, and in its most common usage, to the mass conversion of Dalits to Buddhism in 1956 and afterward, which I mentioned in Chapter 2, as well as to Islam, Christianity, and other religions at various other times both before and after 1956. I use it, however, to describe a number of different dimensions of the Dalit struggle for self-definition and the redefinition of society, for the conversion represents a remarkable attempt to escape from centuries of stigmatization and oppression. The struggle occurred on many fronts in the mid- and late twentieth century, extending far beyond the realm of religious practice and the attendant social prejudices.

I use Dalit conversion, for one thing, to refer to the Dalit entrance into formal citizenship. That step is marked by the abolition of Untouchability in the Indian constitution of 1950, the institution of universal adult franchise, the extension of key legal and political rights to all sections of the Indian population, and the introduction of statutory safeguards and support for specially disadvantaged groups (in the form of "reservations" or reserved quotas in education and a number of public services), with all the consequences this has had for Indian society and politics. I use it also to register a more diffuse, but perhaps no less significant, aspect of the Dalit objective, which may be described loosely as a conversion to the modern, a condition signified by a discourse of individual rights, self-making, science, urbanity, and a democratic public sphere.[1] These are clearly ongoing processes. Indeed, as I have already suggested, one might argue that the most noteworthy feature of the Dalit conversion is that it is a conversion *for the future* to a large extent *in the future* and involving ideally the conversion of all humanity, Dalit and non-Dalit, with the non-Dalit also being recast in that future in a new Dalit mold.

In proposing such a universalist scale for the making of a new citizen and a new consciousness, Dalit and non-Dalit, it is important to consider carefully which commonalities and histories the insurgent discourse privileges and which it denies. What is it that the Dalit (and non-Dalit) need to be converted out of? What practices are they allowed to retain as part of a distinct heritage, or simply as "internal," "customary" matters? In identifying the priorities of the movement, or what used to be called the principal contradiction, what are the contradictions, hierarchies, and privileges that the new Dalit discourse treats as secondary, relatively inconsequential, or even *trivial* (a word that I shall return to later in this analysis)? What does it elide, through the very rhetoric of the *new* citizen that it employs, or through arguments about the needs of this particular historical juncture? This chapter and those that follow attempt to provide a few tentative answers to these questions.

The Double Bind of the Internally Colonized

The question of the Dalit conversion, in the wider sense in which I have used the term, is linked in the India of the 1940s and '50s to the question of decolonization, which in turn is tied up with the real or perceived threat of persistent internal colonialism(s). The matter of internal colonialism was raised directly or indirectly by numerous Dalits, as well as by Muslims and others, in the India of the 1940s and afterward. The charge is not advanced commonly

---

[1] The concept of Dalit liberation (what I am calling conversion) is based to a significant extent, writes Timothy Fitzgerald, on an appeal to "the ethical autonomy of individuals and their ability to transform themselves and their society through collective political action." See Timothy Fitzgerald, "Analysing Sects, Minorities, and Social Movements in India: The Case of Ambedkar Buddhism and Dalit(s)," in Jondhale and Beltz, *Reconstructing the World*, 277. See also Christopher S. Queen, "Ambedkar, Modernity, and the Hermeneutics of Buddhist Liberation," in Narain and Ahir, *Dr. Ambedkar, Buddhism and Social Change*, 99 and passim.

Dalit Conversion

now,[2] but the argument underlying it remains important and provides, in my opinion, one of the more significant frames for a discussion of the Dalit struggle from Indian Independence in 1947 to today.

As indicated in Chapter 1, in the Dalit case, as in that of the Indian Muslims, we are dealing with a population that is widely distributed over a national territory and with disadvantaged communities that have come over time to some kind of mutual accommodation with more privileged, numerous, and powerful groups, although the results are still markedly hierarchical. The political question at issue is what happens to the minority, to Muslims or Dalits in India (or to African Americans or Native Americans in the United States), if the "majority" gains an apparently unfettered right to rule over the minorities and a sense of colonialism persists even after the establishment of formal democracy. The difficulty faced by the "colonized" in this situation is clear, although it has not been widely discussed or theorized. The problem with this kind of internal colonialism is that the colonized cannot escape from the given physical, economic, or even cultural realm. They have no independent territory of their own: they cannot emigrate, and they cannot send the colonizers home. What is more, in some cases they cannot easily lay claim to an independent history and culture – indeed they gain their identity at least in part by their incorporation into the dominant culture or society: African-*Americans*, *Indian* Muslims, Untouchable (Dalit) *Hindus*.

What makes the Dalit example particularly paradoxical is not only the historical location of Dalit groups and individuals on the boundaries of Hindu society – not apart from it, but not quite part of it either – but their identification as Dalits precisely because of that stigmatized marginality. For the Dalit leadership, the first challenge was to have the Dalits accepted as a minority. In the process, the aporia of internal colonialism was further compounded by the need to underline a historically inherited subalternity, for it was precisely their Untouchability within Hindu society that Dalit leaders had to assert in order to try and gain recognition as a "minority," with the safeguards and rights

---

[2] By contrast, of course, the charge of internal colonialism – or outright colonialism – continues to be made by various political leaders and movements in relation to a number of regional nationalities on the northern and northeastern borders of the territory of the Indian state, in Kashmir and the states and territories of the northeast.

64 *A History of Prejudice*

appropriate to a minority in a democratic republic. Moreover, once the principle of affirmative action (through reserved quotas in educational institutions and public services) had been accepted to give the disadvantaged and "backward" classes a fairer chance in the life of the republic, this minority status as an Untouchable community was what Ambedkar and others had to fight to preserve, even after the formal conversion of particular Dalit groups to Buddhism, Christianity, or other religions. Hence Ambedkar's comment in the course of a speech after his initiation into the Buddhist *dhamma* on October 14, 1956 – "Even after conversion to Buddhism, I am confident, I [or "we," the Dalit community] will get the political rights"[3] – and the demands made in recent years by groups of Christian and Muslim Dalits for an extension of the benefits of reserved quotas to them.

Whether the Dalits were Hindus or not became the subject of lengthy and heated controversy in the late nineteenth and early twentieth centuries. As the colonial state's codification and classification of "customary" divisions and practices developed, and the question of numbers gained importance, Hindu leaders and reformers grew active in the effort to "reclaim" the Dalits and "reeducate" them in their identity as Hindus. The assertion of community identity gathered pace at many levels – Hindu, Muslim, Sikh, Nadar, Patidar, Namasudra, Bihari, Oriya, Telugu – and economic and political competition between (and within) these groups acquired a new edge. In this context, militant Hindu leaders and organizations initiated a variety of moves to consolidate the Hindu community.

Among these was the *shuddhi* ("purification") campaign, which had gained significant support among reformist Hindus by the early decades of the twentieth century. *Shuddhi* was a direct rejoinder to Christian missionary attacks on Hinduism and their efforts at converting low- and, to a lesser extent, high-caste Hindus in the nineteenth century. In response, the reformist Arya Samaj movement cast itself, against the grain of orthodox Hindu practice, in the mold of a proselytizing Christian sect. As one of its leaders, Lala Lajpat Rai, put it, "the Arya Samaj, being a Vedic *church*, and as such a Hindu organization, engages itself in reclaiming the *wandering sheep who have*

---

[3] Moon, *Ambedkar: Writings and Speeches*, vol. 17, pt. III, 536.

Dalit Conversion

strayed from the Hindu fold, and converts anyone prepared to accept its religious teachings."[4]

Historians have commented on the impact of the so-called Gait Circular, which directed that separate tables be drawn up in the 1911 census for groups – like the Untouchables and many tribal communities – who were not unambiguously Hindu. The circular "proved a good tonic for the apathy of orthodox Kashi," Lajpat Rai wrote:

One fine morning the learned pandits... rose to learn that their orthodoxy stood the chance of losing the allegiance of 6 crores of human beings who, the Government and its advisers were told, were not Hindus, in so far as other Hindus would not acknowledge them as such, and would not even touch them.... The possibility of losing the untouchables has shaken the intellectual section of the Hindu community to its very depths.[5]

Over the same period, from the later nineteenth century on, many Hindu reformers spoke out against "perverse" Hindu religious notions and practices, "silly" "anti-national" distinctions of caste, restrictions on interdining and travel overseas that were until that time fairly strictly observed, as well as ideas of pollution and the consequent difficulty of reconversion, which ensured that "millions of forcibly converted Hindus have remained Muslims even to this day."[6] Yet the matter was not so easily settled, for, given the inherited Hindu traditions, the organization of different classes and vocational groups into distinct castes, and the overriding concern with issues of purity and pollution, all the indications were that the Dalits would have to remain very *lowly* Hindus – a minority that could not be made part of the majority but that the majority would not treat as a minority either.

The Dalits themselves had an ambivalent, fragmentary relationship with this majority. Were particular Dalit groups Hindu, non-Hindu, animist, or something else altogether? The politics of colonial and postcolonial India gave the subordinated and the marginalized a new opportunity to challenge the inherited structures and relations of power

---

[4] Lajpat Rai, *A History of the Arya Samaj* (Delhi, 1915; reprint Bombay: Orient Longman, 1967), 120 (emphasis added).

[5] Ibid., 124–5.

[6] V. D. Savarkar, *Six Glorious Epochs of Indian History*, trans. S. T. Godbole (New Delhi: Bal Savarkar Rajdhani Granthagar, 1971; reprint 1980), 154–7, 188, 192–3, and passim.

amid which they lived. As the religious communities of the subcontinent went about "purifying" and reconstituting themselves, and as urbanization and migration, educational opportunities, and political consciousness grew, numerous Dalits responded with questions about existing social and political arrangements and demanded greater access to the resources of the modern society and state. Census operations became one of the major sites for an extended contest over status and inherited rights, with attempts by lower-caste groups to rename and redefine themselves and their histories.[7] Another part of this effort, which I referred to earlier, was the attempt by Dalit leaders to redefine the Dalits as a historically distinct community – or minority.

The point about this claim to minority status for the Dalits was to seek safeguards – such as separate electorates and the reservation of seats in legislative bodies and public services – of the kind that had been granted to other minority communities in the early twentieth century. As is well known, Ambedkar and Gandhi disagreed sharply on the matter of separate representation for Dalits. The differences between them reached a climax in 1932, when the British government announced a Communal Award that included the grant of separate electorates to Untouchables in the areas of their greatest concentrations. This award followed negotiations that had stalled – most evidently on the issue of separate electorates for Untouchables – at the Round Table Conferences held in London to work out the details of a revised framework for the continued government of India under British control.

Gandhi, and others in the Congress, saw the grant of separate electorates – and the earlier demand for it by Dalit leaders – as a way of splitting and therefore weakening the Hindu community, a development that would only compound what the British had already accomplished through their institution of separate electorates for Muslims. Ambedkar, by contrast, saw separate electorates as an essential lever in the struggle to advance the downtrodden castes. He was forced to concede in 1932, unable to resist the pressure brought to bear on him

---

[7] See, for example, Mark Juergensmeyer, *Religion as Social Vision: The Movement Against Untouchability in 20th Century Punjab* (Berkeley: University of California Press, 1981); Vijay Prashad, *Untouchable Freedom: A Social History of a Dalit Community* (New Delhi: Oxford University Press, 1999); Dube, *Untouchable Pasts*; and my discussion in Gyanendra Pandey, *Routine Violence: Nations, Fragments, Histories* (Stanford, CA: Stanford University Press, 2006), chap. 7.

Dalit Conversion

by the fast unto death that Gandhi launched against this extension of separate electorates. But the way in which the conflict played out left him deeply embittered, and he seems never to have forgiven Gandhi and the Congress for what he saw as their betrayal.[8]

The issues involved in the clash between Ambedkar and Gandhi were brought into even sharper focus with the acquisition of citizenship by all the inhabitants of the country, and the statutory abolition of Untouchability in the 1950s. At one level, what was at stake in the Dalit struggle before and after Independence was the question of differential access to the state and its resources. Equally at issue, however, was a question of pride and human dignity, the question precisely of being *equal citizens* in a modern, democratic society. What this required was a restructuring of Indian, especially Hindu, society from top to bottom.

Converting the Converter

Consistently through the 1940s and '50s, Ambedkar and other Dalit leaders and activists called for a transformation of Hindu practices. In the context of claims to establish the new democratic society, they put forward the demand that the judges first judge themselves, the converters look to their own conversion. "Those who want to conserve must be ready to repair," Ambedkar said during the debate on the Hindu Code Bill. "If you want to maintain the Hindu system, the Hindu culture, the Hindu society, do not hesitate to repair where repair is necessary." Hindus were the "sick men" of India, he wrote on another occasion, in 1944. It was necessary to generate a new life in Hinduism. For this the Hindus could draw on principles found in their own ancient sources.[9] And the surest means of assuring progress and the greatness of the country, and of the wider world, was to embrace the faith of the Buddha and its fundamental principles – Liberty, Equality, and Fraternity.

Inequality was the "official doctrine" of Brahmanism, Ambedkar declared; Buddhism opposed it root and branch.

---

[8] See Ambedkar's writings of the 1940s, especially B. R. Ambedkar, *What Congress and Gandhi Have Done to the Untouchables* (Bombay: Thacker, 1945).

[9] Moon, *Ambedkar: Writings and Speeches*, vol. 14, pt. I, 283; vol. 1, 26, 77–8.

68   *A History of Prejudice*

The Shudra could never aspire to be a Brahmin in the Vedic regime but he could become a Bhikshu [or Buddhist mendicant] and occupy the same status and dignity as did the Brahmin.... Similar change is noticeable in the case of women. Under the Buddhist regime she became a free person. [S]he could acquire property, she could acquire learning and what was unique, she could become a member of the Buddhist order of Nuns and reach the same status and dignity as a Brahmin.[10]

"Indians today are governed by two different ideologies. Their political ideal set out in the preamble to the Constitution affirms a life of Liberty, Equality, and Fraternity. Their social ideal in their religion denies them." Thus Ambedkar in 1954. It was necessary to radically reform Hindu society to generate new life in it. Hindus would have to convert to the religion of the Buddha "for their own good."[11] "When [in the early years after Christ] Christianity was struggling for existence, the poorer people became its first converts and the upper folks ignored it," Ambedkar declared in an interview with journalists on the day before he and a large number of his followers embraced Buddhism on October 14, 1956, "The same thing will happen here also.... In the course of time all Hindus will become Buddhists."[12]

There is something ironic in the determination shown by a law minister who had vowed not to die a Hindu to do everything he could to bring about fundamental reform in Hindu society for the progress of "the country as a whole": "I have to do the work of conversion."[13] It was in this context that Ambedkar placed the extraordinary emphasis he did on the Hindu Code Bill of 1951. This attempted codification of a multitude of inherited practices related to marriage, divorce, adoption, and inheritance in Hindu households was a wide-ranging piece of legislation. Ambedkar declared it to be "the greatest social reform measure ever undertaken by the Legislature in this country." He went on to explain why he thought this was so: "To leave inequality between class and class, between sex and sex which is the soul of Hindu society untouched and to go on passing legislation relating to

---

[10] Ambedkar, "Revolution and Counter-revolution in Ancient India," 57; and Ambedkar, "What Is Saddhamma?'" 302.

[11] Moon, *Ambedkar: Writings and Speeches*, vol. 17, pt. III, 503, 505; vol. 14, pt. I, 283; vol. I, 26, 77–8.

[12] *Hitavad*, October 14, 1956.

[13] Moon, *Ambedkar: Writings and Speeches*, vol. 17, pt. III, 503.

economic problems is to make a farce of our Constitution and to build a palace on a dung heap. This is the significance I attach . . . to the Hindu Code."[14]

It goes without saying that in the years preceding and following Indian Independence, many other Dalit groups and individuals far less visible than exceptional political leaders like Ambedkar did what they could to bring about meaningful changes in the country's social and political practices. An excellent illustration of contemporary thinking among young, educated Dalits comes from the career of a junior bureaucrat who served in the Indian Administrative Service (IAS) for five years, from 1959 to 1964. Balwant Singh's autobiography, written in the years after his resignation from the IAS in May 1964 and published in the 1990s, tellingly entitled *An Untouchable in the I.A.S.*, provides a detailed account of the circumstances that led him to quit what was in the 1950s and '60s, and for some time afterward, the service of the educated middle class's, and even more emphatically the Dalit graduate's, dream.

"In an independent country, the responsibilities of the administration are not confined merely to law and order, for [the maintenance of] the status quo," the author declares. "In a welfare state the man in the street also has something at stake and his progress and development are of paramount importance." Like Ambedkar, he speaks of the need to purge the Hindu religion of its social evils, "for a house built on discrimination and hatred cannot stand and this ancient religion should ensure a life of dignity and respectability to its poor and low brethren. . . . That is not possible until it is free from the stigma of high and low and [as long as it is] without equality, liberty and fraternity."[15]

Young men like him joined the IAS, the successor to the famed Indian Civil Service of British colonial times, Singh observes, in the hope that in a democratic, independent India this "prestigious service would be responsive to the common man and provide relief and succour by alleviating his sorrows and sufferings." However, five years in

---

[14] Moon, *Ambedkar: Writings and Speeches*, vol. 14, 1325–6.
[15] Balwant Singh, *An Untouchable in the I.A.S.* (Saharanpur: Balwant Singh, n.d.), 216, 199. It is no accident that the book is dedicated to Nelson Mandela, president of South Africa, "the champion, crusader and liberator of the insulted, humiliated and discriminated mankind."

70   *A History of Prejudice*

the service "totally disillusioned" him. "The I.A.S. was still the protector of the rich and the socially privileged and the man in the street did not count much in their scheme." The old order had enormous power. Caste and communal bias persisted among the high-caste officers, and "one was reminded of the taluqdari system [a particularly oppressive form of high landlordism upheld by the British in Awadh and certain other parts of northern India] where law was the rod or the whims of an individual and social equality was out of [the] question."[16]

Singh's brief career in the IAS ended soon after he recorded a combative statement against persistent caste prejudice, derision, and discrimination in public life. The statement appeared as part of his judgment in *State v. Bhaiyan*, a case in which a poor wayside barber showed his disinclination to cut the hair of a Dalit customer and finally cut his hair outside, rather than inside, the shop, and at an inflated cost. The facts of the case were quickly established: "Sri Shyam Lal went for a hair-cut to the shop of Sri Bhaiyan. . . . [H]e was refused the service on account of his being a Barar. . . . Sri Bhaiyan demanded a very exorbitant price for a simple hair-cut and to add further insult he also asked Sri Shyam Lal to sit out[side] the shop to get his hair-cut by which Sri Bhaiyan thought he was giv[ing] a befitting status to Sri Shyam Lal, the unfortunate untouchable in the society." Given the facts, the young magistrate could have proceeded immediately to pronounce his judgment and sentence the accused.

However, Balwant Singh felt the need to comment on the wider social forces and prejudices at work in the course of the judgment:

In the eyes of a Hindu even a dog can be allowed to enter the shop but not a human being who by force of circumstances and ill-luck happened to be born in so called scheduled castes. The Hindu society is a society of defeat and degeneration and it can inspire no confidence in the mind of a sensible human being. . . . It is a society of meanness and a store house of degradations. . . . Every conservative Hindu house is a South Africa [a domain of apartheid] for a poor untouchable who is still being crushed under the heels of Hindu Imperialism.[17]

The fallout was predictable. According to Balwant Singh, the judgment was followed quickly by a series of charges and complaints against

---

[16] Ibid., 221–2, 216.
[17] Ibid., 224–7.

Dalit Conversion

the Dalit official for his acts of commission and omission. He was accused by the local Congress member of the state legislature of lying in connection with his efforts to maintain peace on the occasion of a hunger strike by a Hindu Mahasabha worker. He was described as unduly sensitive by the chief secretary, the senior-most civil servant of the province: "My friend, your work is not the consideration. You are supersensitive and not settling down." By Singh's account, he was also told by the same worthy to "shut up" and not "talk like a clerk or a tehsildar" (lower-level officials, unworthy of the status and standing of the IAS!) when he sought an explanation for the effective "demotion" he was being given through a posting as assistant commissioner.[18]

The distinction between "their" administration and "the man in the street" is a recurrent motif in the Dalit bureaucrat's reminiscences, and he lines up not with the administration but with the oppressed people: "For officers from the low castes things were ... complicated. They were acceptable if they accepted the prevailing ... social norms." Balwant Singh might have made the point more strongly still, for it is probably fair to say that such officers were tolerated if they accepted upper-caste ways and attitudes and yet never fully accepted as social peers.[19] Low-caste officers suffered from much social indignity and humiliation. Expressions of grievance on their part were commonly met with the response that these were "trivial," "inconsequential" matters.[20] However, it is perhaps precisely the history of the *trifling* that those who write from a feminist, subalternist, lower caste and class, or other minority perspectives need to track. Just how frequently do trivial or inconsequential insults have to be repeated before they are seen as historically or politically significant?

---

[18] Ibid., 210–17.

[19] One could adduce all kinds of evidence to show this. Among striking examples that I came across in my own interviews are the recollections of a retired upper-caste IAS officer's wife that in the bureaucratic circles of her husband, an ex-Untouchable officer (whom she recalled clearly) was superficially treated as a friend, but "*hamesha heya drishti se dekha karte the* (he was always looked upon with some revulsion)"; and the recollections of Meera Kumar, the major Congress leader and long-term cabinet minister Jagjivan Ram's daughter, later herself a central government minister and Speaker of the Lok Sabha or lower house of Parliament, about her experience of being visited at home by several school and college friends but never being invited to their homes in return.

[20] Singh, *Untouchable in the I.A.S.*, 196–7.

72   *A History of Prejudice*

A Statutory Reinscription of Difference

It will help to turn at this point to a rather different class location for another example of the Dalit struggle for citizenship in the
wake of Independence – the neglected, "trifling" history of efforts by
Punjabi Dalit laborers and poor peasants to change their circumstances
after they were forced out of areas of West Punjab (which became
part of Pakistan) and found themselves being resettled in East (Indian)
Punjab following the partition of the subcontinent in 1947. At this end
of the Dalit spectrum – that of men and women without any formal
education, legally recognized assets, or obvious political connections –
there were similar struggles and similar contradictory outcomes, sometimes with clearly more punishing consequences.

I should first note that in the received historical account of the famed
Punjab village community – made up, as the received account has it, of
sturdy peasant proprietors and village brotherhoods, in a mixed population of Muslims, Hindus, and Sikhs – the place of the Dalits has gone
largely unacknowledged: the menial and artisanal groups of the lowest
caste status have appeared only tangentially, as nondescript "village
servants." Thus, although there is considerable evidence of bitter and
extended struggles over land and property that accompanied the evic-
tion of Muslims and non-Muslims from different sides of the Punjab
during Partition, little attention has been paid to the struggles of the
Dalits or ex-Untouchables in the course of the forced migrations or the
attempted restoration of "normalcy" on both sides of the new border.
We know very little, too, about the local conflicts that arose when it
came to the official resettlement and rehabilitation of refugees, and
how the contest between local refugees and refugees coming in from
distant districts, and between refugees and more stable and privileged
(or lucky) groups, affected the lower castes and classes as it affected
other sections of the populace.

"We were neither Hindu nor Muslim, so we were not affected," a
number of Dalits are reported to have said in talking about Partition.[21]
The records of the time and the more detailed recollections of these
interviewees themselves, however, tell a somewhat different tale. A

---

[21] For one example, see the interview with Maya Rani in Urvashi Butalia, *The Other
Side of Silence* (New Delhi: Viking Press, 1998), 256.

Dalit Conversion

contemporary report on the needs of rural refugees who had found their way from West to East Punjab provides the following description of the kinds of groups that migrated. There were the well-publicized yeomen farmers, including many (we are told) whose families had migrated to the canal colonies of West Punjab from East Punjab a couple of generations earlier. Next, there were numerous noncultivating landlords, especially from the Rawalpindi and Multan divisions, who held a certain amount of land cultivated largely by Muslim tenants but whose primary income was derived from village trading and moneylending. There was also a not insignificant category of larger landholders in the Multan division, the canal colonies and a couple of other districts. Finally, as this summary statement has it, "mention may be made of sections of [the] non-Muslim population who lived either by labour or by tenant-farming... or by devious pursuits such as those of Bazigars [sic!]." This last group is specifically identified as consisting of Harijans, Raidasi Sikhs, and Bazigars – all Dalit groups.[22]

What is clear is that, partly because of local pressures and partly because of the efforts of the Indian government and various Hindu propagandists working with it, the forced migration of Dalits occurred on a large scale. According to the best estimates we have, some 6% to 7% of the Hindus and Sikhs who migrated from West to East Punjab were from such "untouchable" communities. This would add up to the bulk of the Dalit population of the western districts.[23] It is the aftermath of this displacement that I want to consider here.

Many Punjabi Dalits saw in 1947 an opportunity to right past wrongs. In this they were supported by a few of their more enlightened social and political allies. With the departure of Muslim artisans and the wider choice of occupations for Dalit workers, caste, these groups argued, would no longer be tenable as a hereditary basis for occupation.[24] "The Harijans [Gandhi and the Congress's favoured term for a description of Dalits], who generally comprise landless labourers and village artisans, have become fully conscious of their

---

[22] India Office Library and Records (hereafter IOR) Mss Eur F152/178, F. L. Brayne, "Economic Rehabilitation of Rural Refugees."

[23] See Kirpal Singh, *The Partition of the Punjab* (Patiala: Punjab University, 1989), 188.

[24] Mss Eur F152/178, Brayne, "Economic Rehabilitation of Rural Refugees."

74 *A History of Prejudice*

rights as citizens," M. S. Randhawa, an Indian Civil Service (ICS) official responsible for rural rehabilitation in East Punjab, wrote in the early 1950s. "There is considerable urge among them to acquire the respectable status of landowners, as ownership of land, however small in area, confers dignity and status."[25]

The reconciliation of the interests of different castes and classes among the refugees was, however, never going to be easy. Although the number of Muslims fleeing from East Punjab, and of Sikhs and Hindus coming into the province, was roughly comparable, the land and property they left behind was not. Officials estimated that whereas the economically better-off Sikh and Hindu refugees had left behind some 60 lakh acres of land in West Punjab, the Muslim evacuees from East Punjab and adjacent princely states had left only 45 lakh acres.[26] Landholding and property-owning groups among the refugees, demanding "full compensation" for their own losses, saw no justice in the argument that the contemporary dislocation offered a convenient opportunity for reform.[27] They were supported by influential elements in the administration who wanted to see the maintenance of the "village community" and, with it, rural order.

According to the policy initially laid down by the regional government, the 45 lakh acres left by Muslim evacuees from East Punjab would be allotted to landowners among the incoming refugees, "as distinguishable from mere tillers of the soil [such] as Harijans."[28] As Chaudhri Chotu Ram, a leading spokesman of the Punjab *zamindars* and erstwhile minister in the Unionist government of undivided Punjab put it, the low and menial castes could not be included in the list of statutory agriculturists, as this would adversely affect the protection given to "agricultural castes" under the Punjab Alienation of Land Act.[29]

---

[25] M. S. Randhawa, *Out of the Ashes: An Account of the Rehabilitation of Refugees from West Pakistan in Rural Areas of East Punjab* (Chandigarh: Public Relations Department, Punjab, 1954), 213–14.

[26] One lakh = 100,000.

[27] Mss Eur F152/178, Brayne, "Economic Rehabilitation of Rural Refugees."

[28] National Archives of India, Rajendra Prasad papers, File 5-R/48, col. 3, letter no. 977, Ministry of Relief and Rehabilitation, Harijan section, Rameshwari Nehru to Rajendra Prasad, Congress President, 3 May 1948.

[29] Ishwar Das Pawar, *My Struggle in Life* (Chandigarh: I. D. Pawar, 1982; 3rd edition, 1993), 51. Dalit spokespersons and their allies campaigned actively for the repeal of

Dalit Conversion

75

There are conflicting reports on how much was done for the Dalits in the rehabilitation program, an important arena in the new nationalist desire for "scientific" planning of the economy and society. The temporary allotment of evacuee lands was begun in September 1947 to provide initial refuge and work for the mass of refugees. Many of the larger landholders, noncultivating landlords as well as the bigger farmers, refused to accept these temporary measures. On the other hand, numerous landless groups, including Dalits, appear to have taken advantage of the scheme.[30] Officials were also instructed to pay special attention to the needs of rural artisans and village servants in the matter of jobs, loans, establishment of cooperative societies, and allotment of houses in the countryside. Again, numerous Dalits benefited from these initiatives.[31]

Against this, however, a detailed analysis from May 1948 speaks of 250,000 Dalit refugees in East Punjab, 90% of them agriculturists, "living a life of misery and idleness" in makeshift camps and depending on the "free but inadequate rations" supplied by the government.[32] Around this time, in the first flush of freedom, with the sympathy it generated for democratic aspirations and social justice and motivated further by Gandhi's martyrdom in January 1948, Gandhians like Rameshwari Nehru, Vinoba Bhave, and Rajendra Prasad turned up the pressure on the East Punjab government to take some concrete action, however gradual, to rehabilitate the Dalit refugees as full citizens.

the Land Alienation Act, and it was finally repealed by presidential decree in 1951; (IOR) Mss Eur F158/641B, Indiagram 11 April 1951.

[30] "It will be a problem of considerable size," an official noted in 1948, "to [re-] settle 42,000 families of non-landholders who are at present holding temporary allotments"; see Mss Eur F152/178, Brayne, "Economic Rehabilitation of Rural Refugees." See also Tai Yong Tan and Gyanesh Kudaisya, *The Aftermath of Partition in South Asia* (London: Routledge, 2000), 129.

[31] Rameshwari Nehru papers, Subject File no. 1(a), pt. III, "Harijan Welfare in Punjab," published by the Public Relations Department, Punjab (n.d.; information and statistics cover the period to December 1952). The report notes, for example, that by December 1952 there were twenty-four cooperative societies for shoemaking, weaving, basket work, and so on. These had been granted loans adding up to a total of Rs. 84,200.

[32] Rajendra Prasad papers, File 5-R/48, col. 3, letter no. 977, Ministry of Relief and Rehabilitation, Harijan section, Rameshwari Nehru to Rajendra Prasad, Congress President, 3 May 1948.

76 *A History of Prejudice*

At a conference in June 1948, they urged Gopichand Bhargava, the premier, to give the 50,000 Dalit families still in refugee camps 5 lakh (i.e., 500,000) acres of land to cultivate. "If no land was allotted to the landless Harijans they would once again be relegated to the status of . . . [*kamins*]."[33] The East Punjab government responded cautiously. After the minimum needs of "landowners" had been met, they said, Dalits could perhaps be allotted the estimated remaining $2\frac{1}{2}$ to 3 lakh acres. By August, they had reduced the amount they could hand out to the Dalits to "say, 75,000 acres," about a quarter of what they had suggested two months earlier. Premier Bhargava explained the government's reasoning: "all Harijans were not agriculturists." Many were artisans and should be absorbed in industrial channels, and a good number worked as day laborers. Hence, "they could not legitimately be allotted land."[34]

Indeed, the actions of the landowning castes, refugee and local, to appropriate as much land as possible went further. Throughout East Punjab and the neighboring princely states, there was a rush to partition common lands (*abadi* and *shamilat zamin*) owing to landowners' fears that these areas would be entrusted to newly constituted village *panchayats*, or democratic councils of local self-government. This further eroded the rights of Dalits and other village workers. Ishwar Dass Pawar, the first Dalit to be appointed to the Punjab Judicial Service, visited several villages in the Sonepat subdivision in connection with cases that had been brought before him and found that "Harijans had lost all the small plots of land already in their possession from long generations. . . . In some cases, for example, of weavers and rope-makers, they had no place to carry on their professions as they needed . . . long stretches of land to serve as rope-walks."[35]

Another notable development was the attempt to push several Dalit communities back into the status of criminal tribes. The Punjab Criminal Tribes Act had classified numerous Dalit castes and subcastes as Criminal Tribes and placed restrictions on their movement out of

[33] Rajendra Prasad papers, File 1-C/48, col. 1, Rajendra Prasad to Gopichand Bhargava, 7 May 1948; and minutes of informal conference convened by Dr. Rajendra Prasad, New Delhi, 25 June 1948 (signed Rameshwari Nehru, Head of Harijan Section).

[34] Ibid.; and Rajendra Prasad papers, File 5-R/48, col. 5, Partap Singh, Rehabilitation Minister, East Punjab, to Rajendra Prasad, Congress President, 23 August 1948.

[35] Pawar, *My Struggle in Life*, 91.

designated villages and settlements, with members singled out by the administration for sundry reasons (such as their being unemployed) being asked to report regularly at police posts. In the aftermath of Partition, some segments of the so-called Criminal Tribes who had earlier escaped such classification, or at least some of its worst consequences, appear to have been forced back into the category. Witness the following petition from the Dalit refugees who came from the agricultural settlement of Bauriya Criminal Tribes at Kot Khalsa in Tehsil Khanewal, in the Multan district. As many as 3,500 non-Muslims of the settlement were massacred in August 1947, the petition tells us:

There were 98 landholding hereditary Patedars tenants of the Government in the above mentioned Criminal Tribes settlement with agreements [that is, *pattis*, records of rights in land; hence Patedars or, more accurately, *pattidars*] for 15 years.

About 91 of the total landholders had been murdered, only 7 of us the undersigned survived. . . .

Having suffered so much we come to understand that the Pakistan Authorities have not sent our Jamabandi Records [records relating to rent and revenue payment]. . . . We could not bring the patta deeds enacted with Government for 15 years as hereditary tenants to serve as documentary evidence.

Over and above all this, the Criminal Tribes Dept. has imposed upon us restrictions of giving attendance every day and leaving station with Police permits which we or our parents and ancestors were absolutely exempted from.[36]

I do not know what came of this petition. What is clear is that the issue had become part of a wider struggle over the matter of access to democracy, citizenship, and law and order.

Rameshwari Nehru protested in September 1949 against an act of police firing in Jaipur State that resulted in a number of casualties from among the poor tribal group of Meenas. The government refused to institute an independent inquiry into the incident, apparently because the Meenas "belonged to the so-called criminal tribes, their lives were

---

[36] Rameshwari Nehru Papers, Subject File no. 1 (a), pt. I, petition of 7 residents of village Qutbewal Arain, Tehsil and District Ludhiana, through Shri A. S. Satyayarthi, Regional Working Secretary, Displaced Harijans Rehabilitation Board (Central Government Agency), Civil Secretariat, Jullunder (n.d., but received on 5 August 1950, according to a note on the file).

78   *A History of Prejudice*

supposed to be cheap and it was not considered necessary to institute any inquiry." Nehru noted that the Criminal Tribes Act was being repealed piecemeal: "It is not understandable why this heinous Act is being repealed province-wise. An all-India measure to wipe out this blot is the urgent need of the day."[37]

More than three decades later, however, Pawar would write in his autobiography: "The only thing done so far is that the pernicious law has been repealed, and now they are termed as *Vimukt-jatis*, the 'liberated castes.'"[38] In many places, this is a designation that has served only to perpetuate the segregation of these groups and mark them out for continued discrimination.

A Law Minister from the Wrong Caste

The evidence presented here should suffice to indicate the major trans-formations contemplated, and to some extent set in motion, in the India of the 1940s and '50s. It should tell us something about the extraordinary hopes and expectations of the time and the sense of betrayal and consequent bitterness felt by many among the depressed castes and classes. Yet, as the preceding sections have indicated, the consequences of inherited prejudice were not confined to the poorest and the most downtrodden among them.

It is instructive to juxtapose the preceding accounts of continuing caste discrimination with reports of Ambedkar's experience as law minister at the hands of his fellow parliamentarians in the course of the debates on the Hindu Code Bill. I have already stressed the importance of this piece of legislation for Ambedkar. Let me reinforce the point by adding that he resigned from the union cabinet in October 1951 in large part because of the failure of the Congress government to enact the measure at this time in a form that he deemed adequate to the needs of the country.

A number of remarkable exchanges took place in the course of the debate on the Hindu Code between upper-caste members of Parliament and the distinguished Dalit leader, a member of the central cabinet in the first government of independent India, hailed as the architect of

---

[37] Rameshwari Nehru, letter to *The Hindustan Times*, September 10, 1949.
[38] Pawar, *My Struggle in Life*, 54.

Dalit Conversion

79

the Indian constitution, and acknowledged by now as an outstanding scholar and writer on a wide range of subjects. One is struck repeatedly – even on the basis of the written record alone – by the deep-seated caste prejudice and spite displayed in this most public and supposedly most advanced of Indian political forums. A few extracts from the proceedings of September 20, 1951, will suffice to make the point.

Presenting the bill, Ambedkar argued that the much vaunted adaptability and absorptive capacity of the Hindu social order had not helped to democratize it. It had failed to assimilate the Buddha's preaching of equality and would "never give up its social structure [designed] for the enslavement of the *Sudra* and . . . of women. It is for this reason that law must now come to their rescue."[39] Ambedkar referred to the charge that reforms like the Hindu Code Bill were simply an attempt to bring India in line with Western nations that insisted on monogamy and liberal provisions for divorce. Those who made this charge, Ambedkar noted, "have said that our ideal should be, what? Somebody said Ram; somebody said Dasaratha; somebody said Krishna. . . . I do not wish to comment upon any of the ideals which have been presented to the House, and I do not." At this point, he was interrupted by Shyamnandan Sahay, who declared: "You will be well advised not to do so."[40]

I should note that some Muslim members of the legislature, a particularly vulnerable group in the wake of Partition, had also suffered such injunctions not to speak on matters relating to Hindu tradition. But the animus displayed in further comments directed at the Dalit leader was of a different kind. The law minister noted that the constitutionally guaranteed liberty and equality of citizens necessitated the extension of greater rights to Hindu women in questions of marriage and inheritance: "That is the reason why we are proceeding with this Bill and not because we want to imitate any other people or [because] we want to go in for our ancient ideals which are to my judgement, most archaic and impossible for anybody to practice." The second part of that statement, which I quoted earlier in Chapter 2, was of course not going to remain unanswered.

---

[39] Moon, *Ambedkar: Writings and Speeches*, vol. 14, 1160.
[40] Ibid., 1160–1.

Dr. C. D. Pandey: We are ready to support the Bill, but we do not want these invectives. How far the Hon. Minister is justified in dealing with this subject [in this way?] and resorting to such invectives . . .

An Hon. Member: Why vilify the Hindu religion?

Dr. Ambedkar: Now, I come to the specific amendments that have been tabled by various Members to clause 2.

Shri Krishnanand Rai: The House is for divorce and monogamy, but not for this kind of abuse.

Dr. C. D. Pandey: We are for these provisions, but we do not want these abuses and invectives.

At this point, the prime minister, Jawaharlal Nehru, intervened with a comment on the "tender skins" of some members. Many sharp comments had been made in earlier speeches against the Bill without objection from anyone, he observed. He couldn't understand why people were responding so heatedly to Dr. Ambedkar's statements. However, an agitated Pandit Lakshmi Kanta Maitra proceeded with another interjection: "We have been listening with rapt attention to Dr. Ambedkar, but what we do not want is these invectives and reflections on some of the best ideals which we cherish. The provisions can be defended without injuring the religious susceptibilities of Members." "Side conversations" and disturbances, as they are described in the official record, continued for a while before the house settled down to hear the rest of the law minister's statement on this clause.[41]

Earlier in the debate, when Govind Malaviya remarked that Hindu society prescribed "rights and privileges" for the Chandala (among the lowest of the so-called Scheduled Castes) as much as for the Brahman, various members, including the deputy speaker, raised objections on the grounds that the use of any name suggesting Untouchability was now "unconstitutional." To the further argument that the reference was "only to history," the deputy speaker responded by saying, "all history is not very good to mention." The exchange that followed is extraordinary:

---

[41] Ibid., 1162–3.

Pandit Malaviya: I was referring to it [the word Chandala] not as to an individual, but as to a system in the past. However, I will abide by what you [the Deputy Speaker] have said.

Dr. Ambedkar: Why should you?

Pandit Malaviya: The Hon. Law Minister asks, why I should. Only because I am a law-abiding Member and not the other name that I had been mentioning.[42]

The scarcely veiled reference to Ambedkar's origins in an Untouchable community, presumably among people who could easily act like Chandalas (that is to say, scum) rather than like law-abiding citizens, was perhaps the lowest point in the debate. But the controversial question of the ability of ex-Untouchables to speak for Hindu society, and more broadly democratic India, runs through the exchanges like an undercurrent.

There was some ambivalence in the Dalits' relation to Hindu society, almost inevitably as I have noted: they were defined by it, and at the same time part and not part of it. The ambiguity of this position affected not only Ambedkar but also the caste Hindus who opposed the Hindu Code Bill he was piloting through Parliament. Did someone from a once Untouchable community, denied the right to study or interpret the sacred texts of the Hindus, have the knowledge and heritage appropriate to a reformer of their laws? More than one legislator challenged the right of the Dalit leader to seek to don the mantle of Manu, Yajnavalkya, and other renowned Hindu lawmakers.

One referred to vast "traditions which [the Law Minister] perhaps does not know," reflective of the "collective wisdom," the antiquity and greatness of India and its people.[43] The comment points to more than the limits of an individual's capacity. It seems to me to point also to the illegitimacy of an "untraditional" interpreter, an ex-Untouchable to boot, seeking to define and overhaul Hindu tradition (or for that matter Indian democracy). It is another example of those trifling slights and incidents referred to earlier in this chapter that are brushed aside as inconsequential – of prejudices that remain pervasive

---

[42] Ibid., 1112.
[43] Ibid., 1280.

82 *A History of Prejudice*

and pernicious, and yet unacknowledged, and thus all the more difficult to contend with.

This was the context in which the call for religious "conversion" gathered renewed strength in several Dalit quarters.

The Question of a Religious Conversion

As already mentioned, the matter of religious affiliation was one over which Gandhi and Ambedkar clashed sharply. For Gandhi, the crusade against Untouchability was an internal affair of the Hindus. Ambedkar saw the issue instead as one of civil rights – even during the years in which he argued for the Dalits' right to enter Hindu temples and public tanks. Gandhi was opposed to attempts to translate "the problem of untouchables" into the language of modern politics. Such translation, he argued, would prevent the "natural growth" of the Dalits in the "organic community" of Hinduism and prevent the upper castes from making honorable amends. "The evil [of Untouchability] is far greater than I had thought it to be," he wrote in May 1933. "It cannot be eradicated by money, external organization and even political power for Harijans, although all these three are necessary. . . . To be effective, they must follow . . . self-purification."[44] His advocacy of a cultivation of the harmonious village community, the simplicity of village life, and the ideal Bhangi (the respected and self-respecting sweeper) was in line with this belief in the essential goodness of an organic Hinduism.

Ambedkar, born in a lowly Mahar family and discriminated against as a Dalit in spite of his PhDs from Columbia University (New York) and the London School of Economics and his professional and political standing, had little time for the village pastoral and the nostalgic view of the past that arose with Indian nationalism. He argued that the Mahars and other Dalits had to look to the future and to their own inner strength. They had to trust themselves rather than look to the mercy and benevolence of the upper castes and classes. In what was to become a battle cry for his followers, Ambedkar advocated

---

[44] Cited in D. R. Nagaraj, *The Flaming Feet: A Study of the Dalit Movement in India* (Bangalore: South Forum Press, 1993), 19. The paragraph draws heavily from Nagaraj's argument.

"Education, Organization and Agitation" in the struggle for equality. Finally, in 1935, he took the Gandhian (and the general upper-caste Hindu) position head on when he announced his decision to leave Hinduism.

The fact is that the matter of ritual impurity and religion could not be separated from economic dependence and political powerlessness of the lower castes and classes in India. One student of caste and religion in a south Indian district writes: "There is no evidence that the Harijans' status is more clearly defined by their religious role as funeral servants, than by their economic role as labourers."[45] The converse may perhaps be said with equal validity. Hence Ambedkar's insistent identification of caste, as another scholar has it, as "the most powerful vehicle of dominance – ritual as well as political and economic – in India."[46] Or, as he put it angrily when asked by reporters whether the economic conditions of his followers would improve if they embraced Buddhism, "I am willing to go hungry [rather] than to lose my self-respect. Honour comes first and foremost."[47]

The anthropologist R. S. Khare noted that the Dalit (Chamar) rickshaw pullers he studied in the city of Lucknow spoke repeatedly of the "cobweb" of caste, which they had to work "sometimes along and sometimes across."[48] The cobweb is a significant metaphor. The Hindi word for it, *jaala*, is related to *jaal* (net). It is not easy to escape from either, but the cobweb is more insidious, invisible, scary. "Hinduism is not ours," a group of Punjabi sweepers told Mark Juergensmeyer. It is a religion of oppression, the religion of the rich and the upper castes. At the same time, as they went on to say, because the concept of Untouchability was a religious one, a change of religion would have to accompany economic and social progress to bring about its end.[49] It is for this reason that the question of conversion has been central to the Dalit struggle.

---

[45] D. Mosse, "Caste, Christianity and Hinduism: A Study of Social Organization and Religion in Rural Ramnad," PhD thesis, Institute of Social Anthropology, Oxford University, 1985, 247, cited in Deliege, *Untouchables of India*, 67.

[46] N. B. Dirks, *Castes of Mind: Colonialism and the Making of Modern India* (Princeton, NJ: Princeton University Press, 2001), 7.

[47] *Hitavada*, October 14, 1956.

[48] R. S. Khare, *The Untouchable as Himself: Ideology, Identity, and Pragmatism among the Lucknow Chamars* (Cambridge: Cambridge University Press, 1984), 147.

[49] Juergensmeyer, *Religion as Social Vision*, 1.

84   *A History of Prejudice*

Much of the writing on religious conversion deals with it as an individual act,[50] following on something like a vision or an individual awakening. Against this, what we are concerned with in the Dalit case is a question of collective or mass conversion. One might venture the suggestion that this is what has happened in most instances of conversion in human history. But I want to underscore two other aspects of the moment of the Dalit conversion. First, it is preceded by serious and extended deliberation. Second, it is perhaps best seen as only a stage in a process: not the culminating point of a period of agitation or distress (a culmination reached through a sudden revelation, as it were) but in some senses a beginning, one step in an ongoing transformation and self-making.

The conversion of subaltern groups and peoples cannot be undertaken "in a fit of absent-mindedness"; there is quite simply too much to lose.[51] What follows from this is the express need for deep and extended reflection in the process of the Dalit conversion. The point is illustrated well by Ambedkar's own preparation before his formal conversion to Buddhism in front of a huge gathering of his followers in Nagpur in 1956. He had declared his intention of leaving the Hindu fold in 1935. Yet it was only 21 years later, just two months before his death, that he entered the Buddhist order. He spent the intervening years studying a variety of religious traditions that he saw as possible alternatives to Hinduism, talking to their practitioners and missionaries in an attempt to understand them better. Between 1951 (when he appears to have decided to adopt the Buddhist *dhamma*) and 1956, he wrote at length about his understanding of "the Buddha and the future of his religion," the title of an important 1951 article. Toward the end of his life, when he knew he was very unwell, he was writing frenetically to try and complete his major work on the subject, *The Buddha and His Dhamma*. "I am in a great hurry and I want the book

---

[50] Thus, even in Gauri Vishwanathan's recent study, which stresses the social and political context of nineteenth- and twentieth-century conversions in Britain and India, it is the conversion of the individual that remains the central object of investigation; see Gauri Vishwanathan, *Outside the Fold: Conversion, Modernity, and Belief* (Princeton, NJ: Princeton University Press, 1998).

[51] I have borrowed Ranajit Guha's phrase as applied to acts of subaltern insurgency generally; see Ranajit Guha, *Elementary Aspects of Peasant Insurgency in Colonial India* (Delhi: Oxford University Press, 1983), 9.

Dalit Conversion 85

to be published by September [at] the latest," he wrote.[52] That deadline was determined by his decision to formally embrace Buddhism in October 1956, for he wanted to make available to his followers a clear and elaborate statement of his reasons for choosing the Buddhist path, or more precisely his version of it.

The widely publicized conversion of several thousand Dalits to Islam in and around Meenakshipuram (Tamilnadu) in 1981–2 provides another dramatic illustration of the prolonged deliberation that often accompanies the conversion of subaltern groups. This set of conversions was preceded by a sharpening of regional and national debates on the inequities of caste and the need for positive discrimination, by violent clashes between caste Hindus and Dalits in Maharashtra in 1978 and a militant agitation in Gujarat in 1981 to protest against "reservations" for the Scheduled Castes in medical colleges. They were preceded, too, by continual discussions and planning among local Dalits. In Meenakshipuram, young Dalit converts reported that village elders had been "thinking of converting to Islam for the last twenty years." They had considered the option "time and again." "Since there was no support and unanimity three times earlier, they did not convert." The December 1980 killing of two Thevars – a low (but "clean") landowning caste to which several of the local revenue and police officers belonged – brought "a new wave of police torture and harassment" on the Dalits. In a gathering of Dalit villagers a short time afterward, a proposal to convert, made by one of the young men who had converted to Islam earlier, was finally accepted. "This conversion came as a collective decision of converts," writes Abdul Malik Mujahid in his closely detailed account of this set of conversions, "albeit in three installments."[53]

Similar claims to human dignity and self-respect had been made through other conversions to Christianity, Islam, and Sikhism, in the recent as in the distant past.[54] The mass conversion to Buddhism at Nagpur in 1956 followed in this track but was perhaps even more deliberate, and certainly more organized and widely publicized. The

---

[52] Keer, *Dr. Ambedkar*, 488.

[53] Abdul Malik Mujahid, *Conversion to Islam: Untouchables' Strategy for Protest in India* (Chambersburg, PA: Anima Books, 1989), 55 and passim.

[54] For some indication of the process, see Deliege, *Untouchables of India*, 157ff; and Juergensmeyer, *Religion as Social Vision*, 26–7, 181ff.

86   *A History of Prejudice*

event increased the number of Buddhists in India by half a million, a dramatic jump from the 141,426 Buddhists recorded for the country in the census of 1951; and the total increased to 3,206,142 by 1961. Most of the new converts were members of Ambedkar's Mahar community. The conversions have continued since and extended to many other Dalit constituencies: Buddhists numbered nearly 6 million by the 1990s, and the numbers have grown further since.[55]

Implications of the Dalit Conversion

It is necessary to underline the polyvalent, religious/secular character of the discourse that goes with the Dalit movement for conversion. The watchwords of Dalit discourse from the middle of the twentieth century have been liberty (for every individual), equality (of all citizens), and fraternity (of all those belonging to a community, a village, a town, or regional, national, and even international society). Even if in Ambedkar's later writings these ideals came to be described as deriving from the teachings of the Buddha, they appeared in the developing Dalit struggle for freedom as *self-evident truths*: the fundamental principles of modernity and civilization, a religion for our epoch – secular and sacred at the same time!

It is not coincidental that in Dalit homes, Buddhist *viharas*, and at pilgrimage sites and celebrations associated with Ambedkar and the new Buddhist identity the image of Gautam Buddha is found juxtaposed with, and even superimposed on, the image of Babasaheb Ambedkar. (See Figure 1 below.) While Ambedkar himself is most commonly represented as the quintessential modern leader and intellectual, as we have noted, he is also described as a modern-day bodhisattva. What kind of religious thinker, or guide, do we have here?

Ambedkar's *bhikku* is more social worker than traditional holy man, observes one scholar.[56] The same kind of understanding comes through in the Dalit Buddhist poetry of Maharashtra. Here is Daya Pawar's Buddha, as depicted in his 1974 poem with that title:

---

[55] Viswanathan, *Outside the Fold*, 225; Narain and Ahir, *Ambedkar, Buddhism and Social Change*, 12–13; and Jondhale and Beltz, *Reconstructing the World*, 12.

[56] See Johannes Beltz, "Contesting Caste, Hierarchy, and Hinduism: Buddhist Discursive Practices in Maharashtra," in Jondhale and Beltz, *Reconstructing the World*, 247.

Dalit Conversion

87

> I see you
> Walking, talking,
> Breathing softly, healingly,
> On the sorrow of the poor, the weak;
> Going from hut to hut
> In the life-destroying darkness
> Torch in hand...

The most common argument put forward by Dalits interviewed about their embracing of Buddhism, as I noted in Chapter 2, was that it gave them the chance of living with honor and dignity:

> I am the daughter of Bhima [i.e., Bhimrao Ambedkar]
> And the granddaughter of Gautama.
> . . . .
> Gautama's *dhamma* is like no other;
> A man finds humanity there.
> There are no different gods, no different castes;
> High or low, all are equal...[57]

What kind of "god" is it who discriminates against particular groups of human beings, another anonymous Dalit woman's song asks:

> What kind of Srihari is he
> Who hates some human beings?[58]

Sharankumar Limbale makes the same point in his account of how an uncle in his future in-laws' home spoke out on his behalf when a marriage proposal for him was put in jeopardy by talk of his "impure" blood: "There is no high or low in our Buddhist religion. I will give my daughter to him."[59]

A Dalit woman's recollections of the conversion ceremonies in which she participated helps to elaborate the argument. Shantabai Krishnaji Kamble, who was born in 1923 and began teaching in a

---

[57] Eleanor Zelliot, "New Voices of the Buddhists of India," in Narain and Ahir, *Ambedkar, Buddhism and Social Change,* 196 (the middle verse of these three is also cited in Chapter 2, this volume). See also the poem by Namdeo Dhasal, and Zelliot's commentary on it, that appears in ibid., 203.

[58] Cited in Rege, *Writing Caste/Writing Gender,* 61.

[59] Sharankumar Limbale, *Akkarmashi* (1984; 2nd edition, 1990), translated from the Marathi by Santosh Bhoomkar and published under the title *The Outcaste: Akkarmashi* (Delhi: Oxford University Press, 2003), 88.

88 *A History of Prejudice*

District Board school in 1942, was the first Dalit woman teacher in her district. Shantabai's son, the well-known writer and Dalit Panther activist Arun Kamble, urged her to write her life story when she retired from teaching in 1981, and the memoir, *Mazhya Jalmachi Chittarkatha*, was published soon afterward. In it she describes the conversion ceremony in her husband's village, Kargani. "The year 1957. The people in our community had decided that people from seven different villages would convert to Buddhism at Kargani."[60]

Upper-caste villagers in Kargani threatened a boycott of the Dalits when they heard about this move. The Dalits responded by calling a meeting of concerned castes from 32 surrounding villages and drawing up a plan of action to go through with their intent. On the day fixed for the initiation by specially invited Buddhist monks, people from many villages gathered at a central site in the village, under blue flags, with placards reading "If you want to live as humans, convert!" and shouting slogans of "*Ambedkar Zindabad*" and "*Bhagwan Gautam Buddha ki jai.*" The Buddhist monks garlanded photographs of the Buddha, Ambedkar, and Phule (the renowned non-Brahman leader of the nineteenth century, now seen as a precursor of Ambedkar in the inauguration of a Dalitbahujan movement) and lit candles and incense sticks. Following this, the assembly took the Buddhist vows as composed by Ambedkar – taking refuge in the Buddha, the *dhamma*, and the *sangha*, accepting the *panchsheel*, or five ethical principles of Buddhism, and rejecting brahmanical Hinduism.

From that moment, the local Dalits abandoned the demeaning tasks traditionally assigned to them: dragging dead animals out of the village, performing compulsory labor for the upper castes, running between villages to deliver news of deaths, and so on. "How long would we rot like this? That is why we embraced Buddhism. Dr. Ambedkar showed us the new path.... We began to live as human beings after having embraced Buddhism."

The moment of conversion is invoked as a magical time in account after account by ordinary Dalit converts, as I have noted already.

---

[60] In what follows, I use Maya Pandit's translation of certain passages as cited in Rege, *Writing Caste/Writing Gender*, 186–8, while adding a few details from the original Marathi in Shantabai Krishnaji Kamble, *Mazhya Jalmachi Chittarkatha* (3rd edition, Pune: Sugawa Prakashan, 1998), 107–8.

Dalit Conversion

89

From this point of view, the conversion to Buddhism may indeed be said to mark a supernatural, *religious* transformation, one suffused with the promise of new and fuller lives and linked with the purest and most inspiring of ideals – embodied in the Buddha and Babasaheb Ambedkar. "How did millions of illiterate people follow one man?" Baby Kamble asks about Ambedkar, though her question – and answer – could equally apply to the Buddha:

He was a man who believed in himself. He had courage and fortitude. . . . He never changed his positions; nor did he ever compromise his principles for selfish gain. Money, prosperity, fame – nothing could tempt him. . . . His heart was soft and tender, full of love for the downtrodden. . . . His character was spotlessly clean, without any blemish.[61]

I would go a step further and suggest that this moment of joy and purity associated with the *dharmaantar* is an aspect of the rescripting of the Dalit body. In the elaboration of the making of the Dalit as a full-fledged citizen, Dalit leaders have laid quite exceptional emphasis on this rescripting. They have underlined the importance of education, of refined speech (*sadhu bhasha*) and manners, and of modern dress and cleanliness. On occasion, Ambedkar spoke of the need to look and act like the upper castes and classes. A striking illustration is found in a 1942 speech in which Ambedkar congratulated his mainly Dalit audience on their growing political awareness, progress in education, and entry into state institutions like the army, the police, and the legislatures, and added: "the greatest progress that we have made is to be found among our women folk. Here you see in this conference these 20,000 to 25,000 women present. See their dress, observe their manners, mark their speech. Can any one say that they are Untouchable women?"[62]

---

[61] Baby Kamble, *Prisons We Broke*, 120–1.

[62] *Report of Depressed Class Conference, Nagpur Session* (Nagpur: G. T. Meshram, 1942), 28–9, cited in Zelliot, *From Untouchable to Dalit*, 131. See also the autobiographical memoir written at the end of the 1930s or in the 1940s, in which Ambedkar refers to the first train journey that he and three other children of his extended family took to Goregaon, where his father was stationed as a cashier in the army. "We were well-dressed children," he wrote. "From our dress or talk no one could make out that we were children of . . . untouchables"; see Valerian Rodrigues, ed., *The Essential Writings of B. R. Ambedkar* (Delhi: Oxford University Press, 2002), 48–9.

References to spotless white occur again and again in Dalit accounts of the Ambedkarite movement. The family memoir of a leading Dalit intellectual, Narendra Jadhav, recalls the army of local leaders and activists who emerged in Bombay in the 1940s and '50s, inspired by Dr. Ambedkar, all of them with two things in common – "immaculately clean attire and impressive oratory." Jadhav writes of huge processions on Ambedkar's birthday, in which activist women "dressed all in white" played a major part, and he recalls how his own working-class parents, affected by the Ambedkarite struggle, while thrifty about clothes, "insisted that we always wear shoes." They "brooked no compromise in this regard... their idea of being 'up-to-date' was firmly linked to wearing shoes."[63] Again, we are told that the cloth stores in Nagpur ran out of white saris at the 1956 initiation of Ambedkar and his half million followers, and that some of the women among the initiates actually wore men's white dhotis.[64]

The Dalit stress on books and formal education, "cultured" speech and urban manners, and clean clothes and shoes in the construction and presentation of the Dalit self speaks to the common sense of the modern and of course makes good sense in the struggle to transform attitudes of inferiority or superiority – among the Dalits as well as among their opponents. If rationality, science, and a belief in progress was to provide the spirit of a modern, democratic society, and adult franchise, elected legislatures and governments, a free press, universal laws, and an independent judiciary its political institutions, then education, articulate speech, and self-confidence reflected in dress and manners were clearly necessary conditions of their use.

"Decolonization is the veritable creation of new men," Fanon has written, "the 'thing' which has been colonized becomes man during the same process by which it frees itself."[65] Rationality, social morality, and the possibility of individual choice were, from the Dalit standpoint, the need of the hour. The city was their location. D. R. Nagaraj writes of the motif of escape from persecution and the journey to the Promised Land: "[T]his time the promised land is the modern city."[66] In direct

---

[63] Narendra Jadhav, *Outcaste: A Memoir* (Delhi: Viking Press, 2003), 228–30.
[64] See Rege, *Writing Caste/Writing Gender*, 56.
[65] Fanon, *Wretched of the Earth*, 36–7.
[66] Nagaraj, *Flaming Feet*, 58.

opposition to the Gandhian advocacy of the harmony and simplicity of village life, as I have mentioned, Dalit leaders have stressed the need for Dalits to look to the future and to move to the towns where they could escape from some of the worst disabilities of the caste system as experienced in the countryside.

"I am ... surprised that those who condemn Provincialism and communalism should come forward as champions of the village," Ambedkar observed. "I hold that these village republics [he uses the Gandhian phrase, borrowed from colonialist writings, with some irony] have been the ruination of India.... What is the village but a sink of localism, a den of ignorance, narrow-mindedness and communalism?"[67] "In this republic there is no place for democracy. There is no place for equality. There is no room for liberty and there is no room for fraternity. The Indian village life is the very negation of a Republic."[68]

Ambedkar was hardly alone among Dalit thinkers in his condemnation of the caste-ridden, traditional village community. Traditionally, Dalits were expected to perform functions – to follow paths, literally and metaphorically – that were symbolic of their very low status in ritual and social life, especially in the villages. Given the weight of this history, politically conscious Dalits have in one instance after another called for rejection of the very instruments and expertise – say, in music or in particular handicrafts – that they have inherited as a mark of their lowly status. Nagaraj wrote of an activist friend, Krishna, for whom "the art of playing drums is linked with the humiliating task of carrying dead animals. The joy of singing oral epics is traditionally associated with the insult of the artist standing outside the houses of upper caste landlords with a begging bowl." He will have none of these, even when it is friends and activist colleagues who are celebrating. "I want to forget all this," he screamed one night, "I want to forget their gods, their folk epics, their violence."[69]

The discarding of the demeaning dress and speech and deference of that earlier humiliating condition is thus a necessary part of the Dalit

---

[67] Rodrigues, *Essential Writings of B. R. Ambedkar*, 486.

[68] Moon, *Ambedkar: Writings and Speeches*, vol. 5, 26, cited in G. Aloysius, *Nationalism without a Nation in India* (Delhi: Oxford University Press, 1997), 166.

[69] Nagaraj, *Flaming Feet*, 74–5.

92 *A History of Prejudice*

struggle for full citizenship. To Gandhi's choice of the loincloth, and his advocacy of vegetarianism, manual labor and the simple village life, Dalit spokespersons respond with the statement that they already have these; indeed they have had too much of them. What they need instead is the hat and the three-piece suit, the pipe and the spectacles. It is not an accident, Timothy Fitzgerald suggests, that the dominant mode of representing Ambedkar in sculpture and painting, in calendar art, and in little images found in Dalit homes and offices and fairs all over the country is "not as a mendicant with [a] begging bowl, or as a meditator [bodhisattva] beneath a *bodhi* tree, but as a middle-class intellectual, wearing glasses, a blue suit, and carrying a book which symbolizes the Republican Constitution and the power of education and literacy."[70] (See Figure 1.)

But there is more. The representation of Ambedkar as the immaculately attired, unambiguously rational, learned, imperturbable, and unshakeable modern leader, no less than his representation in the garb of a bodhisattva, returns to the proposition of indomitable courage and fortitude, unselfishness and compassion – the spotlessly clean character, without blemish. The struggle of the subaltern citizen proceeds on many fronts.

A Different Sameness

Religious conversion classically involves the making (or embracing) of a new society and community, a new relationship with other human beings and the world, whatever one's conception of the latter – seeking, even if never attaining, perfection. This is all the more so with the Dalit conversion in India, which takes place in the context of a national, democratic struggle to establish a just, fair, and egalitarian society, and in an era that emphasizes the making of the self through the making and remaking of the modern world.

I have argued that the Dalit conversion aims at the making of the new citizen, the rational, deliberative individual, associating with others in the making of a new Dalit self and calling on non-Dalits to join in the refashioning and improvement of the world. What Dalit discourse fails to do satisfactorily, however, is to recognize what might

[70] Fitzgerald, "Analysing Sects, Minorities, and Social Movements in India," 270.

FIGURE 1. Dr. B. R. Ambedkar and the Buddha (calendar art; purchased at Nagpur, 2008)

be called the "internal" challenges of constituting the new Dalit self and the new Dalit citizen – in spite of talk of the "first case" of genuine conversion and the long process of deliberation and discussion that would go into effecting it. It takes Dalit unity, or shall we say the *spirit* and *irreducibility* of Dalit unity, much as upper-caste leaders of the Indian national movement took Indian national unity, or the *oneness* of India, as a transcendental presence, and it fails to deal robustly with questions of gender oppression, or discrimination between different castes (or subcastes) and classes within the Dalit constituency.

Let us return for a moment to Ambedkar's attempt to unpack the category of caste. It was class conflict that lay at the root of caste and Untouchability, he argued: the Untouchables were "broken men," Buddhists of old who came to occupy the bottom of the social hierarchy when the Brahmans defeated the Buddhists after a long and bitter conflict. While this challenging account clearly points to the fluidity and changeability, shall we say the historical *production* and *perpetuation*, of caste, what it does not capture adequately is the hold that notions of purity and pollution, and hence touchability and untouchability, came to have in Indian society: the consciousness and prejudice that have limited (and organized) social interaction in very specific ways, both between Untouchables/ex-Untouchables and caste Hindus and among the Untouchables/ex-Untouchables – those who would be Dalits – themselves.

Consider the experience of caste discrimination on the ground within the Dalit constituency in Ambedkar's home province of Maharashtra, as recorded by a leading Dalit writer from northern India two and a half decades after Independence. Looking at Maharashtra's Dalit neighborhoods in the 1970s filled his heart with sadness, Om Prakash Valmiki wrote in his autobiography, referring to the part of the country where the Ambedkarite movement, and hence the advancement of education and upward mobility and Dalit assertiveness, had been most pronounced. On account of the Dalit movement, members of Ambedkar's own Mahar caste had taken to education *en masse*. But other important Dalit castes in the region, Matangs (or Mangs), Chambhars (Chamars), and Mehtars among them, remained largely illiterate. The feeling of caste differences persisted, even among Dalit activists. Although they talked about overcoming the discrimination between these different castes, "internally they were caught in the clutches of these beliefs.... One could clearly perceive the hesitation of the activists [most of them Mahars] when they entered

Mehtar bastis." On the other hand, the Mehtars, "placed at the very bottom of the social ladder...were suspicious of the Dalit leadership."[71]

Similarly, recent accounts by Dalit women have brought to the fore the cruel forms of exploitation and torture, physical and psychological, that Dalit men have inflicted on Dalit women. As one account has it, "Dalit men did not hesitate in chopping off the nose[s] of those Dalit women who according to the former failed to abide by the patriarchal norms."[72] It is important to record the dissonant voice, even as we note the existence and value of the loud and clear call to end the Brahmanical oppression of women, which is articulated repeatedly in the discussion of the long, drawn-out contest between Brahmanism and Buddhism in India's history. For, in a paradoxical way, that historical analysis seems to suggest that problems like gender discrimination, domestic violence, male alcoholism, and exploitation of females are not particularly relevant to Dalit society, or at any rate will sort themselves out as this society gains in education, economic security, and political consciousness: a long-standing part of modern common sense.

In the turn I have described, the Dalit argument works to underscore the statement of an already existing Dalit unity and solidarity in beliefs, practices, and aspirations: insurgent Dalits on the one hand, the declining upper castes on the other. In treating this changeable and yet *substantial* caste identity as their overriding concern, the ready ground of a political struggle aimed at changing that ground, Dalit leaders are not only caught in the eternal bind of the subaltern, the outsider within, but also shackled in the range of issues that they believe necessary to tackle in order to produce the new citizen. Like progressive male (masculinist) thinkers in other spheres, they thereby arrive at a position in which questions of gender, and often class, and other internal divisions come to be treated as epiphenomenal – problems that will be overcome "automatically" by the forces of progress in the unfolding of world history.

---

[71] Omprakash Valmiki, *Joothan: A Dalit's Life*, trans. Arun Prabha Mukherkjee (Calcutta: Samya, 2003), 109.
[72] Gopal Guru, "Afterword," in Kamble, *Prisons We Broke*, 166.

In this respect, Dalit discourse produces a somewhat reduced and unhistorical view of the Dalit movement. I consider some of the consequences of this reduction in Chapter 6. Before I do that, however, it will help to take a break from India and examine another movement for "conversion" – the struggle for democracy in mid-twentieth-century USA.

4

"Double V"

The Everyday of Race Relations

The last chapter should have shown how Dalits used the idea of conversion out of the dominant religion of India to claim their rights as citizens and to call for an altered social and political arrangement in the country. For people of African descent in the USA, the idea of conversion (or of opting out) has had a rather different history. Physically removed from the African part of their heritage, they were converted to the new religion of Christianity, or various forms of it, in the late eighteenth and nineteenth centuries. (As we know, different kinds of conversion, not least to a new form of Islamic solidarity, continued strongly in the twentieth century, but these were less pervasive.) Over that time, it became increasingly obvious to African Americans that they were as American as any other immigrants to the country, and they demanded their rights as Americans. To do so, they appropriated the reigning political slogan in the United States, the idea so eloquently and loudly proclaimed in the constitution of 1788 and since, of the common rights of all inhabitants of the land, "We the people..." – not to mention a central proposition of the Bible, "All men are brothers...." Quite self-consciously, then, and with increasing militancy over the middle decades of the twentieth century, it was for African Americans a matter not of opting out but opting in.

I need to reiterate that opting out and opting in are not polar opposite, irreconcilable options, for there is no clear-cut *out* or *in* for most subordinated groups in a society. It is necessary to emphasize that, as with the Dalits, there was no single strategy or platform that African

98 *A History of Prejudice*

Americans as a body adopted for the amelioration or advancement of their social, political, and economic condition. Through most of the second half of the nineteenth century and all of the twentieth, there were those who worked for integration in order to eradicate racial and caste privileges, and there were black nationalists who spoke of the need for a separate geopolitical space for African Americans – most notably represented, it is said, in the Garveyite call for a return to Africa (although even in Garvey's case what was at stake was the redemption of Africa, and by that means the redemption of people of African descent everywhere).[1] There were other perspectives, too, built, for example, around the notion of a black working class and the primacy of labor struggle, aimed at a radical social transformation. Yet, as scholars have noted, these competing paradigms – integration, nationalism, transformation – were not exclusive, but overlapping, braiding, and shifting even in individual cases.[2]

Amiri Baraka captured the convergence and the common ground well in a 1972 address on "The Pan-African Party and the Black Nation." "Nationalists," "repatriation," and "separation" people must understand, he said, that "we," African Americans, "ain't going anywhere." "Back to Africa" was certainly the right slogan, but it applied "wherever we are." "We must move to have self-determination, self-sufficiency, self-respect and self-defense wherever we exist in large numbers – whether it is Chicago or Johannesburg."[3] That claim to sameness, to equal rights and opportunities, and an end to discriminatory practices, pre-judicial and judicial, was the common ground for the African American freedom struggle as it has been called, of civil rights and Black Power.

One important feature of the history of American democracy and American liberty has been a claim to universalism, the applicability of these ideals to one and all, both at home and abroad – in spite of the obvious limits evident in the exclusion of women, blacks, and Native

---

[1] Cf. Randall K. Burkett, *Black Redemption: Churchmen Speak for the Garvey Movement* (Philadelphia: Temple University Press, 1978), especially "Introduction," 8, and passim.

[2] The preceding summary statement is taken from Manning Marable and Leith Mullings, eds., *Let Nobody Turn Us Around: Voices of Resistance, Reform, and Renewal* (Lanham, MD: Rowman and Littlefield, 2000), "Preface," xviii–xxi.

[3] Ibid., 497, 498.

Americans from equal access in the United States. From the moment of the American Revolution down to World War II, and indeed up to now, there has been a continuing American urge (and repeated American actions) to spread capitalism and "democracy" to the "backward" nations of the world. The justification of World War II for the US and its allies lay in an argument about democracy and freedom for all the people of the world; the end of colonialism and imperialism (in its current incarnation of white men's rule over the darker peoples of Asia and Africa); and the end of all notions of racial supremacy, Aryan or other. The call for "Double V[ictory]" – victory against the opponents of democracy and freedom, and for the end of colonialism and racism, at home and abroad – appeared in this context, given the denial of basic democratic rights to African Americans (Native Americans, women, and other second-class citizens, or noncitizens, were not a prominent part of the national debate at this time).

I take the African American call for Double V as a centerpiece in this chapter for a number of reasons. The record of this period of struggle indicates, as I hope my discussion of the Dalit drive for conversion has done, the very lengthy (and often hidden) history of the fight for civil rights and citizenship, and the many fronts on which it was waged. The campaign reaffirms several of the most fundamental propositions and tendencies of the black struggle from the days of the fight for the abolition of slavery to today – issues of human dignity and self-respect, equal political and economic opportunities, and a stake in government. At the same time, it reveals another, perhaps inadequately stressed, aspect of the American experience and American discourse – the unusually strong link between masculinism, militarism, and citizenship in this history.

Military service and citizenship are commonly coupled in the rhetoric and history of modern nation-states. Yet, the connection seems to have been especially strong in the USA, perhaps because it is a young nation that, almost to the very end of the nineteenth century, was still seeking by military force to expand its borders and secure the unchallenged writ of government. Political rights here were long assumed to be gained by defending the land – which is one of the main reasons why women were excluded from citizen status. The conservative judge Thomas P. Brady's rant, in a speech on "Black Monday: Segregation or Amalgamation," delivered in Greenwood, Mississippi, in 1955,

A History of Prejudice

was perhaps unusually blunt, but certainly not uncommon in its logic. Talking of how America "came of age" in the years between 1620 and 1936, Brady declared: "Thirteen pathetically weak colonies oppose the greatest military power on earth, Great Britain. They were not without assistance, and after almost seven trying, bloody years, victory is won at Yorktown, and a nation is born." And then to the punchline: "It is ridiculous to assume that the American negro played any part in this struggle, though he had been in this country approximately one hundred and fifty years. He made no contribution whatsoever." Next stage, 1812: "Like the war of 1776, the War of 1812 was a just war, and the United States emerged victorious." Followed again by the punchline: "It is ridiculous to assume that the American negro played any part in this struggle, though he had been in this country almost two hundred years."[4]

Much has changed since the fabled frontiersmen, pioneers, and Lone Rangers fought the wars of 1776 and 1812, or the 1840s (annexation of New Mexico and California), or 1890 (the attack on and killing of over 300 Native Americans camped at Wounded Knee, South Dakota). The example of recent wars (Vietnam, Iraq, Afghanistan) indicates that, in our day, to have class and racial privilege often means, precisely, to be excused from military service.[5] For all that, in one of those unquestioned paradoxes of modern nationalism, the close intertwining of military duty and citizenship, and the attendant celebration of the nation's military forces, remains daily on display. Even after the heated debate over the legitimacy of U.S. intervention in Vietnam and Iraq, it is the one expression of national duty that remains sacrosanct: one questions "the men and women of the armed forces" – and hence military action? – at one's peril.

The exceptionally close tie between masculinism, militarism, and citizenship is important for my analysis. Civil rights has provided the framework for much of the investigation of American democracy in the twentieth century. All of African American history – and with

---

[4] Clayborne Carson et al., eds., *The Eyes on the Prize: Civil Rights Reader. Documents, Speeches, and Firsthand Accounts from the Black Freedom Struggle, 1954–1990* (New York: Penguin Books, 1991), 84, 85. In fact, African Americans did serve in both wars – when the military needs grew dire.

[5] See Christian G. Appy, *Working-Class War: American Combat Soldiers and Vietnam* (Chapel Hill: University of North Carolina Press, 1993).

that, much of U.S. history – has been written around the struggle against racialized stigmatization and exploitation: slavery and segregation. However, if the racism of American democracy and society was called, loud and clear, by the African American struggle at the time of the Second World War (as well as before and after), the masculinism of the African American (and the wider American) discourse of the time has not been sufficiently noticed – by contemporaries, or by subsequent analysts. We need to bear this in mind as we work through the history, the twists and turns as well as the achievements, of Double V and the longer civil rights movement in the struggle for full citizenship.

The Double V Campaign[6]

In the extended history of civil rights, one might suggest, the time of the most rapid expansion of the province of these rights has been a time of war – the Civil War, World War I, World War II – to which one might add the campaigns in Korea and Vietnam, the military expression of the Cold War, as it were. The Civil War, with Frederick Douglass's famous call to arms as the path to citizenship, was perhaps the crucial moment in establishing the link between African American military service and African American rights. But it has been followed by others. "The emerging black freedom movement of the twentieth century . . . was cataclysmically moved by the guns of August 1914 and the onset of 'the great war'," writes Vincent Harding. The American establishment's call "to make the world safe for democracy served to heighten the already vivid consciousness of Afro-Americans concerning the tragic contradictions endemic to their own native, alien land." Again, World War II "seemed like déjà vu, a reenactment of all the tendencies of 'the war to make the world safe for democracy', with many elements now intensified and magnified."[7]

---

[6] The *Pittsburgh Courier*, February 14, 1942, introduced the phrase "Double V" for "victory over our enemies at home and victory over our enemies on the battle-fields abroad."

[7] Vincent Harding, "We the People: The Long Journey Toward a More Perfect Union," in Carson et al., *Eyes on the Prize*, 3, 17, 18, 29. For important comments on the enormous impact of the Second World War, see Glenda E. Gilmore, *Defying Dixie: The Radical Roots of Civil Rights, 1919–1950* (New York: W. W. Norton and Co., 2008), especially pt. III, 297–444; Richard M. Dalfiume, "The 'Forgotten Years' of the Negro Revolution," in Bernard Sternsher, *The Negro in Depression and War:*

The New York journalist and war correspondent Roi Ottley's 1943 book on African American history as seen from Harlem, *New World a-Coming*, underscores the imbrication of military and political campaigns in the black struggle, as in all U.S. history. Although the declared objective of the Civil War was the preservation of the United States as a unit, he observes, abolitionists quickly recognized it as a critical moment for the campaign against slavery. African American leaders offered Lincoln's federal government three regiments of troops, fully equipped and maintained by the black population. While that offer was declined, blacks were subsequently allowed into the Union Army. The alternative, Lincoln observed, would have been to abandon the Union and the Constitution. The Emancipation Proclamation, issued in September 1862 and effective from January 1, 1863, "decreed that all persons held as slaves . . . [in the rebellious Confederate states] were to be freed, and those of suitable condition were to be 'received into the armed service of the United States.'"[8]

It was a similar kind of military/political necessity that opened up the opportunity for an expansion of the struggle for black rights in World Wars I and II. The U.S. entry into the First World War led to a dramatic increase in the demand for industrial and military forces. "Large numbers of white men left industrial pursuits for military service both in the United States Army and in the armies of their native lands," Ottley notes. What followed was a "mad race" to get hold of southern black labor. Aided by the federal government and railroad entrepreneurs seeking increased profits, agents went to the South and recruited large numbers of blacks over the objections of southern whites.[9]

"At no time since the days following the Civil War had the Negro been in a position where he stood to make greater gain or sustain

---

Prelude to Revolution, 1930–1945 (Chicago: Quadrangle Books, 1969), especially 299; Morton Sosna, "More Important than the Civil War? The Impact of World War II on the South," in *Perspectives on the American South: An Annual Review of Society, Politics and Culture*, vol. 4, ed. James C. Cobb and Charles R. Wilson (New York: Gordon and Breach, 1987); and Carol Anderson, *Eyes off the Prize: The United Nations and the African American Struggle for Human Rights, 1944–1955* (Cambridge: Cambridge University Press, 2003).

[8] Roi Ottley, *New World a-Coming* (1943; reprint New York: Arno Press and New York Times, 1968), 19–20.

[9] Ibid., 33–4.

"Double V"

greater loss in status," James Weldon Johnson noted in his 1933 autobiography, *Along This Way*:

The exodus of Negroes to the North, pulled there to fill the labor vacuum in the great industries, was in full motion; the tremors of war in Europe were shaking America with increasing intensity; circumstances were combining to put a higher premium on Negro muscle, Negro hands, and Negro brains than ever before; all these forces had a quickening effect that was running through the entire mass of the race.[10]

And when, in the middle of that war, two days of organized white attacks in East St. Louis, Illinois, left two hundred blacks dead (indiscriminately shot, burned, and hanged) and thousands homeless, the NAACP and other black leaders in Harlem organized a demonstration of 15,000 African American men, women and children, who marched silently down New York's Fifth Avenue, carrying banners that said: "Mr. President, Why Not Make America Safe for Democracy?"[11]

The sentiment was radicalized, deepened, and greatly extended during World War II, to make Double V a central slogan of the African American struggle. African Americans were quick to seize on the argument that active participation in the defense of the country gave them a claim on equal citizenship. The black press's commentary on the war illustrates very well the shared faith in a militaristic nationhood as well as the idea that *all* citizens had the duty to fight for the country. Consider the response of the *Atlanta Daily World*, the South's only African American-owned daily, to Georgia governor Ellis Arnall's "work or fight" directive. "Work or fight" orders, first introduced in World War I, directed that able-bodied individuals of military-service age (now described by federal Defense official Anna Rosenberg as being on "loan" from the military to civilian life during wartime!) accept "useful occupations" or risk being jailed. During World War II, starting in late 1942, a series of "work or fight" ordinances came into force in different southern states in response to the need for labor on rural farms and a shortage of domestic servants. The *Louisiana Weekly* appropriately dubbed them "work or jail" orders since even a refusal

---

[10] James Weldon Johnson, *Along This Way: The Autobiography of James Weldon Johnson* (1933; reprint New York: Viking Penguin, 1991), 308, 315, and see also 330, 332.

[11] Ottley, *New World a-Coming*, 37–8; Johnson, *Along This Way*, 319–21.

to take on domestic positions could lead to imprisonment. In 1943, before the harvest season, Arnall ordered all sheriffs to enforce "work or fight" regulations for men and women throughout Georgia.[12] While expressing some misgivings that local officials might misuse the power, as they had in the past, pushing African Americans into unsuitable lowly positions, the *Atlanta Daily World* endorsed Arnall's order in ringing terms: "In these critical hours in our history and amid the acute shortage in man and womanpower, it is not only unpatriotic for able-bodied citizens to go loafing about the city streets, but it is down-right sinful."[13]

In an earlier piece entitled "The Case for the Negro," the Atlanta daily had cited the *Kentucky Irish American* to say: "The war is helping to do away with racial and religious prejudice as men and boys of different races are united in the fight for freedom and liberty.... The Negro is a beneficiary of this situation as he is again demonstrating proof of his loyalty and patriotism."[14] Long before then, the Committee for Participation of Negroes in the National Defense, a pressure group formed in 1938 by African American army officers who had served in World War I, had written an open letter to President Franklin D. Roosevelt that said: "[W]e are expecting a more dignified place in our armed forces during the next war than we occupied during the [First] World War." The great labor leader Asa Philip Randolph amplified the argument in January 1941: "We loyal Negro-American citizens demand the right to work and fight for our country."[15] By the end of World War II, nearly one million African American men and women had been recruited into the armed forces, and nearly half of them had served overseas. Indeed, although it is often overlooked

[12] Albert A. Blum, "Work or Fight: The Use of the Draft as a Manpower Sanction during the Second World War," *Industrial and Labor Relations Review*, 16, no. 3 (April 1963), 367; Charles D. Chamberlain, *Victory at Home: Manpower and Race in the American South during World War II* (Athens: University of Georgia Press, 2003), 62, 80–1; and Risa L. Goluboff, "The Thirteenth Amendment and the Lost Origins of Civil Rights," *Duke Law Journal*, 50, no. 6 (April 2001), 1656–9.

[13] *Atlanta Daily World*, September 8, 1943.

[14] *Atlanta Daily World*, May 17, 1943.

[15] David Levering Lewis, *W. E. B. Du Bois: The Fight for Equality and the American Century, 1919–1963* (New York: Henry Holt and Co., 2000), 465; and Dalfiume, "'Forgotten Years' of the Negro Revolution," 305. See also Appy, *Working-Class War*, 21.

"Double V" 105

completely, the women's work in auxiliary services gained them some legitimacy in their political struggles. The consequences for the wider democratic struggle were hardly small.

Ruling classes and governments should not expect a colonized, unfree people to go to war to defend freedom in other parts of the world. The Indian National Congress had made the point categorically by refusing to support Britain's war against the Axis Powers until India itself was promised freedom. African Americans, not quite so obviously colonized, but segregated, ghettoized, impoverished, criminalized, and treated at best as second-class citizens, made the same argument. If no part of the world could be denied the chance of democracy and self-government, every part of the United States, and every part of its population, was entitled to no less (and, as many African American and other antiracist commentators pointed out at this time, the American South, too, was part of the USA!). African Americans made the case even more stridently because no one (or practically no one) now argued that they were not "Americans," whatever their social, economic, or political disadvantages. World War II – with its loud proclamations about the preservation of liberty and democracy – provided the opportunity to argue strongly for an expansion of their part in the national economy and military forces, and the right to be treated as full Americans. And the fact that large numbers of African Americans fought in the war reinforced the case immeasurably.

The NAACP had made the point simply even before the United States had formally declared war: "[T]he hysterical cries of the preachers of democracy for Europe leave us cold. We want democracy in Alabama and Arkansas, in Mississippi and Michigan, in the District of Columbia – *in the Senate of the United States.*" A discharged black army corporal from Alabama put it more bluntly after the war: "I spent four years in the army to free a bunch of Dutchmen and Frenchmen, and I'm hanged if I'm going to let the Alabama version of the Germans kick me around when I get home. No sirree-bob! I went into the Army a nigger; I'm coming out a man." Ottley sums up the argument: "Negroes are . . . insistent that, if they must die as equals, then they must be treated as equals."[16]

---

[16] Dalfiume, "'Forgotten Years' of the Negro Revolution," 302 (emphasis original); Robin D. G. Kelley and Earl Lewis, eds., *To Make Our World Anew*, Volume II:

106   *A History of Prejudice*

The African American struggle grew exponentially during this period of democratic resurgence, as did other labor movements such as the Communist Party of the USA. The NAACP expanded from its 355 branches and 50,556 members in 1940 to 1,073 branches with just under 450,000 members in 1946.[17] Even before America's entry into battle, and more emphatically after that, the Second World War brought a rush of new opportunities for African American and other depressed sections of the American population. Langston Hughes noted how Roosevelt's Executive Order 8802 brought "more than a million Negro workers into contact with machinery" for the first time and allowed thousands of African American women to escape from "the underpaid servitude of white kitchens and laundries." It was in 1941 (after the Japanese attack on Pearl Harbor) that "the war broke out," he wrote in his column in *The Chicago Defender* in January 1943. "Before that there wasn't no defense work much. And the President hadn't told the factory bosses that they had to hire colored.... Now, it's 1942 – and different. Folks have jobs. Money's circulating again. Relatives are in the Army with big insurances if they die."[18]

Ottley's synoptic account of the making of the president's Executive Order 8802 of June 1941, whereby the Roosevelt administration outlawed racial discrimination by companies and unions doing war work on government contracts, and established the Fair Employment Practices Committee (FEPC) to enforce the order, illustrates the intensification of African American aspirations and organization at this time. In the months before the Japanese attack on Pearl Harbor, he writes, "Negro communities in the urban areas were seething with resentment." The Depression, which had hit both white and black folks hard, was over, and the economy was expanding once more. But over one million African Americans (out of 5.4 million of working age) were unemployed. A government survey found only 142 blacks among 29,215 workers employed in ten war plants in the New York area. Fifty-six war-contract factories in St. Louis, Missouri, employed

---

A History of African Americans from 1880 (New York: Oxford University Press, 2005), 174; and Ottley, *New World a-Coming*, 312.

[17] Dalfiume, "'Forgotten Years' of the Negro Revolution," 306. The phrase "period of democratic resurgence" comes from Ralph Ellison's 1944 review of *An American Dilemma*; see Ellison, *Shadow and Act*, 317.

[18] *Chicago Defender*, April 20, 1946 and January 9, 1943.

"Double V" 107

an average of three blacks each. In Michigan, 22,042 of 26,904 defense jobs were reserved for whites. It was not only skilled jobs that were denied to African Americans: the survey found that 35,000 of a total of 83,000 unskilled jobs were also closed to them.[19]

It is well known that Roosevelt's executive order followed A. Philip Randolph's brilliant organization of a March on Washington Movement. Joe W. Trotter, Jr., suggests that the idea of the movement actually came from a black woman participant at a meeting of civil rights groups in Chicago, who said angrily:

We ought to throw fifty thousand Negroes around the White House, bring them over from all over the country, in jalopies, in trains and any way they can get there, and throw them around the White House and keep them there until we can get some action from the White House.

"I agree with the sister," Randolph is reported to have said, as he offered the resources and leadership of his organization, the Brotherhood of Sleeping Car Porters, for the movement.[20]

The March on Washington Movement spread rapidly, set up offices in all the major industrial centers of the North and West, and joined forces with the NAACP, the National Negro Congress, and Urban League, as well as local churches and other associations. In short order, writes Ottley, buses and trains were chartered, and a demonstration of over 50,000 African Americans (revised upward from an initial goal of 10,000 to 20,000 and then 50,000) was planned for July 1, 1941. Alarmed by the audacity and scale of these developments, Washington sent several emissaries, including first lady Eleanor Roosevelt, to appeal to the leaders to call off the movement.

Four days before the threatened march, the leaders of the movement were called to Washington and the order against discrimination in federally funded defense employment was issued. The policy of the government, it declared, was

to encourage full participation in the national defense program by all citizens of the United States, regardless of race, creed, color, or national origin, in the firm belief that the democratic way of life within the Nation can be

---

[19] Ottley, *New World a-Coming*, 289–90.
[20] Joe W. Trotter, Jr., "From a Raw Deal to a New Deal, 1929–1945," in Kelley and Lewis, *To Make Our World Anew*, vol. II, 164–5.

defended successfully only with the help and support of all groups within its borders.[21]

A year later, in the summer of 1942, Roosevelt sent the following message to the NAACP's annual convention: "I note with satisfaction that the theme of your significant gathering read, 'Victory is Vital to Minorities.' This theme might well be reversed and given to the nation as a slogan.... 'Minorities are Vital to Victory.'"[22] It was an extraordinary acknowledgment, the first great victory of civil rights, could one say, since the abolition of slavery and the citizenship and voting rights amendments of the 1860s?

The Geography of Prejudice

Old habits die hard, however. Although Executive Order 8802 opened up many opportunities for African Americans and other colored Americans, it also led to conflict with sections of organized labor that had an established policy of excluding blacks, and with "southern politics" more generally. More than a million African Americans joined the military during the war, as already noted. Only 5% of the army in summer 1941, they comprised 10.3% of it, roughly equivalent to their proportion of the total population, by December 1942. And the question of where these forces should be posted, trained, fed, and allowed to sleep or travel was the cause of considerable tension and misgiving.[23]

Ottley refers to a few of the many demonstrations of deep-rooted prejudice. Alabama's governor, Frank Murray Dixon, a decorated World War I veteran, refused to accept an army contract for tent cloth because it contained a clause against racial discrimination. Numerous white spokespersons defended the exclusion of blacks from

---

[21] Ottley, *New World a-Coming*, 291–3.
[22] Ibid., 320.
[23] See Donald L. Grant, *The Way It Was in the South: The Black Experience in Georgia* (Athens: University of Georgia Press, 1993), 361; Robert J. Norrell, *The House I Live In: Race in the American Century* (New York: Oxford University Press, 2005), 123, 126. See also Ronald Takaki, *Double Victory: A Multicultural History of America in World War II* (Boston: Little Brown and Co., 2000).

"Double V"   109

trade unions and complained that the federal government was forcing employers to hire blacks in jobs that had always been reserved for white men. Fearing the consequences of blacks working alongside whites in offices and factories, one retired politician proposed a "state-wide, South-wide, nation-wide League for White Supremacy" to combat this "menace to our national security and our local way of life." In a letter to the Army chief of staff, Alabama senator John D. Bankhead declared that the federal government was doing "a disservice to the war effort by locating Negro troops in the South in immediate contact with white troops." If black soldiers had to be trained in the South, he added, it would be better to place southern blacks there – since they knew the social rules – and keep "Northern Negro soldiers in the North." The Southern Governors' Conference reinforced the point, asking the War Department to "send no Northern blacks to the South and to refrain from placing black soldiers where they might mingle with white soldiers."[24]

Even outside the South, all was hardly smooth sailing. Events in Detroit, now hailed as the military "arsenal of democracy," illustrate the point well. As Ottley reports it, 2,000 whites attacked 500 blacks to prevent them from moving into the Sojourner Truth housing project, "built with public funds for Negro war workers." "At secret meetings, Ku Klux [Klan]ers received orders to keep the Negro workers from entering their new homes.... The National Workers' League, a pro-Nazi group whose officials were later indicted, cooperated with the Klan in preparing and staging the subsequent riot in which scores of people were injured."[25] While the facts of the violence in 1942 were more complicated and investigators learned that several Detroit officials had come out in favor of the very poorly housed African American workers, Ottley's account clearly reflects what many blacks were feeling and saying during this period. The "epidemic of interracial violence" the following summer, in Detroit, Harlem, Washington, and other places, only served to confirm such feelings.[26]

---

[24] Ottley, *New World a-Coming*, 302–3, 311–12. For the governors' plea, see Grant, *The Way It Was in the South*, 361.

[25] Ottley, *New World a-Coming*, 319–20.

[26] The phrase "epidemic of . . . violence" comes from Harvard Sitkoff, "Racial Militancy and Interracial Violence in the Second World War," *Journal of American History*,

A History of Prejudice

When the Fair Employment Practices Committee (FEPC) first announced hearings in Birmingham, Alabama, a newspaper in the neighboring town of Gadsden declared: "A bunch of snoopers, two of whom are Negroes, will assemble in Birmingham, June 18 [1942], for a three-day session to determine whether the South is doing right by Little Sambo." Another referred to the FEPC as "dat committee fer de purteckshun uv Rastus & Sambo." The self-professed "liberal" Mark F. Ethridge, a member of FEPC and editor of the Louisville (Kentucky) *Courier-Journal*, said that he would never have accepted membership on the committee had he thought its purpose was to destroy segregation. And further: "there is no power in the world – not even in all the mechanized armies of the earth, Allied and Axis – which would now force the Southern white people to the abandonment of the principles of social segregation." In essence, he was saying nothing different from what a white railroad mechanic in Macon, Georgia, said at the end of the war: white feelings toward blacks were "like the affection one has for a dog, we love 'em in their place."[27]

On the other hand, as we have seen, fewer African Americans were now willing to take such views lying down. Earl B. Dickerson, one of the black members of the FEPC, responded to Ethridge: "I am unalterably opposed to segregation, whether in the South or North." The South was no more entitled to its own special regulations than any other region, he asserted, for it was "still a part of the geographical boundaries of the United States."[28] William Holmes Borders, minister at Wheat Street Baptist Church in Atlanta, and a leading advocate for civil rights already in the early 1940s, put the matter in Christian terms in a series of "Radio Sermonets." Along with the need to defeat Japan and Germany across the seas, and to liberate India and China and Africa, it was necessary to spread democracy everywhere. Peace and democracy at home and abroad may well require "ten thousand years of Christian discipline." Justice under God would be ours only

---

58, no. 3 (1971), 674. The Detroit "riots" of that summer were among the worst in the history of the United States: 34 people were killed, 25 of them black; over 700 were injured; and over 1,800 were arrested, perhaps 85% of them black.

[27] Mark F. Ethridge, Oral History interview by Richard D. Mckinzie, June 4, 1974 (Harry S. Truman Library and Museum); Gilmore, *Defying Dixie*, 362; Ottley, *New World a-Coming*, 302–3; and Grant, *The Way It Was in the South*, 362.

[28] Ottley, *New World a-Coming*, 303, 312.

when we "crush Hitler in Germany and Hitlerism in Georgia," for "democracy, like charity, begins at home."[29]

The depth of feeling among leading African Americans is clear from the outrage occasioned by Zora Neale Hurston's reported (or misreported) remark, in February 1943, that "the Jim Crow system works." This was not the time for publicity-seeking people to come up with such "arrant and even vicious nonsense," declared Roy Wilkins, secretary of the NAACP. It is evident also in Hurston's own response to contemporary events: "We are being foolish . . . ," she wrote to Alain Locke after the Detroit violence of June 1943, "if we let it rest as we have done other riots." Race prejudice and violence was not a sectional, southern matter; it was national, and needed to be recognized and confronted as such. The North was simply more hypocritical, she noted, reiterating the argument that was misread as her justifying the Jim Crow South for being more honest. Northerners used the Negro vote to get into power, and "then bar us from jobs and decent living quarter, and if there is any protests [sic], riot, and terrify Negro workers away from town and jobs, and then . . . brush it off with folklore about the south." Once they realized that the "THEM SOUTHERNERS DONE IT" argument was not going to be accepted, they would have to think twice.[30]

Hurston's statements on the worldwide hypocrisy, racism, and violence of the whites, or Anglo-Saxons, as she called them, reflected a heightened global perspective in African American political commentary at this time. Racism and violence went with the Anglo-Saxons, she wrote: "The Anglo-Saxon is the most intolerant [sic] of human beings in the matter of any other group darker than themselves. Did the southerners colonize Africa and India, and put over the outrages based on race there?" "I can think of [Truman] as nothing else but the BUTCHER OF ASIA," she writes in a letter of July 1946: "Of his grin of triumph on giving the order to drop the Atom bombs on Japan. . . . Of his slighting the Inauguration of the new nation of the

---

[29] William Holmes Borders, *Seven Minutes at the 'Mike' in the Deep South* (1943; reprint Atlanta: B. F. Logan Press, 1944), 94, 98, 99. I owe thanks to Randolph Burkett for drawing my attention to Borders's work.

[30] Carla Kaplan, ed., *Zora Neale Hurston: A Life in Letters* (New York: Doubleday, 2002), 439–40, 491–2. On the traditional assumption of southern exceptionalism, see Matthew D. Lassiter and Joseph Crespino, eds., *The Myth of Southern Exceptionalism* (New York: Oxford University Press, 2010).

112   *A History of Prejudice*

Philipines [*sic*] by not bothering to be present." There had not been a word of protest from the black press, she noted: "Is it that we are so devoted to a 'good Massa' that we feel that we ought not to even protest such crimes?"[31]

In December 1945, indeed, Hurston published an essay entitled "Crazy for this Democracy," in which, as her biographers have noted, she restated several of the political propositions that her publishers had insisted on weeding out of her 1942 autobiography, *Dust Tracks on a Road.* She wondered if she had misheard when Franklin Roosevelt talked of the United States as the arsenal of democracy. Did he perhaps mean "arse-and-all," given American support of English, French, and Dutch campaigns to recolonize millions of people in Asia? "I thought when they said Atlantic Charter, that meant me and everybody in Africa and Asia and everywhere. But it seems like the Atlantic is an ocean that does not touch anywhere but North America and Europe." She's all for trying out this "gorgeous thing" called democracy, Hurston says in an echo of Gandhi.[32] The thing that keeps her from "pitching headlong" into it is the existence of the Jim Crow laws in America. The need of the hour, in her judgment, is simple: "the repeal of every Jim Crow law in the nation here and now . . . complete repeal of All Jim Crow laws in the United States once and for all, and right now. For the benefit of this nation and as a precedent to the world."[33]

Hurston had long avowed that she was not interested in politics, in the sense of making grand political statements one way or another on major political issues; she would rather live courageously, and let the individual example show the world what she thought of its judgments and arrangements. Even if her comments between 1943 and 1946 are seen as a defensive reaction to the charge of betrayal made against her, they are also a sign of the greatly heightened emotions of the time. Something of that emotion is reflected in a letter

---

[31] Kaplan, *Zora Neale Hurston*, 474, 491, 546.

[32] When asked what he thought of Western civilization, Gandhi famously said: "It would be a good thing."

[33] Zora Neale Hurston, "Crazy for This Democracy," *Negro Digest* (December 1945), reprinted in *I Love Myself When I Am Laughing . . . and Then Again When I Am Looking Mean and Impressive*, ed. Alice Walker (New York: Feminist Press, 1979), 165–8; Valerie Boyd, *Wrapped in Rainbows: The Life of Zora Neale Hurston* (New York: Scribner, 2003), 380–1; and Robert E. Hemenway, *Zora Neale Hurston: A Literary Biography* (Urbana: University of Illinois Press, 1980), 294.

she wrote to Walter White in November 1942, before the interview on Jim Crow that was used against her. In it, she wrote of conditions in the Signal Corps school in St. Augustine, Florida, that had been established, under pressure from black leaders, for the training of African American officers. Hurston wrote of the unsatisfactory living quarters and the poor quality and quantity of the food. "The dissatisfaction is *tremendous*." The black officers, most of them college graduates from middle-class backgrounds, were continuously insulted by the head of the school, who would ask them when they had ever had three meals in a day before they got there. "Well, the Negroes have been bitched again!... Remember that this is the ONLY [training school] for Negroes in the U.S., though the whites have several. I feel that the whole body of Negroes are being insulted and mocked."[34]

There were other dramatic illustrations of the depth of African American sentiment. Consider the sign displayed by an African American doctor in Harlem on the back of his car in 1942 or '43:

> IS THERE A DIFFERENCE?
> JAPS BRUTALLY BEAT
> AMERICAN REPORTER
> GERMANS BRUTALLY BEAT
> SEVERAL JEWS
> AMERICAN CRACKERS
> BRUTALLY BEAT
> ROLAND HAYES & NEGRO SOLDIERS[35]

Recall that Roland Hayes (1887–1977), a child of former slaves, was the first African American to win international fame as a concert performer, with an inaugural international performance in London in 1920. He and his wife had a home in Brookline, Massachusetts, as well as in Curryville, Georgia, where they owned a 600-acre farm. In July 1942, Hayes's wife and daughter were thrown out of a shoe store in Rome, Georgia, for having sat down in its "whites-only" area. When Hayes confronted the store clerk, he and his wife were arrested by the local police and Hayes was beaten up. In response to the incident, Governor Eugene Talmadge warned blacks who opposed segregation to stay out of Georgia. All this now made national headlines.

---

[34] Kaplan, *Zora Neale Hurston*, 469–70 (emphasis Hurston's).
[35] Ottley, *New World a-Coming*, 307.

114 *A History of Prejudice*

One result of traditional white fears and the growing black determination to reconstruct American social and political life was a polarization of strong positions on both sides. The problems that confronted returning Georgia veterans reflect the challenges faced widely by southern black soldiers. This was a new stage in the fight for "tradition."

The War Comes Home

African Americans had been cruelly disillusioned at the end of the First World War, as wartime promises evaporated and political and social life on the ground returned to normal – or worse. The year 1919 brought a wave of black-baiting and lynching that had not been witnessed for some time, as well as "riots" (in the South and the North) that were quite unprecedented – in part perhaps because, unlike on many former occasions, black communities now fought back. "The Red Summer of 1919 broke in fury," wrote Johnson. "The great majority [of colored people] had trustingly felt that, because they had cheerfully done their bit in the war, conditions for them would be better. The reverse seemed to be true. There was one case, at least, in which a returned Negro soldier was lynched *because of the fact* that he wore the uniform of a United States soldier."[36]

Langston Hughes captured the cynicism and anger of many black spokespersons, not to mention ordinary African Americans, in a piece he wrote in 1934 entitled "Negroes Speak of War": "When the time comes for the next war . . . remember the last war," he wrote. "Does any Negro believe . . . that the world was actually saved for Democracy?" After the Chicago riots, the Washington, D.C., riots, the East St. Louis riots, and the "lynched black workers hanging on trees all around Tuskegee, . . . is it some foreign army needs to be fought?"

[W]hen the next war comes, I want to know whose war and why. . . . There's plenty of perils right here at home that needs attending to: what about those labor unions that won't admit Negroes? And . . . all them factories where I can't work even if there was work? And . . . the schools I can't go to, and the states I can't vote in, and the juries I can't sit on? . . . And what about a voice in whose [*sic*] running this country and why – before I even think of crossing the water and fighting again?

[36] Johnson, *Along This Way*, 341 (emphasis in original).

"Double V" 115

Who said I want to go to war? If I do, it ain't the same war the President wants to go to. No, sir, I been hanging on a rope in Alabama too long.[37]

A good part of the vehemence of the Double V campaign came from a sense of the unfulfilled promises of World War I. The end of World War II was to bring renewed frustration among African Americans, and with it greater agitation and a new assertiveness.

I have cited the comments of the "liberal" editor Mark Ethridge and an unnamed white mechanic from Macon, Georgia, on the subject of keeping blacks in their place. Many whites had openly expressed the fear that, after the war, black soldiers would return with the idea that now that they had fought for their country they were owed the same rights as whites and that, because they had learned to use guns, they would use them. "Negroes were the shock troops of the future Jewish-communist revolution," and "the Americans [sic] who had died in Europe had not given their lives so that niggers could marry American white women," Emory Burke, president of a newly formed fascist organization called the Columbians, told an Atlanta audience in November 1946. Eugene Talmadge, longtime governor of Georgia; Frank M. Dixon, governor of Alabama until 1943; Senator Theodore G. "The Man" Bilbo and Congressman John E. Rankin, both from Mississippi; and other prominent white supremacists, made the same point repeatedly.[38]

Not surprisingly, the end of the war in Europe and Asia brought numerous aggravated racial clashes at home. There were many instances of collective racial assaults in the Midwest and the North, but the South – where 70% of the African American population still lived – bore the brunt of the violence. "Race riots" were reported from Columbia, Tennessee, in February 1946, and from various places in Alabama, Mississippi, Louisiana, South Carolina, and Tennessee

---

[37] Langston Hughes, *Good Morning Revolution: Uncollected Writings of Langston Hughes*, ed. Faith Berry (New York: Carol Publishing Group, 1992), 40–2.

[38] J. Wayne Dudley, "'Hate' Organizations of the 1940s: The Columbians, Inc.," *Phylon*, 42, no. 3 (1981), 262, 268; and Norrell, *The House I Live In*, 143. See also Manning Marable, *Race, Reform and Rebellion: The Second Reconstruction and Beyond in Black America, 1945–2006* (Jackson: University Press of Mississippi, 2007); and Jason M. Ward, *Defending White Democracy: The Making of a Segregationist Movement and the Remaking of Racial Politics, 1936–1965* (Chapel Hill: University of North Carolina Press, 2011).

116   *A History of Prejudice*

between July and September, and there were other cases of serious racial violence. Thus, to take a few examples from Georgia, a 21-year-old military veteran was beaten up by a masked gang at Atlanta Municipal Airport in February 1946. Willie Dudley, a member of the American Federation of Labor, was flogged by four men wearing Ku Klux Klan masks in June 1946 for his refusal to give up his trade union work. Macio Snipes, a military veteran and the only African American in Taylor County who voted in the Democratic primary, was shot dead while sitting on the porch at his home three days later, on July 20, 1946. He had not heeded the signs posted on many black churches warning African Americans not to vote: "The First Nigger to Vote Will Never Vote Again."[39]

In the months of July and August 1946 alone, as many as nine African Americans were lynched in the South, and there were almost certainly other attacks that went unreported. Several of the incidents made national headlines. One of the most widely publicized was the case of the retired army sergeant Isaac Woodard, who was imprisoned, beaten, and blinded by the police in Batesburg, South Carolina, while he was on his way home from the war, for his temerity in asking the bus driver to let him use the toilet when they stopped at a drug store. Because Woodard was a veteran, because he was assaulted and permanently blinded by an officer of the law, and because he survived to tell the tale, writes Kari Frederickson, he became "an emblem" of the racial order that still prevailed in America, especially in the South.[40]

A quadruple lynching that occurred in Georgia on July 25, 1946, received something of the same national attention. On that day, a mob of some twenty armed men lynched George Dorsey, a discharged soldier recently returned after five years in the army, including service in Australia and North Africa, along with his wife, Mae (or May) Murray Dorsey, and his sister and brother-in-law, Dorothy and Roger Malcolm. Their bodies were riddled with dozens of bullets, and in one

---

[39] Dudley, "'Hate' Organizations of the 1940s," 263–4; Grant, *The Way It Was in the South*, 366; Kari Frederickson, "'The Slowest State' and the 'Most Backward Community': Racial Violence in South Carolina and Federal Civil-Rights Legislation, 1946–1948," *South Carolina Historical Magazine*, 98, no. 2 (April 1997), 179–80; *Atlanta Constitution*, July 26, 1946; and *Atlanta Journal*, July 27, 1946.

[40] Frederickson, "'The Slowest State' and the 'Most Backward Community,'" 184 and passim.

"Double V"

or two cases their faces blown up and unrecognizable. The murder of the two couples at Moore's Ford Bridge in Walton County, near the town of Monroe, Georgia, was a return to a form of collective violence that had apparently declined in the preceding years, even decades. It was the first multiple lynching in Georgia since 1918, and one of the instances in which women, too, were lynched. It may help to examine the context and fallout of this event in some detail for what it tells us about the contemporary stage of the struggle for democracy.[41]

Relying on the testimony of J. Loy Harrison, a prosperous white farmer, who reported the lynching, local newspapers reconstructed the sequence of events that led to the lynching as follows. Harrison was driving the four African Americans back to his farm from Atlanta, after having obtained the release of one of the men, Roger Malcolm, on bail. By his account, his car was stopped and surrounded at the wooden bridge spanning the Appalachee River, which divided Walton and Oconee counties, and he was held at gunpoint while an armed mob dragged the four men and women down a side road and blasted them in three fusillades of shots from rifles and shotguns. The talk among members of the crowd suggested that they had come for Roger. Seeing two black men in the car, they seized both. When the women began shouting and one of them evidently recognized one of the attackers, they were pulled out as well. Harrison himself was spared, he told investigators, because he did not recognize anyone among the attackers.[42]

Malcolm had been arrested eleven days earlier for stabbing and wounding Barney Hester, a young white man on whose farm he worked as a sharecropper. The arrested man's wife, Dorothy, worked for Loy Harrison. She and her mother, who lived on his farm, entreated Harrison to stand surety for Roger Malcolm and get him out of jail. They persuaded him after considerable pleading. Harrison said he agreed because he needed additional farmhands.[43] On July 25, he took

---

[41] I have assembled the "facts" in the following account on the basis of reports in the *Atlanta Daily World*, *Atlanta Constitution*, and *Atlanta Journal* in July and August 1946. For a book-length reconstruction of the event and subsequent investigation, see Laura Wexler, *Fire in a Canebrake: The Last Mass Lynching in America* (New York: Scribner, 2003).

[42] *Atlanta Constitution*, July 27, 1946; and *Atlanta Journal*, July 26, 1946.

[43] *Atlanta Journal*, July 27, 1946.

118   *A History of Prejudice*

Dorothy Malcolm, her brother George, and George's wife, Mae, to Atlanta to obtain Roger Malcolm's release. "I made bond for Malcolm at the courthouse. I came outside and told the Negroes I'd pick them up later on."[44] He did so three hours later – after repairs to his car, he said – and then set off for his farm. They were waylaid *en route*. Investigators suggested that the route chosen by Harrison was not the most direct one to his farm. That he could not identify anyone in the crowd of attackers and couldn't remember the name of the man Dorothy Malcolm had called by name may also suggest foul play. However, local reports also suggested that he was an "unusually good and ... indulgent [landlord]."[45] In any event, no one was able to bring charges against him, or against anyone else, for any part in the crime – in spite of offers of rewards totaling tens of thousands of dollars for information leading to the apprehension of the criminals.[46]

Like Harrison, other residents of the habitations around Moore's Ford, black as well as white, retreated into silence after the lynching. Major William E. Spence, Georgia's Director of Public Safety, who was put in charge of the investigation (working with the Georgia Bureau of Investigation and a hurriedly summoned FBI), expressed total frustration: he was getting no cooperation from the citizens of the area, and his forces couldn't cope with the stonewalling. A letter to the editor of the *Atlanta Constitution* from A. O. B. Bailey of Savannah, Georgia, referring to Spence's reported reaction, described a "conspiracy of silence" among local inhabitants, flowing from the "terror" spread by the perpetrators of the crime, and suggested "martial law," "house-to-house searches," "the closest questioning [of] every male citizen in the area affected," and "a careful ballistics study ... to determine the guns from which the bullets found in the bodies were fired."[47]

If there was resentment among the white inhabitants of the area, there was fear among the poor, rural blacks. One group of visiting

---

[44] *Atlanta Constitution*, July 28, 1946.

[45] *Atlanta Daily World*, August 4, 1946.

[46] It was estimated that the total reward offered for the apprehension of the culprits by government and other organizations in Georgia and other states already totaled $42,000; see *Atlanta Journal*, August 1, 1946.

[47] *Atlanta Constitution*, July 28 and August 1, 1946. The phrase "conspiracy of silence" comes from Stetson Kennedy, "Is the U.S. ready?" *Atlanta Daily World*, July 30, 1946.

journalists wrote: "Fear has Walton County in its grips [*sic*]. Fear of death, fear for relatives and kindred. Stark realization that to squawk to the authorities means certain death. Fear that no one who has not talked to these people of the Appalachee Valley and its environs can imagine."[48] Black families, a later report said, were "frightened and terrified" when approached by FBI agents. "One [white?] farmer fled into a cotton field and had to be chased down, eventually telling an investigator he had been warned not to talk." Boyzie Daniels, a young black man who had struggled to register black voters in the area, recalled that the attempt to continue private investigations in the years after 1946 generated fears among local blacks very like their fears in registering to vote.[49]

For decades, Georgia had been dominated by conservative white opinion in the countryside. Eugene Talmadge, famed for his raw racism, had emerged as the symbol of this white power, serving as governor of the state three times by 1942 and winning the election again in 1946. The Democratic Party ruled pretty much unchallenged, and state elections were largely determined by a whites-only Democratic primary. The poll tax qualification barred many poor whites and most blacks from the privilege of voting, while a "county unit" system reinforced a "politics of rural racism," giving disproportionate weight to small rural constituencies, in spite of dramatic growth in the urban population. In 1946, Kevin Kruse notes, the 132 votes of rural Chattanooga County carried the same weight as the 14,092 votes of Atlanta city's Fulton County.[50] However, a number of developments since the 1930s, and especially during the war, threatened to upset the existing order of things.

Increased migration from the rural areas, new aspirations and agitation generated by the war, continuous mobilization by the NAACP and other organizations around injustices suffered and demands made by blacks, and a number of local political developments in Georgia

---

[48] *Atlanta Daily World*, August 4, 1946.
[49] Wexler, *Fire in a Canebrake*, 231–2; Greg Bluestein, "Ex-governor Investigated in 1946 Lynchings" (Associated Press, updated June 15, 2007), http://www.msnbc.com/id/19251476/; and Kathy Lohr, "FBI Re-examines 1946 Lynching Case" (July 25, 2006), http://www.npr.org/templates/story/Id=5579862.
[50] Kevin M. Kruse, *White Flight: Atlanta and the Making of Modern Conservatism* (Princeton, NJ: Princeton University Press, 2005), 20–2.

A History of Prejudice

converged to produce new pressures on the government. In 1943, Georgia had its first conviction of lynchers since the early 1920s: three local law officials were sentenced to three years imprisonment and a fine of $1,000 for beating a black prisoner to death while he was in handcuffs, and the Supreme Court upheld the conviction in 1945. In 1945 also, Governor Arnall dropped the poll tax qualification for voting, in spite of earlier court approval for it in 1937. In October 1945, following the Supreme Court's pronouncement of the unconstitutionality of the practice in Texas the year before, Georgia's whites-only Democratic primary was invalidated; the ruling was confirmed by an appeals court in March 1946.[51]

At the end of the war, with the proclaimed victory for the "forces of democracy" abroad, these developments served to heighten black expectations of democratic advances at home. Encouraged by the determined efforts of the NAACP, as well as churches and other local organizations and activists seeking to make an impact in the impending primary election for governor, 135,000 African Americans had registered as voters by the summer of 1946. In the city of Atlanta, African Americans now constituted 25% of the electorate, with the number of registered black voters going up from 3,000 to 21,000.[52] White supremacist and fascist elements (including a revived, if flailing, Ku Klux Klan) of course fought back. With blacks voting, Eugene Talmadge declared, the laws protecting *our* schools, hotels, trains, even *our* women, would disappear. These laws had to be protected, if necessary by force.[53]

Tempers let loose by the closely fought gubernatorial primary clearly added to other causes of tension leading to the Moore's Ford violence. There were rumors that George Dorsey, recently returned from the war, was "uppity" beyond his station, flirting with white women, perhaps secretly dating one – just as there was a story that Roger Malcolm had attacked Barney Hester because he suspected

---

[51] For the preceding, see Kruse, *White Flight*, 23, 33; Grant, *The Way It Was in the South*, 360–3; and Dora Apel, *Imagery of Lynching: Black Men, White Women and the Mob* (New Brunswick, NJ: Rutgers University Press, 2004), chap. 5.

[52] Grant, *The Way It Was in the South*, 364; and Kruse, *White Flight*, 23. It was reported that 100,000 African Americans voted in the Georgia primary in July; see *Atlanta Daily World*, August 16, 1946.

[53] Kruse, *White Flight*, 24.

Hester of making sexual advances toward his wife, Dorothy. Talmadge is reported to have visited Monroe a day after the fight in which Malcolm wounded Hester. He met the brother of the stabbed farmer and apparently offered immunity to anyone who "took care of the negro." His visit was connected with the Democratic Party primary, which was held two days later: Walton and other small rural counties were critical in the election.[54] Several days afterward, reporters saw a car at the scene of the Moore's Ford lynchings with a sticker that said "Elect Talmadge, he keeps his promises." And Talmadge himself, on a post-primary vacation in the West, when told of the July 25 massacre, offered no more than the comment "Such incidents are to be regretted."[55]

Under the circumstances, there was widespread fear in Monroe and its environs in the aftermath of the lynching, especially with Talmadge winning the primary (and hence, effectively, reelection as governor). The fear even affected the funeral services that were held for the Dorsey and Malcolm couples. In the case of George Dorsey and his sister Dorothy Malcolm, relatives and family members failed to appear at the time of the church service in the town of Bishop. They were "too scared," and the ceremony had to be delayed until a few of them could be assembled.[56] However, as the preceding account indicates, that fear was now only one part of the social and political equation.

The Everyday of "America"

Three words appear again and again in the long and animated debates surrounding the violence of these years (at home and abroad): Christianity, civilization, and democracy. To these we might add the cluster America, American, and un-American, into which they were often translated. The nation was on trial. The denial of justice to its African American minority, and especially to its returned African American military heroes, was un-Christian, uncivilized, and undemocratic; in a word, un-American. This was not the language of churches and

---

[54] Apel, *Imagery of Lynching*, 169; Kruse, *White Flight*, 24; Grant, *The Way It Was in the South*, 366; Lohr, "FBI Re-examines 1946 Lynching Case"; and Bluestein, "Ex-governor Investigated in 1946 Lynchings."

[55] *Atlanta Daily World*, August 4, 1946; and *Atlanta Journal*, July 27, 1946.

[56] *Atlanta Daily World*, July 30, 1946; and *Atlanta Constitution*, July 29, 1946.

A History of Prejudice

ministers alone; it was also the "secular" language of the young nation of pilgrims established on these shores not so long ago, a nation that had pledged to welcome all comers, all hard-working and God-fearing men (and with them women), into what was to be a bastion of democracy and the land of the free.[57] African Americans, liberal whites, and even some conservative white politicians were now forced to think of the concept of "America" in a new, more challenging, and more international context.

James Weldon Johnson had written in 1933 of how the fight against southern racism, lynching, and Jim Crow was a fight to save "black America's body and white America's soul." The poet Langston Hughes wrote five years later of the need to convert America to "Americanism": "O, let America be America again – The land that never has been yet – *And yet must be....*" And further: "O, yes, – I say it plain, – America never was America to me, – And yet I swear this oath – *America will be*!" He reiterated the sentiment many times during the war, and at its termination in 1945. The call to "make America mean what America is supposed to mean"[58] was more open and widespread now than ever before.

"When a Mayor and a City Marshal can take a negro Sergeant off a bus in South Carolina, beat him up and put out one of his eyes, and nothing is done about it by the State authorities, something is radically wrong with the system," President Harry S. Truman, no great champion of the rights of the common people, declared. Even J. Strom

---

[57] Cf. Gunnar Myrdal's comments on what he, following many others, called the American Creed – Christianity, civilization, and democracy; liberty and equality (and, one might add, private, individual enterprise, which supposedly depended on the former two). "Americans" continuously invoked the Creed, Myrdal observed, "lamenting [the nation's] want of conformity to it"; it represented "the national conscience." See Myrdal, *American Dilemma*, vol. 1, 22, 23. Du Bois had made the same kind of point as early as 1903: "Deeply religious and intensely democratic as are the mass of the whites, they feel acutely the false position in which the Negro problems place them. Such an essentially honest-hearted and generous people cannot cite the caste-levelling precepts of Christianity, or believe in equality of opportunity for all men, without coming to feel more and more with each generation that the present drawing of the color-line is a flat contradiction to their beliefs and professions"; see Du Bois, *Souls of Black Folk*, 207–8.

[58] Johnson, *Along This Way*, 318; Langston Hughes, "Let America Be America Again" (1938), emphases added; and Hughes in *Chicago Defender*, June 23, 1945. See also Langston Hughes, "My America" (1944), in Marable and Mullings, *Let Nobody Turn Us Around*, 280–6.

"Double V"

Thurmond, governor of South Carolina from 1947, himself a war veteran, was moved to say that "mob rule" was "against every principle for which we have so recently sacrificed so much." And Colonel William H. Davies of Newton, Massachusetts, wrote to the *Atlanta Constitution* in August 1946: "After over three and a half years overseas in England, France, Luxembourg and Germany with soldiers from all over our nation who thought they were fighting for something that Robert E. Lee and Abraham Lincoln stood for, my heart sickens when I wonder how our friends and enemies will construe the ghastly happenings at Monroe."[59]

Protests over the Monroe lynchings occurred in New York, Philadelphia, San Francisco, and Chicago, along with extensive coverage in the national and international press, and determined efforts at organization, education, and mobilization around the issue by black churches, schools, and numerous community organizations that could only be described as being deeply invested in civil rights. There was evidence of a sharp urban–rural divide. With the increasingly urban character of the black population all over the US, this meant that there was considerable protest activity, even in Georgia and other southern states.

William F. Knowland, Republican senator from California, touched off an angry Senate debate when he condemned the Moore's Ford lynchings and insisted on inserting a news dispatch about the incident in the Congressional Record (violating state rights, as various southern senators charged). More than 5,000 people "of both races" assembled in Chicago, under the banner of a Citizens' Protest Committee, and contributed $1,555 on the spot to build pressure for federal government action to apprehend the lynchers. A group of 700 women delegates in Washington to attend the Golden Jubilee Convention of the National Association of Colored Women marched in silent protest, holding up banners that said: "America Our Home: Let It Be Known" (Georgia); "Can a Great Nation Afford Lynching?" (Wisconsin); "Down with Lynching. Practice Democracy" and "We Beat Hitler's Mob; Can't We Win at Home?" (District of Columbia). Forty national organizations, meeting in Washington at the initiative of the NAACP, called for united opposition and established a committee

---

[59] See Frederickson, "'The Slowest State' and the 'Most Backward Community,'" 184, 189; and *Atlanta Constitution*, August 6, 1946.

A History of Prejudice

to plan "direct action" against the rising tide of interracial violence. This gathering was addressed among others by the NAACP leaders Arthur B. Spingarn and Walter White; by Isaac Woodard, the war veteran whose beating and blinding in South Carolina had become a cause célèbre in the national press; and Oliver Harrington, public relations counsel and former war correspondent of the *Pittsburgh Courier*, who declared that "the Georgia lynchings were . . . part of the highly organized conspiracy to 'put the returned Negro veteran in his place.'"[60]

President Truman had instructed the civil rights section of his Justice Department to aid the local investigation in every way it could. This was judged by many as being not nearly enough. Calls for federal intervention – and for making lynching a federal offense – came from various quarters, in Georgia as well as outside. "I'm going to ask the Governor to appeal to every Congressman to help pass Federal legislation against mob violence," the director of public safety in Georgia, Major Spence, said within days of taking charge of the investigation. New York Representative Democrat Arthur G. Klein and American Labor's Vito Marcantonio, the Negro Newspaper Publishers' Association in Chicago, leaders of the National Negro Congress, and many others urged direct federal intervention, including the dispatch of federal troops. Klein expressed a common sentiment in saying that something had to be done by the federal government: "[I]t is obvious that we cannot depend upon the state authorities in Georgia and Mississippi."[61]

In Georgia, numerous individuals and groups, churches, civic associations, newspaper editors, and college teachers in Atlanta and other towns expressed their sense of outrage and shame. Churches all over the state – in Atlanta, Athens, and Valdosta, as well as the First Methodist Church in Monroe – spoke out against this barbaric and unChristian act. The editors of the *Atlanta Constitution* wrote repeatedly and urgently of the need for the protection of the constitutional rights of all citizens. Until elementary justice and human dignity was established, said Ralph McGill, the South will continue to be "a national

---

[60] *Atlanta Journal*, July 28, 1946; and *Atlanta Daily World*, August 6, 7, and 14, 1946. The quotation from Harrington appears in Apel, *Imagery of Lynching*, 170.

[61] *Atlanta Constitution*, July 27, 28, and 30, 1946; and *Atlanta Journal*, July 30, 1946.

story . . . with more than 40 of the nation's 48 states looking at us with fear and wondering, with our deeds recited to the nations of the world who join in condemning them." "It is easy to be courageous about what is the matter with China," Wright Bryant, editor of the *Atlanta Journal*, told the Carolinas Advertising Executives Association, "but somewhat more difficult when the editor speaks about controversial issues on his own doorstep."[62]

The *Atlanta Daily World* carried on an even more sustained and vigorous campaign to bring about justice. The newspaper was at the fore in publicizing the national and international outcry against the quadruple lynching and the wide-ranging protests that followed in Georgia and elsewhere – as a mere sampling of headlines in the first half of August indicates: "Wheat Street Meet Tonite To Aid Lynching Families. Statewide Plans for Funds to be Launched Tonite" (August 1); "U.S. Officials Probing Klan Activities" (August 1); "World Reporters Revisit Lynch Scene" (August 4); "Church Lethargy Seen in Monroe Lynchings," a report on a statement issued by a gathering of Protestant ministers in New York (August 6); "700 Women Marched in Lynch Protest Parade" in Washington, D.C. (August 6); "Protests to Georgia Lynchings Continue" in Chicago and Philadelphia (August 7); "National Organization Plans Joint Action on Wave of Terror in South" (August 14); "Big Wheat Street Mass-Meet Tonite" (August 16). It joined the call for new kinds of government action, demanding the immediate establishment of one or more Negro units of the National Guard in the state, for instance. It also participated actively in the drive for funds to aid the criminal investigation and prevent attacks of this kind in the future, declaring on August 16, the day of a long-planned mass meeting at the Wheat Street Baptist Church in Atlanta: "There is nothing which should prevent those 100,000 Negroes who voted in the Georgia primary last July 17 from . . . giving One Dollar each to make life and limb safe for them and their families."[63]

In and around Monroe, Georgia, while a few church leaders and individuals spoke out, there was too much fear for any large-scale protest to be mounted. Many relatives of the victims stayed away from

---

[62] *Atlanta Journal*, July 29, 1946; *Atlanta Constitution*, August 3, 1946; and issues for late July and early August generally.
[63] *Atlanta Daily World*, August 16 and 18, 1946, and issues from July 27 onward.

(a)   (b)

FIGURE 2. (a) Lynching of John William (Willie) Clark, Cartersville, Georgia, September 1930 (African American Photograph Collection, Box 1, Folder 17; courtesy – Manuscript, Archives, and Rare Books Library, Emory University); (b) Funeral of George Dorsey, Monroe, Georgia, July 1946 (© Bettmann/CORBIS; courtesy Corbis Images, New York)

the funerals, as I have mentioned. Yet for those who attended there were significant new signs, beginning with the way in which George Dorsey's body was prepared for burial. As Dora Apel has noted, the photograph of the lynching that was most widely circulated in the national press showed not contorted and terrified faces but the body of the "fallen soldier" draped in an American flag (Figure 2). "The abject black body of the lynching victim, usually stripped or clothed in rags, was reimagined as a military hero lying in uniform, a citizen of the nation."[64] The wheel appeared to have come full circle.

Difference Redefined

Given the context of the Double V campaign, the authorities in Georgia were pushed into a more democratic and antiracist stance in the years after the war. William Hartsfield, mayor of its capital city, Atlanta, was soon making symbolically significant concessions in the course of

[64] Apel, *Imagery of Lynching*, 170; see also 166.

"Double V" 127

establishing the first genuinely biracial political base for the maintenance of his power in the city. In 1948, he appointed the city's first black policemen: eight were appointed in March of that year, even if their beat was restricted to the African American neighborhoods. By 1950, with over a third of Atlanta's population now black, streetlights appeared on Auburn Avenue, the major black business district, and Hartsfield directed city officials to address black residents as "Mr. __" and "Mrs. __" in all communications. In 1951, when the NAACP held its national convention in Atlanta, he enthusiastically presided over the opening ceremonies. And an attempt by Herman Talmadge, Eugene's son and anointed successor, to restore the whites-only Democratic primary in Georgia in 1947 was defeated by an alliance of black political organizations and black and white churches, which pronounced the plan "contrary to the teachings of Jesus Christ."[65]

New positions were adopted at the national level, too. The outbreak of egregious interracial violence in the United States in the wake of the war to make the world safe for freedom and democracy, and the NAACP's nationwide campaign to publicize the attacks and call for justice, compelled Truman to appoint a President's Committee on Civil Rights in 1946 to suggest means of strengthening the capacity of government, at federal, state, and local levels, to safeguard the civil rights of the people.[66] Indeed, civil rights became a central political issue during the presidential election of 1948. The 1950s and '60s would see that centrality further underlined. But the chief lines of the argument had been clearly established in the campaign for Double Victory in the 1940s – the "decisive first phase" of the Long Civil Rights Movement, as one historian has described it.[67]

The African American claim to equal citizenship during and after the Second World War was based on an argument of sameness – an equivalence in individual potential, ownership, responsibility, and duty that was imputed to all inhabitants, irrespective of race, color, or continent of origin (although not as yet education and gender). We are as American, as nationalist, as masculine, as fine at war, the

---

[65] Kruse, *White Flight*, 34, 36, 38; and Grant, *The Way It Was in the South*, 366–7.

[66] Executive Order 9808 – Establishing the President's Committee on Civil Rights, December 5, 1946.

[67] Jacquelyn Dowd Hall, "The Long Civil Rights Movement and the Political Uses of the Past," *Journal of American History* (March 2005), 1245.

128   *A History of Prejudice*

argument seemed to go, as any white American. Yet, if the proposition was that black Americans were not to be denied the right to work, to serve in the military and therefore to vote, to freely enter public parks and restaurants, and to share in decision making on the grounds of the universal claims of American Democracy, the rhetoric of the struggle seemed to suggest that it was only half of the African American population that was directly concerned. It was *men* whose citizenly rights were at issue: black men who had served in the military overseas and at home, a black messman who responded to the Japanese attack on American naval ships berthed at Pearl Harbor, black men who were segregated in military training camps and residential quarters, men who were maimed or killed in battle, men who returned as veterans still to be denied the right to travel freely on public buses or to exercise the right to vote. Even the work of women in the auxiliary services of the military seemed to be overlooked.

Curiously, black women were often presented as appearing only in the wings of this unfolding political drama – as supporters, as mothers, as mourners at the grave of the soldier killed in battle; in other words, as reproducers of the citizen and the military hero (black no less than white), not as military personnel, which many of them were, or activists in their own right. Even after the Second World War, when the focus of the protest against anti-black violence shifted "from the tortured body of the black male to the person of the grieving mother," as Apel argues in her analysis of the imagery of lynching, it was still a mother grieving over the fallen soldier, the war hero who had done his all for the nation and democracy. Emmett Till's mother was cast as a war widow in 1955, Emmett Till himself as the son of an American soldier.[68]

It is notable in this context that in explaining his issuance of Executive Order 9808 establishing the Presidential Committee on Civil Rights, Truman highlighted the shameful fact that "even women" were lynched in Monroe, Georgia. Although a number of women had been lynched earlier without any such reaction, the lynching of women was now declared to be simply unacceptable.[69] In illustration of another

---

[68] Apel, *Imagery of Lynching*, 185–8. For details of the Emmett Till lynching in Mississippi in 1955, see Norrell, *The House I Live In*, 174–5.

[69] *New York Times*, December 6, 1946. Close to 200 women were lynched in the South between 1880 and 1930; see Crystal N. Feimster, *Southern Horrors: Women and the Politics of Rape and Lynching* (Cambridge, MA: Harvard University Press, 2009).

"Double V"

facet of American, "frontier society" masculinism, women, even black women, were presented as deserving of protection by the men. That was why, as a white Mississippi man put it in 1920, women should never have the right to vote, even if black men had had it theoretically since Emancipation: "We are not afraid to maul a black man over the head if he dares to vote, but we can't treat women, even black women, that way. No, we'll allow no woman suffrage."[70] Needless to say, the raping, mauling, and physical chastisement of black women continued, unhindered by this twisted patriarchal racial logic.

The discourse of nations and of recognized ("public") political affairs has long been masculinist. So was the idiom of the African American struggle, well into the period of formal civil rights and Black Power in the 1960s and '70s. Publicly at any rate, few commentators invoked what Pauli Murray describes as the "heroic, but formidable" black woman, standing shoulder to shoulder or even one step ahead of the men in every phase of the struggle, and "exhorting her children and grandchildren to overcome every obstacle and humiliation and to 'Be somebody!'"[71] Recall Sojourner Truth and Ida B. Wells, but also the large number of African American women who served in the armed forces during the war and the unnamed woman who urged African Americans to throw 50,000 demonstrators around the White House before Roosevelt's Executive Order 8802.

There was little questioning, too, of militarism and the need for military action – in near and distant lands – in the service of the nation. With Dr. Martin Luther King, Jr., and the rise of the anti–Vietnam War campaign, some of this would change. And with the emergence of a powerful new body of black women as public spokespersons, writers,

---

[70] Cited in Christine Stansell, "A Forgotten Fight for Suffrage," *New York Times*, August 25, 2010. Note that the ratification of the nineteenth amendment to the U.S. Constitution, giving women the right to vote, was almost brought to a halt in 1920 by nine southern states and Delaware. It finally obtained ratification by the required two-thirds majority of state legislatures when Tennessee accepted the amendment by *one* vote, a legislator changing his mind at the last minute on account, as he said, of his mother. Nine southern states did not ratify the amendment until the 1940s or later: Maryland in 1941; Virginia and Alabama in 1952 and 1953, respectively; Florida, Georgia, Louisiana, and North and South Carolina between 1969 and 1971; and Mississippi not until 1984.

[71] Pauli Murray, "The Liberation of Black Women," in *Words of Fire: An Anthology of African-American Feminist Thought*, ed. Beverly Guy-Sheftall (New York: The New Press, 1995), 186.

and interpreters, another stage would open up in the reconstruction of American democracy – beginning with the notion of politics itself, which could no longer automatically exclude the domestic and the personal. I examine some of these issues in the next chapter, on an "ordinary" African American woman's reconstruction of her life and struggles through this period.

5

An African American Autobiography

Relocating Difference

In focusing this chapter on the reminiscences of a relatively unknown woman, mother, sharecropper, seamstress, writer, and religious educator from Georgia, Viola Perryman Andrews, who began writing in the era of the civil rights struggle, my purpose is more than simply to document another ("hidden") aspect of African American history. It is rather to identify two different kinds of history, or perhaps one should say two different perspectives on the history of prejudice and difference, and the attendant matter of civil (civic) rights.

Recall in this context my proposition that the prejudice of the modern requires us to speak in a standard, recognizable idiom, and a standard recognizable manner, to have our words (ourselves?) deemed worthy of attention. I juxtapose an analysis of Viola Andrews's personal account with the analysis of the more public accounts presented in the last chapter precisely because these narratives are constructed very differently and seem at first sight (as I stated in the Introduction) to talk past each other, apparently unable or unwilling to engage one another. In fact, as I shall show, they speak of many of the same issues: of racial privilege and prejudice, of unequal access to resources and opportunities, of the daily struggle to survive and maintain one's dignity. For all that, they speak in rather different voices, with rather different emphases.

Autobiography is history for many sections of the world's people who have not had ready entry into the historical academy and national archives: women, blacks, Dalits, and leaders and participants

131

in all kinds of anticolonial struggles. Across the globe, a good deal of subaltern history-writing has taken the form of life-story, memoir, autobiography, or testimony, as it has variously been called. Analysts have pointed to the distance between the collective and the individual "I" – the difference between the self found in bourgeois (male) autobiographies and memoirs and the community/self that emerges in subaltern life-stories – as the critical difference between classical and subaltern autobiography.[1] "The 'I' in black women's autobiographies often reflects an 'I' that is not simply of this world," writes Johnnie M. Stover, "but exists as a connection between community, individual, and God."[2] Indeed, subaltern and bourgeois life-writings have been seen as oppositional, working to divergent ends in dissimilar worlds. On the one hand is bourgeois autobiography, an articulation of the self in the sense not so much of the display as the very production of a subject and an interiority; on the other is what might be described as subaltern community memoir – a "collective" autobiography, in which the self is less self-centered and egotistical and autobiography also serves as history.

It is important to note that academic and market perceptions and classifications work to underscore untouchability, slavery, humiliation, immiserization, and the struggle to overcome them as the chief conditions of subaltern life and history. When black, ex-slave, ex-Untouchable, or other subaltern elements are offered a chance "to speak for themselves" in the wider economic and cultural market, as it were, it seems clear that there is a preferred, not to say prescribed, language in which they must construct their narratives in order to be published and read widely. African American autobiographical writing becomes a part of something described as Black Literature or Black Studies, as Dalit writings become part of Dalit Studies: a new version of area studies, one might say – exotic and uplifting at the same

[1] Joanne Braxton, *Black Women Writing Autobiography* (Philadelphia: Temple University Press, 1989), 19; Gopal Guru, "Afterword," in Kamble, *Prisons We Broke*; Debjani Ganguly, "Pain, Personhood and the Collective: Dalit Life Narratives," *Asian Studies Review*, 33, no. 4 (December 2009), 433. Sharmila Rege advocates the convenient terms "life-narrative" and "life-writing" for subaltern writings in the autobiographical mode; see her explanation of their advantage in Rege, *Writing Caste/Writing Gender*, n7 and 1–15.

[2] Johnnie Stover, *Rhetoric and Resistance in Black Women's Autobiography* (Gainesville: University of Florida, 2003), 5; cf. 30–1.

An African American Autobiography

time – and not simply another aspect, or new dimension, of literature, autobiography, and memoir.

Hence, while there is force in the argument that subalternist life-writing recounts the tale not of an unusual or unique individual but the story of a subaltern community in general, the proposition calls for further reflection. It is fair to say that the articulation of the self and the will that is found in such writings is seldom flamboyantly autonomous. What we encounter here is a more social, fragmented, and searching "I" than that of the imagined, self-generated, and self-perpetuating human subject of the Enlightenment: an interiority and a self produced in constrained, often damaging, conditions – something that male, upper-class, bourgeois autobiography never acknowledges in full. Yet, even in the case of the latter, the writing itself is often fairly equivocal about the possibility of self-possession. The suggested opposition between individualist and collectivist, bourgeois and subaltern, genres of life-writing may not then be as straightforward as it seems at first sight.

The composition of the self, and the "community" (or world) in which it is located, is decidedly complex in every case. In spite of their differences, as one scholar has noted, both subaltern and classical, or bourgeois, autobiographies seem to share an aspiration to recover the personhood of the protagonist/victim-rebel, an aspiration that is "articulated in the language of 'rights' squarely based on a conception of the 'individual.'" Thus many subaltern autobiographies and memoirs join the political quest for equal citizenship, even as they recognize the impossibility of that quest given what Debjani Ganguly calls the inability of the ideal (with its logic of abstract equivalence) "to address the singular nature of Dalit [or African American, or women's] pain."[3]

I attempt to push the question of the articulation of the "singular nature of [subaltern] pain" further in the following pages through a close investigation of the contexts and modes of a number of Dalit and African American "autobiographies," beginning in this chapter with the voluminous autobiographical writings of Viola Andrews: jottings and life-narrative, letters and fables, "fictional" and "non-fictional."[4]

---

[3] Ganguly, "Pain, Personhood and the Collective," 433.

[4] The writings are held in the Emory University Manuscripts and Rare Books Library (MARBL), Mss 813, Viola Andrews collection. The holdings also include manuscript

134   *A History of Prejudice*

It is hardly necessary to underscore the enormous variation in individual lives and perspectives in the lives of African American women in the South as of any other section of a society or people. Viola Andrews is not Zora Neale Hurston or Alice Walker, to take the example of two southern women who will reappear later in this chapter. Alice Walker, again, isn't Zora Neale Hurston (or Fannie Lou Hamer, or Rosa Parks): she doesn't write like Zora and doesn't follow her political manners, in spite of her extraordinary admiration for Zora. Viola, then, is not "everywoman" of the South, or for that matter every laboring black woman who escaped from the rural South in the Jim Crow era of the early and mid-twentieth century. Nevertheless, what she has to say about her life and times, her particular circumstances, and her struggles has a great deal to tell us about the broader history of African Americans in twentieth-century America – and not just the South, as the last chapter will have reminded us. Through a juxtaposition of her story, as told by herself, with the more widely known story of public encounters, as told by newspapers, public persons, and political activists in the course of the African American struggle, I draw attention to an "inner life" of race and caste conflict, positing this inner life not as a counter to some alleged "outer life" but aiming through it to give the history of race (and caste and gender) – that is to say, of race and caste and gender prejudice, and their consequences – a greater depth and density.

Accessing the "Inner Life"

The issue of the inner experience of historical subjects has been invoked frequently in the ongoing debate on the black freedom struggle and twentieth-century American politics more generally. Thus, Julius Lester criticized William Julius Wilson's important revisionist work *The Declining Significance of Race: Blacks and Changing American Institutions*, published in 1978, for being "divorced from the inner experience of blacks. It relies on economic data, omitting the experiences of the people the data represent."[5] Making much the same point,

---

correspondence between Viola and several of her children, as well as Viola's "fictional" writings, interviews, and documentation of other notable events.

[5] Julius Lester, "The Mark of Race," *The Civil Liberties Review*, 5, no. 4 (January–February 1979), 117.

a reviewer of Thomas J. Sugrue's recent study *Sweet Land of Liberty: The Forgotten Struggle for Civil Rights in the North* argues that "*Sweet Land*'s activists analyze their dilemmas in a cultural and emotional vacuum; they can seem like walking position papers." The challenge is to "animate those damning statistics, and the lives of those who struggled against them."[6] Note that these criticisms are made here even in the case of works that do not set out to chart the realm of interiority. By contrast, other historians have directly attended to the issue of the inner life and how that is affected when groups like African Americans (or Dalits) are treated as a problem rather than a people. Prominent among them are Darlene Clark Hine, who writes of black women creating an "appearance of openness and disclosure" that "shielded the truth of their inner lives," and Nell Irvin Painter, who has focused, in a succession of studies on the American South, on "what historians usually gloss over: personal violence and its psychological sequelae."[7]

My exploration of a relatively unknown – and in that sense "ordinary" – African American woman's life-story in the twentieth-century American South follows from the preceding critiques. That South is often seen as the counterpoint to America as the fabled land of liberty and democracy. Bible belt, province of slavery, conservatism, and the traditional family, strictly controlling sexuality and sin (among the subordinated), the South has also become a symbol for certain enduring old world values – loyalty, obedience, faith, forbearance – clearly related to notions of the proper ordering of society and the appropriate positions of different classes and races. These principles are neatly, if unconsciously, captured in a widespread common sense about the place of a woman, not least her duty to reproduce children and tradition, submission, and obedience, or what one historian has called "the core values of slavery" and "the key words of patriarchy and piety."[8]

---

[6] Scott Saul, "Off Camera," *The Nation* (http://www.thenation.com/doc/20090622/saul).

[7] Darlene Clark Hine, "Rape and the Inner Lives of Black Women in the Middle West: Preliminary Thoughts on the Culture of Dissemblance," *Signs: Journal of Women in Culture and Society*, 14, no. 4 (1989), 912; Hine, *Hine Sight*, 37–47; and Nell Irvin Painter, *Southern History across the Color Line* (Chapel Hill: University of North Carolina Press, 2002), 10.

[8] Painter, *Southern History across the Color Line*, 18; see also 93–133 and passim. For a wide-ranging exploration of the idea of southern exceptionalism, see Lassiter and Crespino, *The Myth of Southern Exceptionalism*.

How do these values and principles affect the inner lives of specific historical actors in the century after the formal abolition of slavery?

I consider the autobiographical writings of Viola Andrews to complicate what might be seen as commonsense answers to this question. I ask what her telling of her life teaches us about black women in the southern states of the US in the first half of the twentieth century, disenfranchised as they were in sundry ways, the demands placed on women as mothers, and the inheritances (social, familial, and spiritual, as well as material) that women worked with. A number of themes stand out in Viola's manuscript autobiography: the struggle against want (economic, political, and cultural), black/white relations, and patriarchy (or, more precisely, a woman's struggle in a patriarchal world). Underlying it all is her extraordinary faith in the Word of the Lord, and an unyielding determination. We are left with a story of an unlikely heroine's quest to fashion a new life for her children (and latterly herself), told by the woman and several of her children. Through an analysis of Viola's writings, I seek to examine what one might call the less explored, "intimate" aspects of racial and sexual subordination, race relations, and patriarchal power in the Jim Crow South – and thereby the politics of race and prejudice.

The generosity of several of Viola's children emboldens me to publish this reflection on her life: they responded to an earlier draft by thanking me for introducing their "real" mother to them and helping them to see her "not just as [a] mother but even more so as a woman." "Through your... writing," says Veronica, now in her 60s, "she has come across as a real person to me as opposed to this heroic bearer of countless burdens of almost mythic proportions that I was told about over the years by her and my older brothers and sisters."[9] That response, and Viola's own writings, resist any assimilation of this life into the simple category of the "mythical, heroic, transcendent black woman,"[10] or the downtrodden and helpless victim, and point to a more recalcitrant, and inventive, working through of the unevenness and mutual crisis between citizenship and subalternity.[11]

---

[9] E-mail from Shirley Lowrie, July 28, 2009; letters from Deloris Andrews and Veronica Villa, January 5 and 6, 2010.

[10] Hine, *Hine Sight*, 38, 51, 52.

[11] I elaborate the point about the relationship between citizenship and subalternity in "The Subaltern as Subaltern Citizen," Introduction to Pandey, *Subaltern Citizens and Their Histories*, 1–12.

An African American Autobiography

My account of Viola's life and work is bookended as it were by the writings and reflections of two great heroes of contemporary black and feminist history, Zora Neale Hurston (1891–1960) and Alice Walker (1944–), who are at one with her in their sharp critique of patriarchy, racism, and hypocrisy, as well as pride in their race and individual development. However, Viola probably knew little or nothing about the other two, and Zora and Alice almost certainly knew/know nothing about her. In making this somewhat surprising juxtaposition, my purpose is not to provide an analysis or comparison of the autobiographical writings of these three women or an indication of possible influences one way or another. I am responding instead to a rather different invitation that I see in Hurston's and Walker's work: the invitation to examine the everyday, unnoticed, yet remarkable struggles of ordinary, "everyday" people.

Alice Walker has written eulogistically of Zora Neale Hurston – as we might write of Alice Walker – praising her fierce independence, individuality, creativity, stardom (reckless, individualistic, brilliant, "genius of the South"). Viola Andrews doesn't belong to the club of famous women. Nevertheless, her still unpublished autobiography and the greater ordinariness of her story may be of some interest in the context of Hurston's and Langston Hughes's (and Walker's) celebration of the "common people," "the man farthest down."[12] Indeed, Viola's story seems to me to be a very good example of what Hurston once called America's "best-kept secret," "the average, struggling, non-morbid Negro."[13]

Several features of her autobiography illustrate the point. Most people who write autobiographies, or are invited to write autobiographies, men as well as women, are already distinguished in public view or appear alternatively as examples of a wider and noteworthy political struggle. Viola Andrews's life story fits neither of these categories. It is unusual in being, professedly, a mother's narrative. The subject of this autobiography is perhaps best known outside her family and local community in Atlanta and Madison, Georgia, as the mother of two prominent African American artists, the painter and activist Benny Andrews and the writer Raymond Andrews. Her life as she tells it is that of a mother continuously, obsessively, unforgivingly

---

[12] Kaplan, *Zora Neale Hurston*, 235.
[13] Boyd, *Wrapped in Rainbows*, 406.

committed to lifting up her children – and only late in life herself, her writing, and her career. Hence her comment on her artist sons Benny and Ray's reactions on their reading the first portions of her auto-biography – "'I did not know that,' what did you mean? You did not know that I was once young or I was an individual or what?" – and her comment on the art critics and admirers who greeted her with astonishment at Benny's first solo exhibition at the High Museum in Atlanta in January 1975: "No one had any idea that you Benny had a Mother.... Several talked with me and could not comprehend you having a Mother! Next! They wanted to know what did I do the reason you are an artist!"[14]

Many black autobiographies emerged out of the growing African American struggle against white privilege, slavery, and segregation. Yet, even though she begins writing at the height of the civil rights movement in one of its most important headquarters, and writes throughout those tumultuous years, Viola Andrews claims to pay little attention to race politics. "The reader may wonder," she interrupts her writing, begun in 1963, to say in 1979, "why I am not writing about Race Relations. I am writing as I knew and saw it then and there. In our community, all the colored owned or rented their land...," by which she refers to the fact that large numbers of blacks in the rural South could do neither: "I was young and I knew nothing about Race Relationship."[15] We shall have an opportunity to consider what she meant by this, for much of what Viola writes about is in fact black/white relations. However, one point is clear: for her, the theme of her narrative is her family and its struggle to make good in an exceptionally difficult environment.

Alice Walker says of Zora Neale Hurston's work: "it spoke the language I'd heard the elders speaking all my life... and she did not condescend to them, and she did not apologize for them, and she was them, delightedly."[16] In Viola Andrews's case, it seems to me, there is a small but significant difference. This isn't the language the author hears the elders speaking as she grows up, or one she remembers and recovers as she moves away from, and later returns to, the "elders"; not

---

[14] MARBL, Benny Andrews Papers, Mss 845, Box 115, Viola's letters to Benny and Mary, January 7 and 22, 1975.
[15] MARBL, Viola Andrews Papers, Mss 813, Box 17, FF9.
[16] Alice Walker, *Anything We Love Can Be Saved: A Writer's Activism* (New York: Random House, 1997), 46.

An African American Autobiography

the position of the insider/outsider that Zora and Alice inhabit. This is the "insiders," the "elders," speaking for themselves, as they and their children negotiate the "outside" and grow away from themselves into other selves.

In a note inserted at more than one place in her manuscript autobiography, Viola insisted that the character of her writing, even the untutored and unpolished prose, should not be changed if these words were ever published.

I want my biography to be – to remain on the *level* of the day and the time and the place which it was written. That will make it more interesting. . . . Some of my paragraphs are kinda jumble: its okay to re arrange the words: if you do not put my biography on a higer level.

P.S. *please*, please do not change it and put it on your *Academic* Intellectual Level, please. It will not be *me* (*mine*) if you do: it will be yours. [June? 1978][17]

Her autobiography has not yet been published. And I only hope that my reflections on her writing, and the extracts I cite here, retain something of the "kinda jumble" that she presented as her life and times.

Echoes of a Life in the South

Viola Andrews lived from 1912 to 2006. She was the sixth child in a relatively comfortable farming family of Morgan County, Georgia, which was of mixed black, white, and Indian heritage and part of "a nice prosperous community so far as the coloreds were considered" in that they owned and/or rented their land.[18] Her parents, John Crawford and Lula Allison Perryman, were forward-looking, and determined that their children would obtain education (and salvation) and never become wage-hands. But the severe economic downturn of

---

[17] MARBL, Mss 813, Box 19, FF 8 (emphasis original). In citing from Viola Andrews's autobiographical manuscripts in the following pages, I have kept footnotes brief since the writings are full of repetition and have several different sequences of numbers, as well as several pages inserted at many points in the form of additional material for particular phases of Viola's life.

[18] The information and quotations in this paragraph and the next come from several folders in Mss 813, Box 17. See also Raymond Andrews, *The Last Radio Baby: A Memoir* (Atlanta: Peachtree Publishers, 1990); J. Richard Gruber, *American Icons: From Madison to Manhattan, the Art of Benny Andrews, 1948–1997* (Augusta, GA: Morris Museum of Art, 1997); and J. Richard Gruber, *The Dot Man: George Andrews of Madison, Georgia* (Augusta, GA: Morris Museum of Art, 1994).

the 1920s put an end to some of those dreams. Viola's father went to the lumber mills, ill health dogged them, and the family moved to sharecropping and "one of the poorest made houses I have ever seen."

In 1930, when she had studied to the eighth grade, Viola married someone she had met several years earlier and long corresponded with, George Andrews. George was the son of a white man from a prominent plantation-owning family of Plainview, Morgan County, Jim Orr ("Mr. Jim"), and a beautiful black woman of Indian, white, and black ancestry, Jessie Rose Lee Wildcat Tennessee (who had earlier been married, and technically remained married, to his hired hand, Eddie). The Depression destroyed the Orr plantation. Jim and Jessie lived on in separate houses, hers on a parcel of land he had given to her. Viola and George and the four oldest of their ten children lived near Jessie and Jim, from 1936 in a new two-room house built for them on land owned by Jim Orr.[19] Economically cushioned, they were scarcely independent, even though Jim was away working on the railroad in Virginia until about 1940. George remained under the thumb of his parents, ever a Mama's boy in Viola's view.

Though Jim Orr had supposedly set up home with Jessie, "Southern etiquette dictated that they could not sit down together at the same table," as Viola's writer-son, Raymond Andrews, puts it in a novel constructed around the figure of his paternal grandmother. On Sundays, Mr. Jim always breakfasted with Jessie. When he rode up to her house, she would have his breakfast "steaming and ready." But he always ate alone at the table: "she waited out on the back porch ... until he had finished and left the kitchen, whereupon she'd come back inside and eat whatever was left."[20] At a later stage, finding Jim Orr and his conduct less and less palatable, Jessie moved out of the vicinity. When in Plainview, Mr. Jim then began having his major

---

[19] Viola had nine children with George. An older child, Harvey, who was born while Viola was in high school, lived with Viola's mother until 1934 (see the next section of this chapter).

[20] Raymond Andrews, *Rosiebelle Lee Wildcat Tennessee* (New York: Dial Press, 1980), 12. In an autobiography, Andrews notes that after the death of his mother, who had lived with him, Mr. Jim started coming to Jessie's house for each of his three daily meals. Jessie fixed and served the meals, but Jim always ate alone in the kitchen and no one else entered there until he had finished and left; *Last Radio Baby*, 120–1.

An African American Autobiography

meal in Viola's house, with the same sequence – of cook and cook's family, food, guest diner, and cook's family – following one another in the kitchen, never sharing it together. Viola's children recall Mr. Jim becoming increasingly "white" in his attitude as he grew older: he had no interest in his grandchildren and never knew their names.

In 1943, Viola finally persuaded George to move to a neighboring farm, where he worked as a sharecropper and later in other jobs. The next few years were hard. As the eldest daughter, Valeria, put it, "Benny, Raymond, and I... slept crossways in the bed together... my mother and father and the baby [Shirley] slept in... the straw mattress.... You would lay on it and it would get flat.... We had to sleep crossways... mama had rubber sheets and (if) we wet the bed... it just wet everybody."[21] "We were at rock-bottom," writes Viola. "I had a Pair of Men Shoes that my Sister gave to me. I went Bare foot through the Week and wore the Men Shoes [to Church] on Sunday; [or] if any one came to see me."[22]

George's temper and physical abusiveness made matters worse. Timid, afraid of thunder and lightning, and unambitious, he was extremely courteous and gentle with outsiders, seeking everyone's approval. As if to compensate, he asserted his "masculinity" at home; he was often cruel to Viola and the children, hitting Viola on her head and face for using too much salt or dropping a bar of soap.[23] They quarreled incessantly about whether the children could be spared from the fields to attend high school (she believed they had to be); whether a person could make a living from drawing, which both George and the older children loved and pursued with whatever materials came to hand (he stoutly denied the possibility; without knowing anything about the art world, she insisted one could);[24] and who should use the small transistor radio (George thought only he should since batteries cost money!)

---

[21] Jesse Freeman's interview with Valeria Anderson at her home in Richmond, CA. (Mr. Freeman kindly provided me with a transcript of interviews he conducted between 2003 and 2005 with several members of the Andrews family); see also Gruber, *American Icons*, 18.

[22] Mss 813, Box 18, FF 1; and Box 20, FF 4.

[23] Mss 813, Box 17, FF 7; Box 20, FF 8, for instance.

[24] Both Benny and George were to become fairly well-known "professional" painters; see Gruber's studies of their work cited in n18, this chapter.

142   *A History of Prejudice*

After World War II, the three older boys left home for Atlanta one after another and joined the military successively. Valeria Belle followed in 1951. Together, they began preparing to get the rest of the family out of Morgan County. In 1953, after much secret planning, a pregnant Viola moved to Atlanta with her five younger children. (Gregory, the tenth and last, was born soon after.) George, who had not believed she could leave, refused to give up his connections to Morgan County and his parents. After the move, Viola rejected the few feeble efforts George made to resume their lives together and refused him any further part in her or her children's future. It was a turning point, and the beginning of a new life. "When we moved to Atlanta Feb. 7 (or 8) 1953," she wrote (probably in 1978), "I not only left Morgan County physically, but I left mentally – with no regrets. . . . I had been a Slave all the years I spent with my Husband. The reason that I love atlanta; I have gained my Freedom here."[25]

In Atlanta, circumstances were initially not much easier than they had been immediately before. Viola started with the little furniture she had managed to bring from Morgan County. This was supplemented with a fridge, some more furniture, bedding, dishes, and clothes that Viola received within two weeks of her leaving, on the death of her elder sister Soncie in Madison. Viola and the younger children survived on the government checks and other help her older children gave her, until Viola began work as a part-time nurse at the nearby McLendon Hospital on a night shift after taking courses at the Beaumont School of Nursing in 1955–1956. The hospital was a 10 minute walk from her home: she left at 10:50 and worked from 11 p.m. to 7 a.m. "I slept a little when the children returned from school," she writes, "however, I survived somehow." Later, she worked as a maid for one day a week ("I was not housemaid material") and as a seamstress for many years ("at least it was not servant work").[26]

During these years, Viola lived very alone, avoiding neighbors and even her beloved church – a circumstance that her younger daughters, reading of it in this essay, find incredible. When she resumed occasional attendance at Sunday service around 1957, an acquaintance from Morgan County noticed her depression and suggested she see a Christian

---

[25] Mss 813, Box 17, FF 7; and "Looking Back," Box 20, FF 4.
[26] Mss 813, Box 18, FF 2 and 4.

An African American Autobiography

spiritualist.[27] Grateful for the spiritual solace, if unconvinced by the "therapy," Viola became even more committed to her faith. And the faith watched over her, as she watched over, and prayed for, her children's progress. At Easter in 1961, she writes, she heard on the radio (her own, bought by her older children – another sign of "freedom"!): "He arose, He arose and he arose from the Dead." And: "I believed it.... Yes I believed in the God of the Bible and I trusted in him."[28]

Her own career as a religious educator from the 1970s follows logically. She attended Bible School and in 1971 started teaching at the (white) Lakewood Presbyterian Church. Sister Viola soon became director of the Church Education Department and, in 1980, Staff Religious Editor of the "Metro Atlanta Community Bulletin."

In 1953, when Viola arrived in Atlanta, Harvey, Benny, Valeria, and Raymond had already taken steps toward further education and new careers. In the following years, she put her remaining children through high school, and most through college, and onto secure life and career paths. When Greg, the youngest, finished elementary school, then high school, then college, she writes, she could not believe that after sending children out to study for 42 years she now no longer had a child at school!

At 47 Holly Road, where she lived from 1953 until the end of her life, she now found more time for writing, religious education, and travel. In a 1968 letter, she writes of how, with the children grown up, "I can entertain myself with my Church and playing around with flowers and vegetables! Trying to write a little (because of my [seamstress's] job that goes so slow ...)." And in 1979, when she was teaching Bible classes on Saturday and Sunday mornings and on Tuesday evenings, as well as a class at a white Presbyterian Church "across town," looking after her house and garden, and traveling several times a year to visit her children in distant cities: "I am one of the busiest elderly women I know."[29]

Benny Andrews spoke for many in the rural South when he wrote of New York as "the place I'd always set out to come to" and Georgia

---

[27] Mss 813, Box 18, FF 2; see also Box 18, FF 1; and Benny Andrews collection, Mss 845, Box 114, Viola's letter to Benny and Raymond, August 31, 1957.

[28] Several entries in Mss 813, Box 18, FF 3.

[29] Mss 845, Box 114, Viola's letter of October 27, 1968; Box 115, letter of August 31, 1979.

144   *A History of Prejudice*

as "the place I'd set out to leave."[30] It is important to remember
that this rural South, Georgia, and New York are best thought of
metaphorically, for the themes of race prejudice, feudal and patriarchal
oppression, dreams of the city, and the search for new opportunities,
education, and equality are widely encountered in the twentieth century. How these conditioned the life of Viola Andrews and others like
her, the articulation of a woman's duty, and the organizing of social
relations is a matter of more than local interest.

The Destiny of a Woman

A poor black woman in the twentieth-century American South was
sustained by faith as much as by anything else. Looking back on events,
Viola wrote of how her "greatest Blessing was finding and knowing
God when I was young."[31] She believed in God's miracles: "It's a
miracle how we got this brand new house in a decent community."
Not yet in Atlanta, she was pregnant, without a job, without money
for a down payment, or references. "The bank let me have this new
House; Thats a miracle." Another "miracle" happened with her second
mortgage, when the man who owned it waived the last few installments
on discovering Viola's inability to pay.[32]

Yet, that same religious upbringing required her to accept as God-
given many inherited circumstances, to be resigned to what God had
ordained. One instance of the "ordained" that Viola put up with for
23 years (and lived with for longer) was marriage. Marriage, she had
been taught, was forever. Whatever a husband did – drinking, gam-
bling, philandering, or abusing his wife and children – one had to make
the best of it. "If you make your Bed hard, turn [it] over more often,"
as Viola's mother taught her.[33] Paradoxically, even as she celebrated
her "liberation" from her husband, she lived with long-lasting feelings
of guilt and inadequacy.

Viola saw the move to Atlanta in 1953 as her one chance of building another kind of life. Nevertheless, she writes, she was troubled

---

[30] Gruber, *American Icons*, ii.
[31] Mss 813, Box 20, FF 3.
[32] Mss 813, Box 20, FF 6.
[33] Mss 813, Box 17, FF 12.

An African American Autobiography

about leaving her husband: "the older children would be very disappointed."[34] For the rest of her years, it is important to note, Viola refused to contemplate another marriage, in spite of several opportunities. In 1957, a man she met on the train to Chicago asked if he could come and see her in Atlanta. She declined, she tells us, but for the next eight years, he visited once or twice a year, saw her, and asked about the family. One Easter, he sent her a beautiful orchid, "perhaps from Hawai'i"! Eighteen years later, the Hamptons, old family friends from Morgan County, visited her, and Willie Hampton's brother, Haywood, asked her to marry him. Taken aback, she could only write to him later, saying that it was impossible. He was a "fine looking man," she muses, and she might have considered marriage if he wasn't in another city. It was also in her view "too late" for her to change. Some of her children were also "deadly against the idea," believing that their father needed a partner but not their mother! "That's common among children," she observes.[35]

Given her views, Viola never overcame her ambivalence on the issue. In 1975, she advised her youngest daughter, who was troubled by her in-laws, to accept woman's fate. "The thing is to smile sweetly and go on with one's life, as I did with my mother-in-law and family," she wrote,[36] setting aside in that moment all her struggles against her husband and "in-laws" and the "escape" from them that she so joyously celebrated. In 1977, when her son Benny's first marriage broke up, she wrote that she believed Benny and Mary Ellen should certainly get a divorce, for they were "liberated," twentieth-century people. By contrast, she described herself as "a 19th century Southern Country Black Woman," still living with the belief that man and wife are to be together always.[37] In 1964, when her husband wrote to his children pathetically begging for money and old clothes, she was scathing about him: "I hope that I have forgiven him but, I do not plan to loose [lose] any time thinking about him." Yet a few years later she wondered if this lonely life was "what I have been striving for"

---

[34] Mss 813, Box 18, FF 1.

[35] Mss 813, Box 18, FF 2; Box 20, FF 3 and FF 7. See also Mss 845, Box 114, Viola to Benny and Raymond, August 31, 1957.

[36] Mss 845, Box 115, Viola to Benny and Mary, January 22, 1975.

[37] Mss 845, Box 115, Viola to Benny, March 21, 1977.

146 *A History of Prejudice*

and recalled a verse from the scriptures, "It is not good for Man to be alone."[38]

In 1983, then over 70, she wrote of feeling sorry for "my children's Father. He lost his wife; I hope he find another." And in 1995, when George passed away and she was unable to go to his funeral (she was in southern California, visiting her daughter Veronica, whose mother-in-law fell seriously ill just then), she comforted herself about her decision not to attend: "the – His Children – our children could and would take care of everything. In A way, in A sense, I mourn My Husband's Death. The past can not be changed. So, time goes on."[39]

Another critical dimension of a woman's duty, of affairs settled in heaven and burdens a woman must bear, that Viola wrestles with is the matter of children. Her children, she tells us, were her reason for living: "If I did not have them... life would be completely empty." "What does A woman or how does A woman do when she does not have any children?"[40] Nevertheless, children were a mixed blessing in the rough years after her marriage. Benny, Viola's first child with George, was born in 1930; Valeria Belle in 1932; Raymond in 1934. In 1934, Harvey, her eldest son, born of an unwanted pregnancy while she was in high school, who had been in her mother's care since 1927, also came to live with them. In 1935, Viola was pregnant again (with Shirley). There was nothing like birth control in those days, she writes, "I would have been an outcast if I had inquired."[41]

Viola describes her routine in 1931, when she had only one child, Benny, to look after. The day went in rushing from work on the farm, to cooking, to feeding Benny (left in the care of a young babysitter). George didn't see why it should take her so long to cook or to nurse the child. "The only rest I had was while I ate," she writes. "Other than being Pregnant, giving berth," she wrote later, and attending to the children, her husband also expected her to work in the fields, and she did. "How I lived through those years... Only the Lord know." "My youth was the only way that helped me to survive."[42] And, one might add, her faith.

---

[38] Mss 845, Box 114, Viola to Benny (undated, but 1964); and Mss 813, Box 20, FF 3.
[39] Mss 813, Box 20, FF 9; and Box 21, FF 1.
[40] Mss 845, Box 114, Viola to Benny, November 25, 1965; and Mss 813, Box 20, FF 11.
[41] Mss 813, Box 17, FF 12.
[42] Mss 813, Box 17, FF 12; and Box 20, FF 8.

An African American Autobiography

147

The young mother survived those years, she says in retrospect, by hanging onto the things her mother had said to her: "There is hope between the Stub and the Ground." "All things is possible with God if one keep the Faith." She recalls the spirituals she had heard and sung in church while she was growing up and during her years with George: "I'm so glad that trouble don't last allways." God had delivered the Israelites from Egypt: "what he does for others, he could do for me."[43]

The cycle of pregnancies tested not only the young woman's body; it tested her faith. With a baby coming every two years, Viola realized, she would quickly be worn out. In the spring of 1933, when she already had three children, she used her small savings from working in the fields to order a syringe from Sears. She used this as a douche to prevent pregnancy, "successfully," as she proudly told her mother. Unfortunately, the babysitter discovered and accidentally broke the syringe. Viola couldn't replace it, given the cost and time required to get another from Sears; buying one from the local drug store in Madison "would have been everybody's Business." "Again, I say that I was destined to have ten children."

In this context, Viola's reading – the one love she and George shared with the children – provided an unexpected lifeline. While George and the older boys concentrated on sports magazines and comics, she read many women's magazines, which now increasingly discussed the issue of birth control. Through them, she heard about the rhythm or cycle method of avoiding pregnancy, around the time when her sixth child, Harold, was born, in May 1938. "At that time anything concerning 'Birth Control' was considered sinfull: which I agree in part," she wrote, "but I did not believe that 'the Cycle Method' was sinfull." She decided to try it: "I vowed that I would have no more children. I did not feel sinfull or immoral: I had taken no drugs nor done anything to my body. I was jubilant."

Their decision to abstain from sex several days a month, Viola says with relief, was one thing George didn't tell his mother! In December 1939, Harold was 20 months old, and she was not pregnant, she notes happily: "I hoped to be able to continue reading the cycle method correct[ly]." In December 1940, she was optimistic: "My Baby was 2 years and 8 months old and I was not pregnant." She repeats the sentiment for May 1941, when Harold was three, marveling over the

---

[43] See Mss 813, Box 17, FF 7 and FF 12 for this and the next four paragraphs.

148   *A History of Prejudice*

"cycle method" but worried about the "narrow line" between "do" and "don't." She didn't fully understand the cycle or the risks, but couldn't ask anyone about it: "I would have been considered Immoral, allmost a criminal: everyone would have known, there is no secrets in the country nor small Towns."

In 1942, she was pregnant again – and downhearted. However, when John was born, at the end of August 1942, Harold was four years and three months old. Viola continued to use the cycle method, praying that she would not be pregnant again for a long time. Veronica, her eighth child, was born in April 1948, five and a half years after John. Viola recalls looking at the newborn and thinking that, whatever the benefits of the cycle method, it was her destiny to have children, and they "were *the only, the only* thing that I had" (her emphasis).[44]

Viola lived with an undying sense of guilt and sin because of the child she had before marriage. She writes of how, in getting involved with an unnamed "smart, charming, clever...city boy" while still at high school in Madison, she had "committed the unpardonable moral sin." For some time, she could not bring herself to tell anyone of her pregnancy, and suffered alone. Then she wrote about it to her mother, who stood by her. When the baby was born, "Ma and I prayed together...she said God will forgive my grave mistake."[45]

It is instructive to put Viola's sense of shame and penitence in conceiving a child outside marriage alongside Alice Walker's account of her own discovery that she was pregnant when she returned to college in New York from a trip to Africa, her failure to find an abortionist, and her thoughts of committing suicide. "I did not eat or sleep for three days," Walker notes. "When I thought of my family, and...began to see their faces around the walls, I realized they would be shocked and hurt to learn of my death, but I felt they would not care deeply at all, when they discovered I was pregnant. Essentially, they would believe I was evil."[46] It was when she was contemplating suicide because of her

---

[44] There were two more babies: Deloris, born in 1950, and Gregory – a "disappointment" to Benny and Raymond when they visited from their posts in the Air Force because they hadn't expected that their mother would have more children – in 1953, shortly after Viola and the other children had moved to Atlanta.

[45] Mss 813, Box 17, FF 11.

[46] Walker, *In Search of Our Mothers' Gardens*, 245–6.

An African American Autobiography 149

unwanted pregnancy, she writes, that she "began to understand how alone a woman is, because of her body."[47]

It is this loneliness of the woman's body – when divorced from politics, and torn away from the community of other women by the institution of the modern heterosexual family, segregation, and the insistent demands of childbearing and mothering – that emerges poignantly in large parts of Viola's autobiography. Yet there are other dimensions in Viola's anguish and ambivalence, related to her clear sense of the duties of a black woman and a Christian.

Viola's husband, George, regularly said that he, a "black man," was "nobody," and that no one in a black family should try to be "somebody." By contrast, Viola declares: "I felt I was somebody *even though I had an illegitimate child*." Later in life, when she celebrated the children's success, independence, and self-respect, she still often introduced Harvey as "my illegitimate son." It was a comment on her belief in the responsibilities of a woman of faith, and a mother, an ethical position on childbearing and the sanctity of the body. While she seemed to implicate Harvey in the illegitimacy of his birth by her repeated reference to it in his presence, she also spoke of her duty to her firstborn: "I didn't kill my child. He's a part of me." At other times she referred to him in biblical terms – "He led us out of Morgan County, off the farm"[48] – an appropriate point for us to return to the question of liberation from slavery.

The Problem of the Color Line

I have said little so far about what is considered *the* problem of the South, Du Bois's problem of the twentieth century, the problem of the color line – and thence the African American struggle against it. In part this is because the protagonist of my story in this chapter does not address the history of that struggle very directly in her writings.

Viola Andrews wrote her memoirs between the mid-1960s and the 1990s, from the inauguration of the most visible and effective phase

---

[47] Ibid., 248.
[48] Wendell Brock, "The Amazing Life of Viola Andrews," *Atlanta Journal Constitution*, January 21, 2001, Arts, L 7–8. See also Mss 813, Box 17, FF 12 (emphasis mine). Viola's daughters, Shirley, Veronica, and Deloris, also recall her obsessive fear, during their school-going years, that they might go out with a boy and become pregnant.

of the civil rights movement, in the city where its most important leader was born and lived, a city whose leaders were proud of their achievements in changing race relations. Several of her children became active in the movement: one, Benny, as a leader and organizer of the struggle for the rights of black artists; another, Harold, as a Black Muslim minister. Viola writes about these developments in her children's lives; she expresses some anxiety, for example, about what it means for a son of hers to become a Muslim brother. But she spends remarkably little time on the question of civil rights and the African American struggle in general.

She says little or nothing, for example, about conditions in the armed forces and the treatment of military personnel on their return from duty (including the lynchings after the Second World War that I discussed in the last chapter), although all six of her sons went into the military and used the provisions of the GI Bill to further their education and build careers after they were discharged; the oldest, Harvey, served in the army for twenty years.[49] Viola would probably have seconded what Zora Neale Hurston wrote in the 1920s: "I am not tragically colored.... Even in the helter-skelter skirmish that is my life, I have seen that the world is to [for?] the strong regardless of a little pigmentation more or less."[50]

Viola's artist sons, Benny and Raymond, the first readers of the earliest parts of her autobiography, wrote more than once to ask why she didn't write about the black struggle. "Negroes progress...," she responds in a letter of April 1965, "It is such a big thing and such a miracle. I do believe in miracles.... I saw one of the marches here. Yes the Nuns were with the marchers[,] also quite a few other Whites, which is surprising." She notes the big changes occurring – African American policemen on the streets of Atlanta, bus drivers, firemen, store clerks, nurses – and follows up with proud comments on Martin Luther King, Jr.'s Nobel Peace Prize, the Selma march, and the large numbers of young blacks ready and organizing to help Dr. King. At Grady Hospital in Atlanta, she writes, they'd adopted a "first come,

---

[49] The government should give her a medal for furnishing so much assistance to the country, Viola told an interviewer in 1980; *Time Capsule*, 4, no. 1 (Spring 1980).
[50] Hurston, "How It Feels to Be Colored Me" (1928), in Walker, *I Love Myself When I Am Laughing...*, 153.

An African American Autobiography

first served" system; "so many of the workers are colord. So many of the nurses, maybe most nurses. Really, they [whites?] have no way out." In addition, the federal government had now offered money for public schools, and Viola felt that Atlanta would have to accept the funds – and the consequences. "In a few years there will be no Segregation. The person with the money and Education will be in front."[51]

Yet, in the very same letter, Viola writes that she "never remember[s] to mention" the matter of race relations and black progress in the "biography" she is so meticulously compiling at this time ("from [her] memory bank"). She tries to explain this omission at a later point in the writing of her life-story, in a few sentences that I have already quoted: "I am writing as I knew and saw it then and there. In our community, all the colored owned or rented their land. . . . I was young and I knew nothing about Race Relationship."[52]

When she writes that she has not attended to race relations, Viola is clearly thinking of demonstrations, sit-ins, and other dramatic events of the civil rights struggle in the 1950s and '60s. Yet, although she rarely refers to these developments in her autobiography, there is no escape from the business of race (or color, which has often stood in for race) in the lives of black, brown, or white people in twentieth-century Asia, Africa, and Europe, or in the private lives of rural blacks, or public exchanges in city spaces and governmental institutions in the United States. Notwithstanding her caveat on the matter, then, Viola's writing about the fortunes of the family, and the effort to find the minimum resources necessary for survival and the education of her children, is rarely far removed from what whites and blacks, men and women, rich and poor, had given to them by law and inheritance. Her account of her life in the segregated – conservative, conformist, and Christian – South has a great deal to say about matters that scarcely figured in the public debate on Double V, and not very much in the discourse of the Black Liberation in the 1960s and '70s either: about a woman's reproductive rights, bodily integrity, and the impact of race on all of this, and on the psychological and bodily attitudes and expectations – of whites and blacks.

[51] Mss 845, Box 115, Viola to Benny, April 28, 1965.
[52] MARBL, Viola Andrews Papers, Mss 813, Box 17, FF9.

152   *A History of Prejudice*

"The white man could not loose[lose]," Viola writes in her notes on "growing up," " pryor to 1920," repeating the proposition three times on one page. "The colored man could not win." The whites bragged that they were "Free, White and Twenty-one," young and powerful. "They looked down on everyone else": not only "Niggers" as they called them, but all races, "Orientals, Asians."[53]

In Chapter 2, I cited Viola's, and the local African American community's, skepticism about the religiosity of the whites: what kind of Christians were these who did not heed the Bible's injunction to "treat *every* man as a Brother"? As the young Viola heard it, "the Whites seldom spoke of Heaven." "Actually," muses the older Viola, "they were living Heaven like here on earth." For all that, white men, at least "the wealthy, intelligent, educated ones – never the poor ones," lived a double life. On the outside, the white man had a "clean life," with his wife, children, church, and work. Behind the scenes, "he had his colored concubines." Colored folks knew that "*all* well to do white men had their colored concubines."[54] Occasionally, she notes, the white man lived with a colored woman as his common-law wife, and never married anyone else (as was the case with her father-in-law, Mr. Jim). But the bottom line was that the white man, especially the rich white man, was immoral.

All of this comes together in Viola's reconstruction of her own life with George and his family. "I never heard any Profane Language in our home – nor in our neighbors home." On the other hand, George "used God's name in or with cuss words daily." So did his "white Father," Mr. Jim. Not so his black mother: "never." Viola recalls her father-in-law as being "mean and cruel." When a cow got loose, he cursed Viola soundly. She had to accept this quietly for fear that he would hit her, even if no damage was done. "Anyway he was a white man and I was on his place, also I was Black."[55]

There were times, she says, when she would look at her husband George's "blue eyes, look at his completely white skin and ash Blond hair and know in my heart that I was married to a low moral white man." She believed that he was someone who had absolutely no qualms

[53] Mss 813, Box 17, FF 7 and FF 8; and Box 21, FF 8.
[54] Mss 813, Box 17, FF 10 and FF 7.
[55] Mss 813, Box 17, FF 12.

An African American Autobiography 153

about right or wrong. He never went into church, preferring to sit outside chatting with other men. A Mama's boy, all he wanted was his quota of liquor, hanging out with his mates (and Jim and Jessie's family), and spending Saturday nights "with his girl-friend."[56]

On the question of the children's future, race divided the couple – in unexpected ways. In spite of her racially mixed, Indian-African-Caucasian heritage, Viola was dark, and proud of it. George, born of someone seen as a racially pure "white" father and a very mixed "black" mother, was exceedingly fair, blue-eyed, blonde-haired – and ashamed of it. "He shaved his head rather than let his blonde hair show," his son Benny has written, "he shuffled more, 'yassuhed more', scratched his head . . . because he was *totally* ashamed of his whiteness. He was more of a crushed and defeated man than any out and out black man could ever be."[57] (See Figure 3.)

George was "Deadly against Educated Niggers" and "ashame for his children to be in school especially if they were a little more regular or ahead of others."[58] Viola held the polar opposite view: "*How, how* could a White Man [which her husband was, in her view] . . . be against his child getting an Education. I thought that white . . . men and Education were Related, how could they and it be separated."[59] George believed he was a "nobody," as Viola notes frequently in her autobiography, and that African Americans should never try to be "somebody" – a lesson he had learned, paradoxically, from his black mother rather than his white father.

Jim Orr had wanted all his children to go to Booker T. Washington, the first black public high school in Atlanta. His partner, Jessie, refused. She didn't see why her children should leave Plainview, their little patch of Morgan County: black kids in the country would gain nothing from a high school education since most of them dropped out after a little elementary education and went to work in the fields. In this as in other matters, George followed her views faithfully.

Viola had to fight tooth and nail to ensure that her children went to school, saving every dime and cutting corners wherever possible.

---

[56] Mss 813, Box 18, FF 1.
[57] Benny Andrews, "Forty Years," Mss 845, Box 117 (emphasis Benny's).
[58] Mss 813, Box 17, FF 7 and FF 12.
[59] Mss 813, Box 17, FF 12 (emphasis Viola's).

FIGURE 3. (clockwise from top left) Viola Andrews, Atlanta, Georgia, 1975; George Andrews, Madison, Georgia, 1975; and George's parents, Jessie Andrews and James Orr (Mr. Jim) in the 1940s (courtesy Shirley Lowrie; photos of Viola and George Andrews by Veronica Villa)

In 1944, when Benny was 13, she worked out a compromise with the overseer on the farm where the family worked, whereby Benny could go to Burney Street, the black high school in Madison five miles away, on rainy days or when there was no work in the fields. The overseer

An African American Autobiography

spat, and George sulked, but Benny started high school, and this was the beginning of a new phase in their lives.[60] Benny's entry into high school and Harvey's move to Atlanta, where he lived in the YMCA and found odd jobs to make a living before he went into the army, opened the way for the other children.

For the mature Viola, now in far more comfortable circumstances, the proud mother of children who had gained considerable personal and professional success, and even fame, racial privilege and its attendant prejudices were still impossible to forget. She writes of the appalling conditions in which chain gangs of prisoners were forced to work early in the century ("the chained gang were colored, the [armed] Bosses were White") and about how they sang "Go down Moses, Way down in Egypt Land, tell old Pharoah, let My people go" and other songs of redemption – underlining again that, whatever else they had or did not have, "they had a song." "Yes, one day we Colored Folks will be free.... [T]he Bible says so and God will bring it to pass."[61] And many of her letters, from the 1960s to the 1990s (almost to the end of her life), reveal a deep-seated distrust of southern whites. Only the exceptional younger white man or woman could possibly escape the older generation's calculated investment in racial privilege and segregation. Thus, the archivist who acquired her papers for the Emory University manuscripts library was "very Brave" and "Benevolent" to take such an interest in her writings and to discuss her work publicly "in a Sophisticated place Emory's": "Evidently he is not a Klans-man."[62]

Not surprisingly, the high point of the Andrews saga is reached for Viola when the white folks of Madison, Georgia, recognize the achievements of Benny and Raymond Andrews: a lesson to them about what blacks could achieve, and how her children had placed them on the cultural map of America in a way that "white Madisonians"

---

[60] Mss 813, Box 17, FF 12; Gruber, *American Icons*, 31; Viola's letter to Benny quoted in Andrews, "Forty Years."

[61] "Go Down Moses," *Time Capsule*, 4, no. 1 (Spring 1980). Viola notes that the story "is not fiction," though the editor of the New York artists' magazine ("a northern person") classified it as such; see Mss 813, Box 21, FF 7. The quotations I have used come from the handwritten version found in Mss 813, Box 17, FF 10.

[62] Mss 813, Box 22, FF4, Viola to Kathy and Richard Hawke, March 17, 1999 (see also other letters in this box); also Mss 813, Box 20, FF 13; and Mss 845, Box 114, Viola's letters of June 16 and 19, 1966.

156   *A History of Prejudice*

had never even dreamed of. In May 1978, when Benny's drawings and Raymond's forthcoming book were exhibited at Peachtree Summit, Atlanta, she declared this "a Monument... a Milestone" for the Andrews family, and the climax of her story.[63] In 1980, Viola wrote of "the ultimate" having happened, Benny's "painting [a mural] in the Largest Airport in the world.... The Home Town see and Realize your qualifications. I cannot ask for more." And a couple of years later, when Benny returned to his native Georgia to attend another function in Madison: "To think that he [Benny] could not attend the School that belonged to the white – now – today he is being honored here in the [same] Building he could not attend; and he is the greatest Artist ever from G[eorgi]a.... God moves in A mysterious way."[64]

And here the story returns to the very private. In November 1982, Benny and Raymond were felicitated respectively for their artwork and books at the Cultural Center in Madison, the same building that they were denied entry into as children. The large gathering, consisting of more whites than blacks, included Viola's husband, George, whom her eldest son, Harvey, had brought along. Her comments on the occasion are noteworthy: "That white Man... my Husband! I didn't recognize him.... I see that he is not the strong Dominant Man that he appeared to be when we were together. Looking at that little Man; thinking about how cruel he was to me and the children; how could that little Puny looking Man be so cruel."[65]

And further: "I have overcome the 'Madisonians' my worst enemies." "The White People were very nice; I could hardly believe what had happened after 29 years. We went back in style – on different terms than when we left. This was the Ultimate.... I never dreamed that this could happen. My children (us) left the cotton fields of G[eorgi]a and My children had made good.... WE HAVE ARRIVED."[66]

The Body of History

Viola Andrews came from a relatively comfortable, literate, and proud, though still poor, family of small farmers; her parents sent her to high school and, like her parents and her husband's father (though not her

---

[63] Mss 813, Box 20, FF 4.
[64] Mss 845, Box 115, Viola to Benny, October 1, 1980; and Mss 813, Box 20, FF 11.
[65] Mss 813, Box 20, FF 9.
[66] Ibid.; and Mss 845, Box 115, Viola to Benny, November 29, 1982.

An African American Autobiography

husband), she recognized the importance of education for the younger generation. Both she and her husband had early in their lives cultivated a love for reading, a "hobby" they persisted with and encouraged in their children, even in hard times. While she was growing up and during her years of marriage, Viola would almost certainly have heard of, if she hadn't seen or read, slave accounts of their life in bondage and their exceptional, fortuitous, plucky escapes to freedom. In any event, the motif of slavery and liberation is a central one in her account of her life: "I had been a slave too long." "The reason that I love atlanta; I... gained my Freedom here."[67] The "biography" that she started writing in the early 1960s – journal, memoir, repetitive notes on her life, however we classify it – is clearly marked by this upbringing and this heritage.

The reasons she gives, in the early stages of writing, for committing her memories to paper are several: "I wanted to put some things on paper, if possible; some of the ways of life that I saw, also experienced. there was so much that I could not put in print no matter how hard I tried; anyway, I and my inner self communed together while I wrote." In addition, as she said in a letter written in April 1963, at 50 a person has "sweet memories [sic]." So she wanted to write, if only for the children. "It can be family property and Greg [her youngest son, still barely 10] may rewrite it one day, who knows."[68]

As Viola notes repeatedly, her children were her life. But as the younger children grew, and became independent, she was able to turn more and more to other things. By the mid-'60s, the family already seemed to have turned the corner. "How about us going Republican?" she asked in November 1964. "We are big time folks now." Greg was by this time expressing admiration and envy for his older brother, Harold, who had become a Black Muslim activist. He wanted to be like Harold, noted Viola, and bragged that he (Harold) used to pick cotton![69]

By 1967, Viola was committed to writing: "I have to write." Along with her life-story, she was writing short stories: "AND – I – have – a – big – dream! It might sell. It's possible." In 1981, aged almost 70, she returned to school to learn typing; and unusually for her, given

---

[67] Mss 813, Box 17, FF 7; and "Looking Back," Box 20, FF 4.
[68] Mss 813, Box 18, FF 4; Mss 845, letters of April 20, 1963, and April 24, 1965.
[69] Mss 845, letters of November 20, 1964, and March 17, 1965.

158   *A History of Prejudice*

her thriftiness, she even looked for a paid typist for her work, which her daughters had helped type until then.[70] What I read in all of this is the poignancy of Viola's relation to her writing, and her life: a woman coming into her own in a quite unprecedented way.

For all that, or perhaps one should say because of it, the Andrews' saga is not the familiar rags-to-riches tale of the great American story. The American Dream is skewed in Viola's recounting. In the years after her move to Atlanta in 1953, struggling to get by with several minor children in an alien environment, Viola suffered what would today almost certainly be diagnosed as post-traumatic stress disorder. She kept entirely to herself, even staying away from church, as I have noted. She envied other people's "social life" but believed that kind of life was not for her, an "ex-slave." "Yes. I was free but I still had the marks."[71] She was beset by endlessly repeated dreams of failure, which she writes about over and over again, every few pages at some points in the autobiography: imagining a child left behind in Morgan County who would only be saved if she returned to her husband, and a cow she'd brought from the country but neglected so that the animal suffered greatly. Remarkably, the trauma comes at the very moment of liberation. "I suffered for 30 years more or less in those Dreams."[72]

Expecting her tenth child when she left Morgan County, Viola hardly forgives herself for leaving her husband: "I knew the older children would be very disappointed but I knew that 'even this would pass.'" She had escaped "slavery" but still bore the marks. When she went into downtown Atlanta with her eldest daughter, Valeria, who took her fair color from her father, "Some of the clerks in the stores asked me, was I her nurse? People watched us so much. . . . I started walking behind her!"[73] A "hiding behind" is evident also in those early years in Atlanta in her isolation from her neighbors, and even from the house of God; and, in the longer term, in her refusal to countenance any liaison with men. This is the "soul murder" that Painter has written about, "the violation of one's inner being, the extinguishing of one's identity, including sexual identity."[74]

---

[70] Mss 845, letters of January 1, 1967; March 13, 1968; November 1, 1970; September 3, 1979; March 25, 1981.
[71] Mss 813, Box 18, FF 2 and FF 4.
[72] Mss 813, Box 18, FF 1, and several other files.
[73] Mss 813, Box 18, FF 1, for the preceding quotations.
[74] Painter, *Southern History across the Color Line*, 15, 17.

An African American Autobiography 159

Power in this account is shown to us in its naked, most irreducible form. Recall Viola's comment on the fallout when a cow broke loose on the farm in Plainview and her father-in-law, Mr. Jim, cursed her for the happening. There was nothing she could do about it, as she wrote: "He was a white man and I was on his place, also I was Black." Yet Viola's construction of this history is a little removed from the standard narrative of white oppression and black liberation. To the white man's authority signaled in the sentence just quoted, one would have to add her emphasis on the despotism of a father-in-law and of men more generally. As the autobiographical writings convey it, Viola's sense of being a prisoner and a slave is inextricably linked not only to the legacy of slavery and the oppressions of segregation but to the persistence of patriarchal power. However, the politics surrounding them is scarcely straightforward. Consider the identification of "blacks" and "whites."

Viola's natal family was in her own words "related to the Indians, related to the Afros, related to the Caucasians."[75] George, the son of a white man and a person I've described as a beautiful, part Indian, part white, black woman, looked completely white and wished to be completely black. If the "hierarchy of racism," "white" dominance, and "black" subordination expresses a clear ranking of classes,[76] it clearly has a political – and, for Viola, moral – connotation, too: "How could white men and Education be separated." Patriarchal power, too, is implicated in the historical and political privilege attained by white men over the last several centuries. The private and the public are, in critical ways, one and the same. "I see that [that "low moral," "puny looking" white man] is not the strong Dominant Man that he appeared to be."

Through the later decades of the twentieth century, Viola took increasing pride in her writing, her editing of a religious bulletin, her Bible teaching, and her radicalism! A 1979 letter captures her mood well: "Guess what! I completed My Masterpiece! . . . the first (story) I started. It's the longest one. It was difficult to get rid of My Characters! but I did. Really, I think it is my best. . . . Someday a movie may be made from Ray's work, also mine. Our work is a little Radical for the South but we gotta believe."[77]

---

[75] *Atlanta Journal Constitution*, January 21, 2001, L8.
[76] Painter, *Southern History across the Color Line*, 113.
[77] Mss 845, Box 115, Viola to Benny, August 31, 1979.

160   *A History of Prejudice*

Viola's life-story defies the scholar's attempt to give it political coherence. Her detailed and often repetitive autobiography points to the instability – but not for that reason the reduced force – of assumed identities and the powers and privileges attendant on them. It shows the fragmented, interrupted, "kinda jumbled," and for that reason challenging and enriching articulations that have constituted "ordinary life" – all life – in the twentieth century and beyond. This is perhaps what is at stake when Viola says, "*Please*, please do not change it [my biography] and put it on your *Academic* Intellectual Level."

Scholars analyzing women's autobiographies, and more specifically the autobiographical writings of black women in the segregated society of late nineteenth- and early twentieth-century America, have remarked on their pronounced "uncertainty," "confessional" mode, and strategy of "dissemblance."[78] However, we have another frame for engagement with Viola's account: that of assembling a life that fails to assemble, not because it has no coherence or guiding principle(s) but because it has too many Others, too much common sense, to contend with – a whole variety of powerful forces bent on otherizing *her* life, bending it to their will, and creating clear-cut, well-marked, measurable distances. For Viola, the woman's body, subjected to unrelenting sexual and social labor, is the bearer of the Cross. Yet, like Jesus, it may triumph – with the aid of God and the assistance of God's instrument, Moses, here found in the form of her own children, perhaps above all in that of her "illegitimate" son, Harvey.

There is in Viola's account a refusal to conform to academic and social/racial expectation. There is the struggle to retain control of her body and her sexuality; the location of race relations (and much else of what is called politics) in questions of personal morality, bodily disposition, and the sphere of intimate relations; the challenging of the common sense and inheritances of what a woman – and a woman in the rural South of the mid-twentieth-century United States – ought to be

---

[78] E.g., Patricia Spacks, "Selves in Hiding," and Regina Blackburn, "In Search of the Black Female Self: African-American Women's Autobiographies and Ethnicity," in *Women's Autobiography: Essays in Criticism*, ed. Estelle C. Jelinek (Bloomington: Indiana University Press, 1980); Elizabeth Fox-Genovese, "My Statue, My Self: Autobiographical Writings of Afro-American Women," in *The Private Self: Theory and Practice of Women's Autobiographical Writings*, ed. Shari Benstock (Chapel Hill: University of North Carolina, 1988); and Hine, *Hine Sight*, 37–47.

An African American Autobiography

and to do.[79] Yet, even as she celebrates her liberation from "slavery," there is also her lament about her failed marriage: the Bible says, "It is not good for Man to be alone." And her comment on her husband's death: "In A way, in A sense, I mourn My Husband's Death. The past [cannot] be changed. So, time goes on." And her repeated reference to Harvey – who "led us [Moses-like] out of Morgan County" – as her illegitimate son.

In his illustrations and paintings, Benny Andrews, by then an important black artist and activist, regularly portrayed his mother as the dignified Southern Black Woman of faith. "He always paint me with the Bible," Viola commented jocularly. "[He make] me out to be a missionary!"[80] Viola Andrews would not be constrained in this way, even by the Bible. She comes across, in her own work, as very much more conflicted, "ordinary," historical and heroic. With the overarching presence of God and in an era of great civil rights struggle, she is struggling daughter, wife, mother, seamstress, gardener, traveler, religious educator, author – individual, woman.

Centrally at issue here is the difficult question of the rescripting of the subaltern body. In an earlier chapter, I cited Apel's finding that after the Second World War, "The abject black body of the lynching victim, usually stripped or clothed in rags, was reimagined as a military hero lying in uniform, a citizen of the nation."[81] (See Figure 2.) Viola's description of her every day before, during, and after that war provides another account of how difference lodges in the body of the subaltern woman; her writing serves to bring that body into historical time.

I pursue the matter of rescripting the subaltern body further in the next chapter through an examination of a number of important, and unusual, Dalit autobiographies.

---

[79] Cf. the comment of Janie Crawford's grandmother in Zora Neale Hurston, *Their Eyes Were Watching God* (1937; reprint New York: Harper and Row, 1990), that she never had the opportunity "to fulfill [her] dreams of whut a woman oughta be and to do," cited and used as the title of her work by Stephanie J. Shaw, *What a Woman Ought to Be and to Do: Black Professional Women Workers during the Jim Crow Era* (Chicago: University of Chicago Press, 1996), 1.

[80] MSS 813 Box 1, TV interview on *The Public Affair*, conducted by Angela Rice (produced by Atlanta Interfaith Broadcasters Inc., 1994).

[81] Apel, *Imagery of Lynching*, 170; also 166.

6

Dalit Memoirs

Rescripting the Body

Dalit autobiography emerged as a category in the 1970s, along with a new kind of protest poetry as well as fiction that was not always removed from writings in an autobiographical mode. Many of these writings foregrounded the vicious history of (vernacular, visible) caste prejudice. They did so through a recitation of the practices of othering – discrimination, exclusion, and humiliation – that have been central to the rural (and urban) performance of caste and, not least, through their depiction of the bodies of suffering, laboring lower-caste men and women, bodies that come to bear the distinct marks of such oppression, discrimination, and exclusion. In their description of the Dalit struggle to overcome the history of this oppression and to inhabit a different kind of body, they also tell us a good deal about the play of a less visible, universal prejudice – the common sense of the age, or of the community that says, casually, *that's how it is*, and, implicitly, *how it is meant to be.*

The reminiscences I consider in this chapter belong to the category of what might be described as resistance literature, emerging out of and building on recognized traditions of political and intellectual resistance. The very titles of numerous Dalit life-writings indicate the history of stigmatization, oppression, and poverty against which the Dalit self (individual or collective) is insistently, and perhaps necessarily, articulated: *Joothan* (the leftovers of the upper castes' food that we lived on); *Apne Apne Pinjre* (our own individual cages); *Upara* (outsider); *Uchalya* (thief, or pilferer); *Akkarmashi* (half-caste, or bastard); *Baluta*

Dalit Memoirs

(the services traditionally required of the lowest castes in rural Maharashtra); *Aaydaan* (the weaving of baskets from bamboo, condemned as an Untouchable occupation); *Dohra Abhishaap* (twice cursed).

Translations of these texts into English and other European languages have constrained their location and meaning even more, with their titles focusing almost jarringly on the matter of caste discrimination and Untouchability. Narendra Jadhav's *Aamcha baap aan aamhi* (Our Father and Us) (1993), about which I shall have more to say later in this chapter, is translated into French as *Intouchable* (2002) and into English as *Outcaste* (2003), with the American edition (2005) spelling out the subject further as *Untouchables: My Family's Triumphant Journey out of the Caste System in Modern India.* Vasant Moon's beautifully titled *Vasti* (neighborhood, or community) (1995) becomes *Growing up Untouchable in India: A Dalit Autobiography* when translated and published in English five years later. Om Prakash Valmiki's *Joothan* (1997) gains the subtitle "A Dalit's Life" on its publication in English in 2003. Urmila Pawar's *Aaydaan* (2003), nicely translated as *The Weave of My Life* (2008), now has the added subtitle, "A Dalit Woman's Memoir."

The making of a new Dalit politics and history in the late twentieth century was conditioned by the heightened expectations that came with the establishment of an independent Indian state in the 1940s and '50s, educational advance and social mobility in the later colonial period (which expanded greatly after Independence, assisted by new policies of affirmative action), and the very emergence of Dalit autobiography and memoir as a form of protest literature and a means of documenting the Dalit struggle. The shift followed the gradual collapse of the promise and aspirations of Nehruvian democracy in the wake of independence, the apparent taming (and marginalization) of the philosophical challenge mounted by the mass conversion to Buddhism, and the splintering of Ambedkar's own political movement. A number of political fractions came out of this splintering and accommodated themselves in varying degrees and various ways to the dominant political discourse and dominant political parties. At the same time, however, a newly militant cultural/political movement emerged, led by a first generation of college-educated Dalit intellectuals and professionals and gaining particular visibility (and notoriety) under a loosely organized group called the Dalit Panthers. Although this movement

164   *A History of Prejudice*

was far from being closely coordinated or centralized, and was to suffer serious internal division and disintegration by the 1980s, it left its mark in the form of a body of autobiographical writings that has come to stay and that has had wide impact – in the literary world and in Dalit consciousness.

The outpouring of Dalit autobiographical accounts was particularly remarkable in Maharashtra, western India, the home province of B. R. Ambedkar and the area of his greatest initial influence. The critical acclaim and popularity that attended the publication of Daya Pawar's Marathi autobiography *Baluta* (1978) was followed by a spate of autobiographical writings, especially by individuals from Ambedkar's own caste of Mahars, but soon extending to other Dalit castes and other regions of India, with publications in Hindi, Kannada, Tamil, and other languages. The movement heralded a literary revolution, producing fresh modes of narration, a changed literary consciousness, and novel ideas of history.

With the establishment of a market for Dalit literature in the 1980s and '90s, and the emergence of Ambedkar, posthumously, as a towering national figure and an unparalleled intellectual, visionary, and leader whom Dalits all over India begin to invoke, many life-writings appear in the form of fairly direct political commentary and inducement to Dalit mobilization. The figure of Ambedkar is critical, and the writings take on the character of early modern *charitra* (literally "character") – biographies or accounts of the lives and character of saints, written in order to claim discipleship and an empowering connection with the saint. Ambedkar now becomes a flame that lights other flames: disciples who are chosen individuals in their own right, and who see no distinction between exceptional writers and ordinary people.[1] The meaning of this literary/political revolution requires closer examination, however, for the politics of particular subaltern autobiographical traditions and practices are not, by any means, monochromatic or transparent.

I have argued that subaltern writings in the autobiographical mode are denied the space of the unmarked universal, which is occupied

---

[1] I am grateful to Rashmi Bhatnagar for discussions on this point and for stressing to me the relevance of the *charitra* tradition; for an extended discussion of *charitra*, see Rashmi Bhatnagar, *World and Bhāsa Literatures: Revolutions in Philology* (forthcoming).

by male, upper-class, bourgeois autobiography. They are consigned instead to the local, the vernacular, and the marked: subjects (or, shall we say, objects) that appear as something of a deviance from the "normal" condition of modern existence, the autonomous self, and autobiography. They are also denied their individuality and variety, the very stuff of human life in the liberal understanding. I want to suggest, however, that this is a channeling, a confinement, that owes something to the agenda and politics of specific subaltern constituencies as well as to the compulsions of the market and a wider common sense.

Life-story/autobiography/memoir involves the production, not the presentation, of an already available self, as I have already observed. I suggested in Chapter 3 that in treating caste discrimination, and in particular the treatment of ex-Untouchable castes by Touchable castes, as their overriding concern, Dalit leaders overstated the claim of Dalit unity and understated the force of divisions and tensions "internal" to the putative Dalit community. An important question of political choices arises, then, even in the subset of subaltern life-writing that one might call political autobiography. It is these choices that I set out to explore in the following pages.

The "Inner Cry"

Numerous examples of subalternist life-writing convey the sense of releasing an irrepressible, inner cry. Thus the leading poet of the Harlem Renaissance, Langston Hughes: "Because my mouth/ Is wide with laughter/And my throat/ Is deep with song/ You do not think/ I suffer after/ I have held my pain/ So long?" Or the Dalit Professor of Sanskrit, Kumud Pawde's autobiographical narrative *Antah-sphot* (1981), literally "inner explosion," an inner cry like a volcanic eruption. Is the subaltern memoir an archive of that cry, one might ask? And whose cry? The individual? The collective? The times?

Let us begin with a quick examination of the circumstances of the men and women responsible for this outpouring of autobiographical literary work among Dalits – when and how these accounts are written, in what circumstances, at what stage in the protagonist's life – which helps to indicate some of the more distinctive aspects of this body of writing. When people asked Om Prakash Valmiki, the distinguished Hindi writer and memoirist from Uttar Pradesh in northern India, why he had written an autobiography so early in life, he responded: "Don't compare this narrative of pain with the achievements of others."[2] Aravind Malagatti from Karnataka (southern India) makes much the same point in a note to the reader ("before you read") at the start of his autobiography, published in Kannada under the English title *Government Brahmana* (1994): "I do not have any illusions of becoming a mahatma [a "great soul": the implied reference is apparently to Mahatma Gandhi] by presenting these few pages of my life story. I am quite ordinary.... At the same time, I cannot resist saying that these experiences are those of every ordinary dalit."[3] The politics of this assertion of ordinariness bears reflection.

The memoirs in question are not the works of well-schooled, comfortable, degree-holding, trained or leisured intellectuals, ruminating on life, love, and the mysteries of human being. On the contrary. Early women writers in nineteenth-century Bengal, we might recall, frequently learned to read and write on the sly, against the injunctions of "respectable" society: Shanta Nag, standing silently on the other side of a table at which her older brother was being taught the Bengali primer, which the young girl also cleverly learned to read – but only with the book held the wrong way around; Rassundari Debi stealing a page on which her son had written the alphabet, and using it painfully to decipher individual pages that she removed, one at a time, from the household copy of a religious text – with no one but a few household maids aware of her self-teaching.[4] Although Dalit children in the middle and later decades of the twentieth century were not denied access to schools and textbooks in quite the same way, it was still far from easy for them to gain fluency in the "high," literary languages of the different parts of India and even less easy – for Dalit women, even more than for Dalit men – to become writers.

As with Viola's children, the first question asked about schooling beyond a minimal primary stage was what, if anything, Dalit (or black) children would gain from the effort. And more emphatically,

---

[2] Valmiki, *Joothan*, viii.

[3] Aravind Malagatti, *Government Brahamana* (Chennai: Orient Longman, 2007), 1.

[4] Partha Chatterjee, *The Nation and Its Fragments* (Princeton, NJ: Princeton University Press, 1993), 140, 142. Ashraf-un-nisa Begum provides a striking parallel example from northern India; see Ruby Lal, *Coming of Age in Nineteenth Century India: The Girl Child and the Art of Playfulness* (forthcoming).

Dalit Memoirs

what would they gain from "writing" (or, in the Andrews' case, "coloring and drawing")? What good would it do for their livelihood and survival? Along with the dominant classes, subaltern society frowned on such attempts to ape the upper classes. When it came to women writers, the men (and older women) of their local communities were particularly blistering in their comments. These young, "educated," often urban (or urban-returned) folk were giving themselves airs; they thought they had become pundits (or Brahmans). One outcome is seen in the examples of a female and a male writer whom I discuss at greater length later in this chapter. Baby Kamble kept the writing of her memoirs a secret from her husband and all her relatives, except perhaps an elder brother,[5] for twenty years. So did Damodar Jadhav, who, after his retirement from work in the Bombay Port railway yards, secretly jotted down reminiscences (and short stories) of his early life: his well-educated and now well-placed (middle-class) children, who had given him the notebooks and encouraged him to write, say that they discovered his writings only after his death.

In large part, at least in the early stages of Dalit (and other subaltern) autobiographical ventures – and I use the term advisedly, for the process is a discovery of literacy and of genre as well as of self – the writing, to quote one student of Dalit autobiographies, "has no literary purpose" (or ambition): it is rather "a laborious effort in quest of oneself."[6] In many instances, indeed, in nineteenth-century bhadralok Bengali women's accounts, as in twentieth-century subaltern women's and men's accounts, the writing takes the form of an interaction with an inner self. Recall the mode of Rassundari Debi's narration of her life, *Amar Jiban*, in which the successive chapters read like a series of entreaties to god. Or again, an important reason offered by Viola Andrews for writing about her life: "[A]nyway I and my inner self communed together while I wrote."

Consider in this context the example of Madhav Kondhvilkar, the son of a cobbler, who became a schoolteacher and was sent to his own village to teach in the very building where as a pupil, before Indian

---

[5] Guy Poitevin, "Dalit Autobiographical Narratives: Figures of Subaltern Consciousness, Assertion and Identity," 13, http://aune.lpl.univ-aix.fr/-belbernard/misc/ccrss/dalitautobio.htm.

[6] Ibid., 21.

independence, he was made to sit in a corner and treated as an untouchable. The scholar-activist Guy Poitevin writes of how Kondhvilkar continued to be slighted by the upper castes in the village, as well as "misunderstood and rebuked" by his own caste fellows, and how, as this renewed experience of caste oppression blended with memories of his childhood, Kondhvilkar started keeping a diary, "in a complete social isolation, prompted by an inner urge to write, speak out and cry out." His writing becomes, as it did for Viola, "his confidant, the support of his inward dialogue with himself, the witness to his aspirations and torment, a means to record his expectations when no one else takes him seriously."[7]

The articulation of the subaltern subject – the assertion of humanity, agency, subjectivity – occurs in a fairly untypical manner. The distinction between subject and object often disappears, as in the *charitra* genre of early modern writing of saintly and exceptional lives in the Indic tradition, though in a rather different context. In the former, saint and god, disciple and saint, are merged into one. In Dalit life-stories, the "community" is the omnipresent; hence, the subject who writes and the object of reflection are not easily separated. On occasion, an apparently unconscious slide from first- to third-person narration, and the other way around, signals the particularity of the experience – possibly suggesting also that the first-person voice cannot bear the weight of the life being relived. I shall have occasion to refer to this move in analyzing Baby Kamble's account of her and her community's life, as well as Narendra Jadhav's family memoir, later in this chapter. Here, let me illustrate the point quickly with three quotations from the Bengali domestic servant Baby Halder's *Aalo Andhari*, where subject and object appear as one and the same – sometimes in the same sentence.

As a little girl, sitting quietly after serving visitors in her aunt's home, Halder writes: "I thought of all those people who had praised my work – what would they have said if they had known that ever since she was a small child, Baby had known little other than the hard drudgery of household chores?" Recalling her time in the hospital having her first child: "I – a child, not even fourteen years old – I, Baby, lay there alone crying and screaming. When the other patients

---

[7] All quotations in this paragraph are from Poitevin, ibid.

Dalit Memoirs

began complaining, Baby was moved to another room, where she was put on a table and her arms and legs were tied." "I, Baby, lay there crying"; "she (Baby)" was put on a table with her arms and legs tied. Or again, on the day when she sees her mother, who had left her father, and the children with him, years earlier:

> I wondered again how she could have left such small children and gone away.... Did she even remember that she had managed to get rid of her little girl, Baby, by bribing her with ten paise on the day she left home? Did she remember that she hadn't turned around once to look back? How then could she have known that Baby stood there and watched her until she became a mere speck on the horizon?[8]

Perhaps even more emphatically than in the case of the relatively comfortable middle-class (or bourgeois) individual, the agency, subjectivity, or selfhood of newly literate and still disenfranchised groups is not already available, ready-made as it were. Against the examples of resistance to the first-person singular, in the interest of some larger self, many Dalit commentators have articulated the need for a strong assertion of the long-denied "I." Dalits, "who have for so long been treated as commodities owned by others, must shout out their selfhood, their 'I', when they rise up," Raj Gauthaman observes.[9] The new literature of Dalit selfhood that has emerged in recent decades has sought to establish "the dignity of the untouchable person" through "powerful words," writes Sharankumar Limbale.[10]

At the same time, as Limbale goes on to say, "The experience described in Dalit literature is social, hence it is articulated as collective in character. Therefore, even when the experience expressed . . . is that of an individual, it appears to be that of a group."[11] And elsewhere, in his autobiographical account of the "half-caste" "bastard" produced by the sexual abuse of his Untouchable laboring mother by a high caste, landlord "father": "I regard the immorality of my father . . . [towards

---

[8] Baby Halder, *A Life Less Ordinary*, translated from the Hindi by Urvashi Butalia (New Delhi: Zubaan, 2002), 30, 57, 117.

[9] Raj Gauthaman, cited in Lakshmi Holmstrom, "Introduction," in Bama, *Sangati*, translated from the Tamil by Lakshmi Holmstrom (New Delhi: Oxford University Press, 2005), xv.

[10] Sharankumar Limbale, *Towards an Aesthetic of Dalit Literature*, translated from the Marathi by Alok Mukherjee (New Delhi: Orient Longman, 2004), 26.

[11] Ibid., 36; cf. 31.

my] mother as a metaphor for rape. . . . I grow restless whenever I read about a rape in the newspaper. A violation anywhere in the country, I feel, is a violation of my mother."[12]

Thus, the loudly declaimed subaltern "I" is located in a no less forcefully proclaimed "we." Dalit writing cannot be severed from its relationship with pain, says Limbale.[13] "My mother used to weave *aaydans* [baskets or containers made of bamboo]," writes Urmila Pawar in a 2003 book that sharply critiques both caste society and Dalit patriarchy. "I find her act of weaving and my act of writing are organically linked. The weave is similar. It is the weave of pain, suffering and agony that links us."[14] In a similar vein, the translator and critic Maya Pandit has described Baby Kamble's autobiographical account *Jina Amcha* (1986) as more a socio-biography than the autobiography of an individual.[15] Kamble herself describes it as "the autobiography of my entire community": "The suffering of my people became my own suffering. Their experiences became mine. . . . I really find it difficult to think of myself outside of my community."[16]

We return here to the question of the "singular nature of [subaltern] pain"[17] and of the body as archive for the writing of subaltern history. These are the issues that I pursue in the remaining sections of this chapter, through a focus on two important autobiographical accounts of Dalit life and history in Maharashtra (western India): Baby Kondiba Kamble's life-story, *Jina Amcha (Our Lives)*, first serialized in a Marathi journal in 1982, published as a book in Marathi in 1986, and translated into and published in English in 2008; and Narendra Jadhav's compilation *Aamcha Baap aan Aamhi (Our Father and Us)*, first broadcast as a life-story on regional Marathi radio and published in Marathi in 1993, and translated, or rather rewritten, by the author and published in English in 2003, with a French translation having appeared in 2002 and translations into numerous other Indian languages subsequently.

---

[12] Limbale, *The Outcaste*, ix.
[13] Limbale, *Towards an Aesthetic of Dalit Literature*, 35.
[14] Urmila Pawar, *The Weave of My Life: A Dalit Woman's Memoirs*, translated from the Marathi by Maya Pandit (Calcutta: Stree, 2008), x.
[15] Maya Pandit, "Introduction," in Pawar, *Weave of My Life*, xv.
[16] Kamble, *Prisons We Broke*, 157, 136.
[17] Ganguly, "Pain, Personhood, and the Collective," 433.

Dalit Memoirs

Baby Kamble and Narendra Jadhav both come from Ambedkar's caste group, the Mahars. Both write in the tradition of Dalit life-writing that I have described above. And both write of Ambedkar and the Ambedkarite struggle as an integral part of the family story, so much so that one might say of these accounts what Jonathan Spence says about Zhong Dai's biographical sketches in seventeenth-century China: that they "are also – or could it be 'are mainly'?" about the wider political struggle, the emergence of an unprecedented Dalit movement under the inspiration of Ambedkar.[18] It is this facet of the reminiscences that perhaps explains the juxtaposition of the autobiographical narrative with what we could classify as ethnography and reportage, as well as the easy shift from first-person to third-person narration: this is my/our story, but it is also a broader history.

It is perhaps unnecessary to add that the Kamble and Jadhav memoirs are overdetermined by the broader political trends of the times in which they were written, the early 1980s and the early 1990s, respectively. In the case of the latter, the text was indeed recast and rewritten several times in the decade following its initial publication, and the rewriting was done by individuals who are no longer in anything like a subaltern position, yet remain strongly committed to the principles of the Ambedkarite struggle and the advancement of the lower-caste group they originally came from (and of other castes and classes caught in a similarly disenfranchised position).

Although both Baby Kamble and Narendra Jadhav build on a long tradition of Dalit aspiration and struggle, their work also marks important departures in the history of Dalit autobiography that need to be noted. Kamble's book has been lauded by Maya Pandit as "redefin[ing] the tradition of autobiographical writing in Marathi" in terms of narrative strategy and the description of the community that is at its heart: the Mahar community of rural and small-town western Maharashtra in the period of Ambedkar's national ascendancy in the 1940s and '50s and in the decades that followed. In particular, Pandit notes, *Jina Amcha* gives us one of the earliest and most sustained "internal critique(s)" of patriarchal relations in Dalit society and the consequences

---

[18] Cf. Jonathan Spence, "Cliffhanger Days: A Chinese Family in the 17th Century," *American Historical Review*, 10, no. 1 (February 2005), 1–10.

172   *A History of Prejudice*

of patriarchal practices for Dalit women, who are doubly subalternized – by caste and by gender.[19]

Jadhav's *Aamcha Baap aan Aamhi* has been hailed as providing a significant new turn in Dalit literature, with its end product (and aspiration) being that of the global citizen. It has been characterized as the life-story of "an emancipated de-caste" Dalit family,[20] a "story of success" rather than suffering, of the potential of individuals to overcome all odds, one no longer focused on the issue of caste or the fact of being a Dalit and written (as a number of critics put it) in a "balanced, cultured, civilized" style, without any virulence, bitterness, or invective.[21]

I have chosen to counterpose these two texts here for what they tell us, in their different ways, about a Dalit perspective on democratic rights, discrimination, and prejudice, and because they represent two different, not to say contradictory, possibilities in the matter of rescripting the subaltern body.

The Body as Text

The late Baby Kamble (or Baby Tai as she was affectionately called as an elder, until her death in April 2012; see Figure 4) was born in 1929 in a relatively comfortable working-class family that had prospered modestly under British rule. The details of her personal life, activities, and experiences are directly relevant to the story she tells, so it will help to outline them briefly.

Baby Kamble's maternal grandfather and grand uncles had worked as butlers for various British officials and "spoke excellent English." Her father was a labor contractor, who provided and managed the laborers required for canal building in various parts of Maharashtra, and later in his career worked on the construction of the Mumbadevi Temple in Mumbai and a milk dairy in Pune owned by the central government. He earned a fairly good living, although (she tells us) he saved little; he had "a bungalow for himself" when he worked in Pune, and "no dearth of servants either." Because Baby Tai's father

---

[19] Kamble, *Prisons We Broke*, vii, ix, xi, 160.
[20] Maya Pandit in Pawar, *Weave of My Life*, xvi.
[21] Shailesh Tribhuvan, ed., *Aamcha Baap aan Aamhi: Svarup ani Sameeksha* (Mumbai: Granthali, 2008), 7, 77, 82, 204.

Dalit Memoirs

FIGURE 4. Babytai Kamble, Phaltan, Maharashtra, January 2012 (photo by Pinak Kalloli; courtesy Maya Pandit)

traveled a lot, she and her mother lived until she was eight or nine in her maternal grandparents' home in Veergaon, in the Purandar district in western Maharashtra. The house was "a storehouse of food," she writes, and the only Mahar household in the locality that had and served tea![22]

There are other snapshots of Kamble's pampered life as a child:

> Whenever my father went to Mumbai, he used to buy lots of things for me – thick silver anklets, thin and hollow silver anklets, a silver nose ring with a red bead, gold earrings with red stones, three big silver tassels for my hair, silk for a long skirt and blouse, and a red chunni with a crescent on it. He used to send all these to me through my mawshi [mother's sister].

> In the maharwada of Veergaon, I behaved as if the locality was my personal property. I called all men mama [maternal uncle] and their wives mami [aunt], and their parents aaja and aaji [grandfather and grandmother]. All those fifteen

---

[22] Kamble, *Prisons We Broke*, 45, 51–2, 103, 105. All the information in the following paragraphs comes from Baby Kamble's autobiography, *Jina Amcha* (third printing, Pune: Sugava Prakashan, 2008). Hereafter, page numbers follow direct quotations in the text, which come from Maya Pandit's English translation, *The Prisons We Broke*, except in a few instances (footnoted) where I have felt it necessary to modify her excellent translation.

174 *A History of Prejudice*

or sixteen houses in our maharwada were like family to me.... I used to walk in style with silver tassels down my back, silver anklets on my feet, silver chains clinking above them, my half-tola nose ring, earrings, and silk clothes! (Kamble, *Prisons We Broke*, 6–7)

The move to her father's house in Phaltan, in the Satara district, was a comedown – perhaps not surprisingly. This had to do not only with moving out of the loving embrace of her grandparents' home but also with the coming of "mature" age for a girl. Baby Tai was married at 13: she'd passed the Standard IV examination and was thought already to be getting too old for marriage.

Inspired by the emergence of Ambedkar to regional and national fame, and by his emphasis on education, self-respect, and equality for the Mahars and other Dalit groups, Baby Kamble's father insisted on sending both her and her brother to school in Phaltan (the school had a total of ten girls, counting all castes, high and low). Her uncle Narhari Kakade, not much older than her elder siblings, was the first one from the local Mahar community to go to the high school, situated of course outside the Mahar neighborhood. Her cousin Pandharinath Kakade and some forty other Mahar boys followed suit, and Pandharinath named a building that was given to them as a hostel Harijan Boarding after Gandhi's preferred term for the Dalits. Baby Tai herself attended school for a few years. Her husband, Kondiba Kamble, who studied in the same school as her brother, went longer – up to high school.

Marriage brought new responsibilities and burdens for the teenage girl. Her marital home in Phaltan had "fifteen or sixteen" people living in it, and she had to work nonstop to keep up with the demands made of a young wife and daughter-in-law. Her husband, deeply attached to notions of family honor and respectability, expected her to stay within the bounds of the home, just as her own mother had been forced to do by her father. To make matters worse, he was jobless – until she came up with the suggestion that they start a small trade in groceries, working from a room at the front of the house.

Baby Tai attributes the idea of establishing an independent business, rather than entering another family's service, to Ambedkar's inspiration and advice to the Mahars, and declares her own devotion to the Dalit movement from the age of 7 or 8. With the setting up of the grocery store, she and her husband gained a steady source of income,

Dalit Memoirs

175

and they used their education and their shop for the advancement of the Dalit movement. Along the way, as part of the duties of a married woman in a respectable Mahar household, she had ten children – the same number as Viola. Unlike in the Andrews' case, however, three of Kamble's children died early. The remaining seven, three sons and four daughters, have done well, becoming bank officials, schoolteachers, lower-level government functionaries, and in the case of the two youngest daughters, marrying a rich farmer and a doctor, respectively.

It will be clear that Baby Kamble's family, both in her natal and her married homes, had escaped the extreme condition of poverty and deprivation in which the majority of Mahars lived, especially in the countryside. In spite of this, what her autobiography emphasizes is the poverty and filth that abounded in the community. And in this portrayal the immediate family and the wider caste group are continuously interlinked.

"Roughly speaking," she says of her grandparents' village, Veergaon, "we were fifteen or sixteen [Mahar] households." Save for three or four of them, related to the head of the Mahar caste group, who got 16% of any payments received for traditional services performed for higher-caste villagers (removing animal carcasses, carrying notices of death and other urgent messages to neighboring habitations, guarding the village, sweeping village roads, serving visiting officials, etc.), the rest lived in exceptionally poor houses – "tiny huts really," "eternally stricken by poverty." "Children looked as if they had rolled in mud, snot dripping from their noses in green gooey lines... their bodies... completely bare without a stitch on them. Each hut contained at least eight to ten such kids; some even had fifteen to twenty." The Goddess Satwai, who was supposed to determine the fate of every individual, "had stamped hunger" on every Mahar forehead.[23]

Indeed, Veergaon comes to stand in for the condition of the Mahars at large – in Phaltan, in Pune, and all over Maharashtra. Baby Tai suggests it affected her own family: "Poverty was common to my husband's house and mine." Once her father gave up work because of his increasing involvement in Ambedkar's movement, "we often had

---

[23] Kamble, *Prisons We Broke*, 7, 8, 82. I have modified the translation in the first sentence quoted to underline Baby Kamble's stress on counting all 15–16 Mahar households in Veergaon as *her* community; see Kamble, *Jina Amcha*, 13.

176   *A History of Prejudice*

to go hungry" (ibid., 107, 141). For the rest, "the maharwada [Mahar neighborhood] symbolized utter poverty and total destitution." "All the dirty and laborious jobs were the privilege of the Mahar!" "Poverty oozed out of their house[s]" (ibid., 46, 76, 80).

Occasionally, she writes, after long periods without food, some Mahar laborers would secretly poison a buffalo. When summoned to clear away the remains, she goes on to say in the third person, "the Mahars were more than ready." They skinned the carcass, cut the flesh into pieces, and distributed it among the households. The family of the caste-head got the largest share, others got their allotted shares – some more, some less – "but everybody got at least a basketful." During epidemics, when they heard news of several cattle having died, "the joy of the Mahars knew no bounds."

The Mahars considered animal epidemics...a boon....The inside of some animals would be putrid, filled with puss and infected with maggots. There would be a horrid, foul smell!...But we did not throw away even such animals. We cut off the infected parts full of puss, and convinced ourselves that it was now safe to eat the meat.[24]

Observe once more the easy slide between third- and first-person narrative.

Liberation in this account comes in the form of a miracle wrought by a savior, Babasaheb Ambedkar:

[He] breathed life into lifeless statues, that is, the people of our community. It was he who lighted a lamp in each heart and brought light to our dark lives...he made us human beings...[h]e made it possible for us to receive education....[I]t is because of him that the age-old suffering of millions of people could be wiped out within fifty years. (ibid., 118)

Baby Tai etches this story of liberation, of a move from darkness to light, by underlining the intensity of the ignorance and squalor that existed before. "The entire community had sunk deep in the mire of...dreadful superstitions. The upper castes had never allowed this

---

[24] Kamble, *Prisons We Broke*, 83, 85; Kamble, *Jina Amcha*, 66, 68. Compare Aime Cesaire: "At the hour before dawn, on the far side of my father and my mother, the whole hut cracking and blistered, like a sinner punished with boils.... And the bed of planks from which my race has risen...as if the old bed had elephantiasis, covered with a goat skin, and its dried banana leaves and its rags, the ghost of a mattress that is my grandmother's bed," cited in Fanon, *Black Skins, White Masks*, 71.

Dalit Memoirs   177

lowly caste of ours to acquire knowledge. Generation after generation, our people rotted and perished by following such a superstitious way of life." "The condition of the Mahars was no better than that of bullocks, those beasts of burden, who slogged all their life for a handful of dry grass" (ibid., 37, 80).

The body of the Mahars – unclean, grimy, superstitious, irrational, lacking in human dignity, self-confidence, and self-respect – is the mark of their degradation. *Jina Amcha* presents the marked subaltern body in crushing detail as the archive of this history.

People would be covered in thick layers of dust and dirt, a black coating on their skin. You could see the deep marks where moisture trickled down. Hair, untouched by oil, fell over their shoulders in thick tangles. They looked like rag dolls, nibbled and torn by sharp-teethed mice. The thick tangles of hair would be infested with lice and coated with lice eggs. (ibid., 8)

The majority of Mahars – laborers and servants – were "like insects crawling around in hunger. With no food to eat, at least a couple of people would be ill in each house, lying down in rags...almost lifeless with hunger....They breathed, therefore they were supposed to be alive" (ibid., 103, 104).

The promise of transformation, of self-respect and human dignity and liberty, brought by Ambedkar is in turn visible in the leader's body. For those who had seen him and those who had not, the celebration of Babasaheb's physical appearance accompanied the celebration of his message. "This boy of our Mahar community" had arrived – at this meeting or that, in Mumbai or Jejuri – in his own car, dressed in European clothes, speaking the white *sahib*'s tongue: it was quite incredible. He had studied overseas and returned to Mumbai in a ship, a truly learned (young) man.

In words that Baby Tai puts into the mouths of her grandparents, "My, my, that Bhimrao Ambedkar, that tender young boy! He has returned after getting educated with the sahibs beyond the seven seas." As for his personality, "what can I tell you! So tall, so strong, so fair, with such a high forehead. He dresses like a white sahib and looks like one too. When he got out of his car, it was as if a governor had stepped out. And what a speech that was! As if it was the court of [Lord] Indra!" The grandparents, in common with other elder (and younger) Mahars, go on to retail what Ambedkar is reported to have said on these occasions: "Give up these [disreputable] Mahar ways now. See how our people have progressed in the cities. Start sending your children to schools. Stop carting the filth of the village. Don't eat the flesh of dead animals."[25]

"Suddenly the times changed," says Kamble, summing up the gifts bequeathed by Ambedkar in words I have quoted before: "The struggle yielded us three jewels – humanity, education and the religion of the Buddha.... We began to walk and talk. We became conscious that we too are human beings."[26] Here was the making of the new Dalit – and the new Dalit body.

With all her attention to the miserable, unclean, superstitious, and irrational body of the Mahar "in general," however, the history that Baby Tai recounts also foregrounds another body that is no less marked by its specific oppression – the body of the Mahar woman. I have quoted her comment on the Mahar families' treatment of daughters-in-law in Chapter 2 – "The other world had bound us with chains of slavery. But we too were human beings. And we too desired to dominate, to wield power.... So we made our own arrangements to find slaves – our very own daughters-in-law!" – and cited her account of the confinement of Mahar girls and women, and of their chastisement and punishment for small mistakes and the slightest suggestion of transgression.

Two kinds of subaltern bodies appear in Baby Kamble's narrative, the first is the body of *the poor* (child, laborer, woman) – with runny noses, sweat pouring down emaciated and exhausted bodies, blood and dirt (from meat and refuse) running out of baskets they must carry, and seeping into their hair and down their faces. The second is the body of *the girl/woman*, most dramatically embodied in the figure of the daughter-in-law and the wife – which (and the pronoun is appropriate) is constantly exploited, overworked, disciplined, punished by a jealous patriarchal order that doesn't hesitate to show its manliness by cutting off the noses of women for real or imagined transgressions.[27] Outside the home, we are told, poor, laboring Mahar

---

[25] Kamble, *Jina Amcha*, 52–4.
[26] Kamble, *Prisons We Broke*, 122 (also cited in chap. 2, this volume).
[27] Kamble, *Jina Amcha*, 78 and passim.

women walked on the side of the village roads "with utmost humility so as not to offend anyone. They tried to make themselves as inconspicuous as possible, hiding themselves from all others." Inside the home, they bore other burdens: "A Mahar woman would continue to give birth till she reached menopause. Perhaps, this became possible because of the inner strength that she had.... Hardly a few of the babies would survive.... But somehow the cycle of birth and death would go on" (ibid., 54, 82).

In spite of the careful detailing of the parallel histories of these two subaltern constituencies, however, the woman's body finds negligible place in the account of the struggle that Baby Tai foregrounds. There is a recognition of the marking of that body but little indication of the possibility of its reinscription. What is rewritten is the potential of the universal (male) subaltern body, which may now be imagined in the image of the indomitable leader, Babasaheb Ambedkar: the body of the superstitious, ignorant, "untouchable" (or more generally lower-caste) laboring poor, long deprived of education or opportunity for self-improvement but not to be denied any longer with the coming of Ambedkar and the rise of the Dalit movement.

Women and girls are utterly central to Baby Kamble's narrative. Even in the account of the liberation struggle set in motion by Ambedkar, they appear as major protagonists, and a Mahar woman of course gives birth to Babasaheb. For all that, women do not figure as an independent, guiding force in the community or its struggle. The source of that energy lies elsewhere: "After having undergone the ordeal of fire for ages, [a Mahar woman, steeped like all women in patience and fortitude] finally gave birth to a divine flame." "A small sapling grew out of this... soil [that the Mahars had sustained and enriched with their labor]. It went on to become a huge tree of light and truth. It gave shelter to millions who were suffering. The tree transform[ed] beasts into human beings." This new force was "that ideal human being, our very own Buddha," Bhim Rao Ambedkar (ibid., 62, 102).

In the depiction of Ambedkar's achievements, again the matter of the liberation of women from age-long oppression is underscored, but women, and Baby Tai herself, appear as humble interpreters of a supernatural leader's vision. "The man who gave birth to the Hindu Code Bill [which "tore off the net in which men had trapped women for ages"] was my king Bhim, the son of Morality, saviour of the world. It is because of him that my pen can scribble out some thoughts. It is because of him that I have understood truth" (ibid., 102).

I cited earlier the author's statement that *Jina Amcha* is the "autobiography of my entire community." She was caught up in the Ambedkarite movement from an early age, she says in several places, attending meetings along with her husband and helping to mobilize Dalits in the small town of Phaltan. Following Ambedkar's advice that Dalits should try to set up small businesses rather than look for service jobs, she persuaded her husband to begin selling grapes, buying loose grapes from the surrounding countryside and selling them at a small profit. With that start, they went on to open a small grocery shop (in an additional room built on the front of the house) that quickly became a center of trade and political discussion, located as it was just opposite the Mahar *chawdi* (or public gathering place) of the neighborhood.

It was during her long hours sitting at the shop, waiting for customers, that Baby Kamble began writing her memoirs – *in hiding*. Asked by her translator why she hid her writing for twenty years, she said: "because of my husband. He was a good man but like all the men of his time and generation, he considered a woman an inferior being." She recalls how deeply suspicious her husband was of her littlest moves, and how he beat her repeatedly on flimsy grounds. "In fact," she states, "this was the life most women led. . . . Women are still slaves. . . . (They) used to be afraid of even looking up at their husbands." "Fathers used to teach their sons to treat their wives as footwear! A wife's place was near her husband's feet." Pressed to explain why she never felt the need to write about all this, the memoirist says simply: "Well, he was my husband after all! . . . Besides I had my community to consider, our lack of education, progress. It would be so demeaning." And further, "I had to suffer like many other women. But how do you . . . talk about it when everyone is suffering?" (ibid., 147, 154–7).

Recall that Baby Tai makes exactly the opposite argument in relation to the suffering of the Mahars and the wider Dalit population: "I wrote about what my community experienced. The suffering of my people became my own suffering. Their experiences became mine. . . . I really find it difficult to think of myself outside of my community."

Thus, the self that Baby Kamble constructs is a self-consciously Dalit, anti-upper-caste self, inspired by Ambedkar. The community whose suffering she writes about is distinctly defined by the Dalit struggle, or a certain construction of it. Hence her foregrounding of how she and her husband worked together in Ambedkar's movement, her emphasis on the fresh ideas that the movement brought, and her celebration of the unprecedented sense of freedom and energy. "Times were changing fast," she writes, "Because of Dr. Ambedkar, many new norms were coming into force.... [B]oth my husband and I started doing a lot of social work. That became my life" (ibid., 145). And that becomes the primary theme of *Jina Amcha*, a moving and powerful "socio-biography," now beautifully and sympathetically translated into English by Maya Pandit under the telling title of *The Prisons We Broke*.

Yet, given such complex and contradictory narratives, we have to continue to ask questions about the conditions in which a subaltern will and consciousness, a Dalit self, and Dalit politics are produced. The plainly intractable issues of "natural" community and the autonomy of the individual become even more problematical when it comes to the writings of Dalits who have moved some distance from their original homes (and communities) and established themselves as successful professionals, entrepreneurs, or writers in a very different location. It is one such narrative that we have in the Jadhav family memoir, *Aamcha baap aan aamhi* ("Our Father and Us").

The Indomitable Self

The Jadhav story is marked by rather more dramatic upward mobility than that of Baby Kamble. A tale of three generations, the memoir begins with a family and community caught up in hard labor in the fields of the Nasik district and the railways and slums of Bombay. It documents the family's journey through education, determination, and struggle to high bureaucratic office in India for the second generation (including the vice-chancellorship of a leading university and membership of the powerful National Planning Commission for the youngest son, the distinguished economist and now well-known writer Narendra Jadhav), and goes on to refer to a third generation, which, with its highly privileged education and life in Mumbai and overseas, hardly grows up with a sense of being Dalit. The story is told in several voices (some of which literally appear and disappear in different editions of the text) and is now available in three very distinct versions in three different languages.

Before the published Marathi text, we have the manuscript notebooks of Narendra Jadhav's father, Damodar (or Damu), written in a rural dialect Marathi. Narendra generously gave me a copy of these. He readily acknowledged their importance for the researcher, but warned me that I would find the rural idiom difficult. He was right. The accomplished translator Maya Pandit, who helped me with the translation, also struggled in deciphering and making sense of the narrative at points. Narendra also told me the story of how his father scribbled these notes (along with some short stories) in secrecy from the rest of the family, who discovered the writings only after Damodar Jadhav's death. A familiar motif in subaltern reminiscences, and sometimes apocryphal, it speaks to the power of the written word and of inherited traditions in which writing played no part, in which indeed writing – and book-learning – could be seen as a hindrance to the performance of other, unavoidable tasks.

Next is the literary Marathi of the published form of the memoir, which has now gone through a number of editions. (In what follows, I use the fifth, people's, edition, dated 2007, in the main.) Finally, there is the English transcreation published in Delhi in 2003, not to mention translations (usually of this English version) that have appeared in numerous other languages in India and abroad. These several recensions, and the possibility of tracing the translation (by the lead author Narendra Jadhav himself) from one language to another and one context to another, give us an unusual opportunity to consider how the individual and collective self of a successfully mobile "ex-subaltern" family comes to be narrated.

The available Marathi and English texts of the Jadhav family memoir feed on a number of different genres. We begin in Damu's manuscript notebooks with the recapitulation of a "common" man's common struggles, itself originating in childhood memories, captured in the Marathi of the Mahars of Ozer, soaked in the texture of everyday life (of togetherness in labor and travel, of community, names, colors, smells, petty foibles, and common dangers – including the sighting of a leopard in the fields, the burning of a child's fingers on a *tawa* or hot-plate, and a sleeping child falling off a bullock cart and remaining asleep while the caravan moves on a long way ahead!) – and told in a quite matter-of-fact tone. It is the story of an "I" located firmly in a disparate, scattered "we" of the laboring poor, first in the village and the surrounding farms, jungles, and pathways, and then in an urban working-class neighborhood in the big city of Bombay – environments that are distinctly made by both human and nonhuman forces.

In the published Marathi version, the tale becomes a more emotional family saga. The text includes chapters divisible into autobiographical fragments, biographical commentaries, and social description and analysis.[28] The narrative works through its many authors (father, sons, and in some editions daughters, daughters-in-law, and in the most recent edition a granddaughter, too) to center the "I" (of the father, mother, sons, granddaughter) amid a narration of exceptional family endeavor and achievement, initiated by an extraordinary and invincible father, Dada, as Damu is called by his children.[29]

The family story is now constructed by Narendra Jadhav around an unusual, and unusually rewarding, father–son relationship. The early editions of the Marathi publication begin with a chapter entitled "*Mee, aan maazha baap*" ("My father and I"). In some later editions, this is preceded by a very brief chapter on the father's mother ("*Rahi aai ga!*," a rather Brahmanical diminutive for the grandmother), the title of the chapter on the father is changed to "*Aamcha baap*" ("Our father"), and the chapter writer's name (Narendra Jadhav) is dropped. After a comment on the straightforward, "caustic" language that Damodar favored – hence Narendra's choice of the robust, earthy "*Baap*" rather than the sweet, polite "*Vadil*" for father – the chapter goes straight into a discussion of Damodar's character:

All of us brothers and sisters called him "Dada" ["elder brother," presumably following the form of address used by other elders in the home and vicinity]. Medium height. Dark, asymmetrical face. Stern manner, but with a

---

[28] One reviewer calculates the distribution as 50 pages of biographical accounts, 190 pages of the autobiographical, and 30 pages of social analysis, although one might add up the pages differently and they differ in any case in different editions; see Ramesh Dhongade, "*Pach Pellu*," in Tribhuvan, *Aamcha Baap: Sameeksha*, 71.

[29] In later editions of the Marathi text, there is also a brief chapter on an extraordinary and indomitable grandmother; see *Aamcha baap aan aamhi*, 5th edition, 3–7.

FIGURE 5. Narendra Jadhav with his wife, Vasundhara, and parents, Damu (Dada) and Sonu, Mumbai, December 1979 (courtesy Narendra Jadhav)

mischievous look in his eyes when talking to little children. *Dhoti* [loin-cloth], white shirt, khaki coat and black hat, this was his regular dress. A staff in his hand: only, the staff was used less for support than to intimidate [others].[30] (See Figure 5.)

A few pages later, the fifth edition has several paragraphs that are not found in the first and second editions: "We were six brothers and sisters in all. Our childhood was spent in Wadala [in Mumbai]. Given the economic, social and cultural circumstances in which we grew up, the other boys and girls of the locality fared as one might expect. The sole difference [between them and us] was this, that we had Dada with us!" "Dada's self-confidence was extraordinary [*khupats daandga*]. 'Get me a long enough stick, I'll flatten this circular earth and show you', so he would announce like an Archimedes [the Western trope is Narendra Jadhav's – a conscious, or unconscious, gesture towards scientific modernity?]. Dada was a believer in rational thought

---

[30] Jadhav, *Aamcha Baap aan Aamhi*, 2nd edition, 3; 5th edition, 8.

and the individual's effort, and intolerant of any kind of blind faith." "The Father from the little hamlet of Ozer, involved with the nitty-gritty of everyday struggle for existence, is according to the author eternal because he is not an individual but a striving force," as one commentator observes.[31]

In this transcendental statement, however, whereas the force and presence of the protagonists, the father and the son(s) especially, is greatly enhanced, the presence of the wider community and environment is much reduced. In the case of the father's autobiographical jottings as they appear in the published version, this is signaled in part by a reduction of the dialect (something that is understandable in terms of the requirements of publication and markets) and a greater use of a standardized, literary, and, one might say, elite Marathi.[32] Finally, the English version recounts the story of two generations (plus a third in the "Epilogue") in an uncommon mix of romantic novel, ethnography, and political commentary. The Jadhav story now appears as a tale of individual romance and a rugged, masculine individualism, set in the context of Ambedkar's struggle for Dalit dignity and rights. Related in the form of a rags-to-riches story, it is a celebration of two remarkable individuals, Ambedkar and Damu, and of their heirs.

Very different sensibilities emerge in different versions of the narrative. The point may be illustrated by comparing the descriptions of a few events and individuals as presented in the manuscript notebooks and the published Marathi. Here are two examples, one very small, one slightly longer. The first is a statement about Damu's mother, Rahibai, that appears in the opening paragraphs of the notebooks and in an early chapter of the published Marathi. In the former, she is introduced as the daughter of Bhiu Nimba:

She had ([or] There were) two brothers... and three sisters.... Elder one was Sonu; she was given away at Dindori. She had only one son. The second sister was Reu and she was married off at Gangapur; she had one son, Mohan. The youngest was my mother; her name was Rahibai.[33]

---

[31] Ibid, 5th edition, 14–15; and Vidyut Bhagwat, "*Ek streevadi vatsan,*" in Tribhuvan, *Aamcha Baap: Sameeksha,* 229.

[32] Cf. Dhongade, "*Pach Pellu,*" in ibid., 83–4.

[33] I have not provided page references for citations from Damodar Jadhav's manuscript notebooks since there are several notebooks, somewhat haphazard in their presentation, not fully numbered, and repetitive in many places. Page numbers in the text

186 *A History of Prejudice*

We have here the description of a family, conceived of as a unit, although spanning several generations. The mother was one of five siblings, "two brothers and three sisters"; the youngest of these was the writer's mother. In the published version, the description is altered very slightly, yet the small shift of emphasis serves to center the mother more fully and makes this a statement about Rahibai rather than her natal family. "Bhiu Nimba's daughter, Rahibai. She was my mother. My mother was the youngest [in her family]. She had two brothers. Their names, Chahadu and Haari. Two sisters. Sonu and Reu" (Jadhav, *Aamcha Baap*, 53).

Consider again the account of the part played by Damu's wife and sister, Sonu and Najuka, in a protest over Ganpati celebrations in Mumbai (probably in 1928), as it appears in the unpublished notebooks and the published Marathi. Damu writes of the quiet progress of the procession:

Some people were walking to and fro and I also was keeping an eye, moving back and forth. Suddenly some goondas threw a stone at the procession. There was a commotion. The scouts blew their whistles. People started running. There were a lot of women as well. The sisters-in-law [*nanad-bhavaj*] were also among them. They snatched away the sticks in the hands of the scouts. Some other women also followed their example and chased the goondas away. Our procession went on till Chunabhatti. There we immersed our Ganpati in the water.... Then people praised my sister and wife and put garlands around their necks.

The report is almost exactly the same in the *Aamcha Baap aan Aamhi*, except that the phrase *"patni Sonabai aani baheen Najuka"* ("wife Sonabai and sister Najuka") in parentheses replaces the "they" after the sentence "The sisters-in-law were also among them" (ibid., 97–8). A minor alteration serves to specify the individuality of the women concerned.

The English text goes very much further in its construction of an individualist, not to say liberal, sensibility. The account of Sonu and Najuka's part in the 1928 Ganpati celebrations, presented in Sonu's voice, becomes much more personal, marriage-centered, deliberative, and romantic. To summarize briefly, every locality had its Ganapati

following other quotations refer to the fifth edition of the published Marathi text and to the Indian edition of the English version, *Outcaste* (2003).

image. Some placed Babasaheb's picture by its side, and music and theater performances were held around them. Damu sometimes obtained permission from his mother to take his wife and sister along to the programs. "My man often held my hand and pulled me along, much to my embarrassment," Sonu recalls in this version. He also urged Sonu to take an interest in the lectures that were given and not just in the music and dance. Dalit speakers talked of the Dalit liberation struggle, asking: "Is it a sin to be born a Mahar? Babasaheb has made us aware that we are as human as any other people. We have to unite and agitate against discrimination." Initially, Sonu says, she was bored by all this, but "Before I knew it... all those speeches and my husband's talks had an effect on me. Then an incident occurred that totally changed my passive attitude" (Jadhav, *Outcaste*, 117–19).

On the occasion of the Ganapati festival, the Dalit procession was attacked, stones flew, and a fight ensued. In the melee, a group of men began misbehaving with the girls in the procession "under the pretext of controlling the crowds." Sonu noticed that they weren't wearing the armbands of the Ambedkarite volunteers.

I became so enraged that I snatched a baton from one of the volunteers. Emboldened by me, even Najuka snatched a baton and together we started hitting the miscreants. We hit them so hard that finally the police intervened.... Eventually, our procession continued in a low-key and we immersed the idol. When we returned home, everyone fussed over us and called us brave women and garlanded us.... my husband was very proud of me. "I am so glad that you are not just a pretty face," he said. (Ibid., 118–20)

Many of Damu's childhood experiences are recounted in the English transcreation as part of a budding romance with his very young wife. Several of them emerge in a conversation between husband and wife in the account of one long journey from Ozer to Mumbai in 1930. "When we reached the outskirts of Nasik," Sonu observes, "we had walked continuously for almost four hours" (ibid., 122).

The romance of the couple is matched by the romance of the liberation struggle launched by Ambedkar. In Nasik, Damu learns of Ambedkar's impending arrival and of the upcoming satyagraha at the local Kalaram Temple, and tells his wife, "We will stay... (to) participate in this movement" (ibid., 123). Living in poor railway workers' quarters in Bombay, and surrounded by the politics of the city, the family imbibes the lesson of human dignity and self-respect preached by Ambedkar. A first step in this is cleanliness and good grooming. The women now insist on daily baths, neat and clean clothes, the women's hair tied in a bun, the house kept immaculately clean with pots and pans shining. "We sensed a change in the way we carried ourselves. We proudly proclaimed ourselves Dalits, with our chin up, and we looked everyone in the eye. We began to lose our former servility, associated with being born in a low caste" (ibid., 178). Strikingly, in this recension, Damu's personal memoir ends on the day of Ambedkar's funeral, with Damu and Sonu taking solace in their allegiance to Ambedkar's ideas (ibid., 199).

"As a participant and an observer in the social movement," writes Narendra, "my father was the veritable symbol of a new spark of self-respect ignited among the untouchables by Dr. Ambedkar. Dada would come home electrified by Babasaheb's thinking, and talked about it to us every day" (ibid., 210–11). This is a life-story sparked by the life of a saintly leader, in the image of the saintly leader's life: in the image, one might say, of the biography of saints. And the fifth edition of the Marathi text carries a new dedication to Babasaheb Ambedkar, who was "father [*baap*] to everyone of us in a larger sense" – a remarkable play on the title *Aamcha Baap aan Aamhi* ("Our Father and Us"). For the record, Damodar Jadhav's "Notebooks," written in the late 1970s and '80s, have very little to say about Ambedkar and his struggle, although, as the author/translator/presenter (Narendra) has said to me, he talked a great deal about the leader and the movement over the same period.

Narendra Jadhav describes his mother as less "intelligent" and broad-minded than his father. In later life, he tells us, she told a reporter from an English weekly that the qualities she most admired in her husband were that "He never drank, never abused me. Best of all, he never raised his hand (on) me." "A telling comment," Narendra remarks, "on the meagre expectations of women of her generation" (ibid., 217, 258). For all that, the English version of the memoir has Sonu speaking in tones that suggest a developed bourgeois sensibility and clear consciousness of men's and women's equal rights.

"My man" is a curious mode of address, with all that it implies in English, even if this is a literal translation of the Marathi phrase "*mazha maansa*"; and it is notable that, according to Narendra, his

Dalit Memoirs

mother always addressed his father as "Jadhav" in later life. Yet this is how the exchanges between the two, on the journey from their village home and in Mumbai, are described in *Outcaste*: "In Mumbai, my man and I hardly had any opportunity to talk openly. It would have been a sign of disrespect to the elders, like my mother-in-law. [But] now, my man seemed anxious to share his childhood with me. He continued talking even as we resumed walking." "Now there was no stopping my man." "I discovered that my man looked charming telling stories. His eyes twinkled and his gestures grew livelier as he became absorbed in his narrative." "'I am sure you were a very naughty boy,' I said, leading him on." At other times, for example when he reminisced about a young English girl with whom he had played, "I also had tricks of my own to distract him. I was amazed at my own ability to be coy. I sent him fleeting glances and looked away just when he seemed to have caught my eye" (ibid., 49–51, 103).

And, on another note: "It's always you, you and you . . . Damodar Runjaji Jadhav. What about me? I am the insignificant Sonu, always nodding my head to whatever you say and walking behind you like a shadow." By this point in the narrative, Sonu, too, has learned the lesson of individual reasoning and self-help that Damu has brought to them from Ambedkar. Having lived all her life in accordance with what her husband wanted, she will take it no more: "I have come of age," she tells her sister-in-law, "I [have] learned to think for myself" (ibid., 174, 176).

The Question of Dalit Selfhood

We may return at this point to the question of the political choices that go into the rescripting of the Dalit body and the production of a new Dalit consciousness. Babasaheb Ambedkar's life and work, the great anti-caste movement that has followed in its wake, and the Dalit literature of the 1970s, '80s, and on have mounted an exceptional challenge to the received account of Indian society and history. The writings of Baby Kamble, Narendra Jadhav, and other Dalit thinkers are extraordinary, powerful, and moving interventions in this history, essential to any plausible understanding of the Indian past and present. Yet many of these work with inherited assumptions about the transparency of community and individual, and the motive force of history, that bear further scrutiny.

For a start, the matter of community needs to be recognized as a question of politically legible community. As we know, such community is rather more easily accepted on the basis of claimed religious, racial, or ethnic unity, rather less so when the claim is based on class or gender. Accompanying that circumstance is the long-standing, common-sense understanding of the "natural" domain of the political – supposedly found in a public and institutional location, with the possibility of recourse to the law and the state, not so much in the realm of the domestic and the personal. What follows from these assumptions is an emphasis on already established community and culture, arising out of a shared history and providing the grounds for a politics of resistance, and, with that, on the idea of a preexisting self, implicated variously in, yet separable from, community and culture.

What Dalit memoirs of recent decades, and especially those of women, present as a clash between "feudal" (hierarchical) and patriarchal ideals and practices on the one hand, and bourgeois (modern), democratic (and yet patriarchal) ideals and practices on the other, is at the same time a clash between different kinds of politics. The political contests involved are played out at the level of family and local community, as well as that of the wider society and polity. However, what is striking in the autobiographical works examined above, and in other writings of the same kind, is a persistent tendency to expel the political question from the domain of family and community and locate it instead in the realm of the political party and the state. Such a move involves not a removal of questions about values, appropriate relationships, and acceptable behavior from the realm of the political, but a shifting of them to the domain of constitutional politics. The proposed resolution to problems of poverty and deprivation, patriarchy and caste, is to be found not in personal and familial practices and arrangements but in formal politics and in an embrace of ideas of progress, political action, and political modernity focused on the state.

Shared political perspectives produce important commonalities in Dalit life-stories. Individual circumstances and experiences are nevertheless varied, and there are significant differences between different accounts. Consider the rescripting of the body in the two texts here discussed in detail. Babasaheb Ambedkar in both the Kamble and Jadhav narratives, and Damodar Jadhav in the latter, symbolize the new Dalit body: imposing, rational, self-confident, and self-sufficient – in need of no one else's support ("a staff in his hand [but] used less for support than to intimidate"). But this body is still an ideal – in the future, and indeed in danger of being forgotten, in Baby Tai's rendering of recent events. It seems rather more at hand in Narendra Jadhav's.

Rarely in Kamble's reconstruction of Dalit life do we feel we are face to face with the self-same, self-generated, autonomous individual. The conditions of Mahar life in Phaltan and Satara remain contradictory, unbalanced, troublesome; the narrative troubled, fragmentary, interrupted, and multi-tonal. The agential subject appears very differently, however, with the emergence of a markedly bourgeois sensibility and the centering of the liberal subject in the later versions of the Jadhav family memoir. What the smoothly flowing story of a family's journey from rags to riches, an indomitable, clear-sighted father, and an exceptionally clear-sighted struggle produces, in the latter instance, is rather like the ideal of the coherent, rational, post-Smithian economic individual. What it erases, as in many popular upper-class and middle-class success stories, is any suggestion of incoherence in the self we construct, or of limits to individual capability in given historical conditions.

Let me illustrate the point, and conclude this exploration of Dalit memoirs, with a few brief extracts from the recollections of Narendra Jadhav's daughter, Damu's granddaughter, Apoorva, in which the high point of the individualist presentation is reached. The reminiscence appears as an epilogue in the English edition of the memoir as well as in the latest versions of the printed Marathi text. "When my dad asked me to write about my life," writes Apoorva, "I was skeptical to say the least.... I am only sixteen years old! What 'life' have I had? But I decided why the hell not? *I would get to know myself in the process*" (ibid., 260; emphasis added).

Born in Bloomington, Indiana, and brought back to India when she was two years old, Apoorva returned to the United States at a later stage and was studying there in high school when she wrote this short entry for the family memoir. She came to know that she was a Dalit at the age of twelve, she tells us. "I didn't know what it meant and was confused.... [T]his teacher in sixth grade...recognized my name, I guess, and asked, 'Are you the daughter of Dr. Narendra Jadhav? the Dalit scholar?' I was proud, but confused.... My dad is famous, but what does Dalit have to do with it" (ibid., 261).

A History of Prejudice

Back in the United States, she writes:

No one reminds me that I am a Dalit. I mean, that's who I am – take it or leave it. When I hear about people deliberately marrying into their own caste or sub-caste, it bothers me.... Recently, I was appalled to learn that the relief in the earthquake stricken area in Gujarat was being distributed on caste-basis.... Now I can see why Dad talks about Dalit issues with such fervour.

And further:

Now, I think I know who I am. I am Apoorva, not tied down by race, religion or caste. My ancestors carried the burden of being a Dalit and bowing down to demeaning tasks even after India's Independence. I have the torch they have lit for me and nothing can stop me. (Ibid., 262–3)

In the fifth edition of *Aamcha Baap aan Aamhi* (2007), where Apoorva's account appears for the first time in Marathi, this self-confident, universal, autonomous self becomes even more resplendent. I presume that the translation here is done by Narendra, and so take this as his articulation of the self in his daughter's generation. The Marathi version says:

I am Apoorva. Just Apoorva. A global citizen without any caste or religious label. A global citizen with Indian roots. Now, no one tells me that I am a Dalit. I couldn't care less if anyone suggests that I might be handicapped in some way because of my Dalit background. *They have a problem. They need psychiatric treatment!* [The words here italicized appear in English, written in the Nagri script, in the Marathi text.]

The last lines of Apoorva's ruminations are now presented differently. She speaks of the path cleared for her by the sacrifices and unremitting labor of her Dalit ancestors and then goes on:

I stand on their shoulders, that is why the distant horizon becomes visible, [and] beckons me. Believing in a religion of humanity, I am a global citizen of Indian roots. Dr. Babasaheb has handed on to me a blazing torch. With that I will clean up [brighten] everything all around. I will make my own future! No one can stop me. (Jadhav, *Aamcha Baap*, 287)

In this articulation, the expansiveness, self-confidence, and self-generated quality of the post-Dalit self becomes almost boundless.

In "stand[ing] on their shoulders," we still return to the bodily: the erect, powerful, self-confident, laboring body of the Dalit, the true

Dalit Memoirs

global citizen of the past and the future. However, we have moved away from the palpable physicality of Damodar Jadhav's notebooks (also found in Baby Kamble's memoir), the human-animal-natural environment in which men and women lived and had their being, and indeed the extraordinary toil that went into the making of the world. It is an unmarked, unconquerable, but at the same time disembodied spirit that triumphs in the later versions of the Jadhav saga. Animals, and dirt, and labor disappear from our world: that may be seen as one of the gains of modern life. What Narendra Jadhav (re)produces in the end, then, is the abstract citizen of the Enlightenment, the citizen *without* a body, at any rate without a body that may be felt as a burden.

What is lost, it seems to me, when the writer produces a narrative of bourgeois individuality and individual aspiration, success, and social mobility, accessible to all – irrespective of gender, caste, class, or ethnicity – is a robust appreciation of the concrete material and historical conditions that allow, or deny, access to resources and opportunities to different classes, groups, and sexes in a multitude of different ways. Gone are the specific historical constraints, the confusing, contradictory, generative, and damaging conditions of all life – that of subaltern groups as well as those in positions of privilege and comfort. What is downplayed as well is the singular experience and detail of caste humiliation and inequality, even though these are painted into the picture in bold, broad-brush strokes.

Also reduced is something of the questioning and self-doubt necessary to a different politics and culture and a differently imagined future, and with that the trace of alternative sensibilities and perceptions that is still found in many Dalit writings (emanating from both working-class and middle-class individuals and families), perhaps especially in Dalit women's memoirs: writings that challenge the modern prejudice of the unmarked individual and unambiguous belonging, and the prospect of self-help and progress for all.

I consider these issues further in the next chapter, which examines the persistence of race, caste, and cultural prejudice in the case of African Americans and Dalits who have in social and economic terms clearly moved out of a working-class or underclass, subaltern milieu.

7

The Persistence of Prejudice

What I have attempted to do in this book is to explore some of the circumstances and ways in which the matter of prejudice – "vernacular" and "universal" – has shaped the history of African Americans and Dalits, and by extension the history of the United States and India, over the last century and more. It should be obvious that many of the quandaries and challenges considered here do not apply to these minorities alone, although it will be clear, too, that prejudice and its costs affect different populations, and differently disenfranchised and marginalized groups, in many distinct ways. The proposition is perhaps self-evident. However, its force and its fallout, not always adequately appreciated, may be illustrated simply.

"*Hindustan mein rehna hai, to humse milkar rehna hoga/ Hindustan mein rehna hai, to bande mataram kehna hoga,*" as Hindu right-wing political forces have it, in a slogan that has appeared over and over again in attacks against the Muslim minority in India, in the mouths of political agitators, and on city walls, especially since the 1980s. "Those who wish to live in Hindustan will have to live like us/ Those who wish to live in Hindustan will have to say '*Bande Mataram*' [Victory to the Mother; i.e., the mother goddess, who is also Mother India]." In an echo of the "Jewish question" of the nineteenth and twentieth centuries, Muslims can live in India, as long as they stop being Muslims. Samuel Huntington articulates much the same kind of proposition for immigrants from Mexico who have come to live, work, and die in the United States (in quite significant numbers even in military service, to which the American establishment readily welcomes them). "There is no Americano dream," he writes. "There is *only the American dream* created by an Anglo-Protestant society. Mexican-Americans will share in that dream and in that society *only if they dream in English.*"[1] Here, the suggestion goes, as in the case of Jews ceasing to be Jews, or Muslims Muslims, is another impossibility.

The two slogans just quoted should suffice to indicate some of the demands still being made of minorities, Muslims in India and Latina/Latino migrants to the USA, in these instances, to assimilate, to conform, to change themselves – if indeed they can. Upward social mobility is the presumed route out of conditions of subordination and marginalization the world over. Yet, the implications and rewards of upward social and economic mobility have not always been as straightforward or smooth as narratives of rags to riches, or fortune favoring the brave (or the enterprising), would have it. What is it that thwarts some subaltern citizens for so long from gaining the full benefits of modern, liberal society? That is the question I ask in this final chapter, focused to a considerable extent on the continuing dilemmas of the increasingly visible African American and Dalit middle classes: the "black bourgeoisie" and "Dalit brahmans," as they have been called, white but not quite, groups that are under pressure to be citizens of the modern world (rational, meritocratic, and universalist in their outlook) on the one hand, and to speak for their still underprivileged communities ("not to forget where they come from") on the other.

The focus on middle-class elements tied to communities that are seen historically, but also somehow inevitably (by definition), as communities of lower-class and underclass individuals and families allows me to address two specific questions in these concluding pages. What happens to members of these communities (or assemblages) who inhabit, or come to inhabit, not the positions of the down-and-out where they allegedly belong but those of more comfortable, educated, often professional, middle-class individuals?[2] And, reversing the question, what

---

[1] Samuel P. Huntington, *Who Are We?* (New York: Simon and Schuster, 2004), 256 (emphasis added).

[2] The educated, professional middle-class position has been the major aspiration, and avenue of advancement, for the widest sections of the lower classes, American blacks and Indian Dalits included. As E. Franklin Frazier put it, "Education is the chief means

196 *A History of Prejudice*

does the history of the struggles of Dalit and African American elites tell us about the conditions necessary for the consolidation of particular groups as full rights-bearing citizens – middle class, modern, and unmarked?

The slogans about Indian Muslims and Hispanic migrants to the United States cited above should also serve to underline a point I made in Chapter 1, that the archive for a history of prejudice is almost certain to be unconventional, indeed subterranean. The evidence that identifies or signifies prejudice, even in its more commonly recognizable forms, is fleeting and chancy, scrappy and ambiguous. Hence the common response, and even more common feeling, that Viola Andrews, Baby Kamble, Om Prakash Valmiki, and others like them write of trivial, trifling matters, unscientifically and emotionally, in texts that inhabit the domain of the merely ordinary. "The everydayness and repeatability of untouchability in these texts [as of racial and sexual humiliation in others] place them outside the domain of history."[3]

Prejudice is not proclaimed from the rooftops, I have noted. It is hardly self-conscious. It appears instead as common sense, as the natural order of things: what is, is – and, if all were properly ordered, must be. It is largely in this way that the self-serving idea of the lazy, dirty, inefficient, slow to learn, and yet untrustworthy, aggressive, clannish Dalit or black (or other impoverished denizen of the ghettoes and the slums) has lived on. This "common sense" is articulated in unarchived archives. I draw on two other parts of this curious archive for purposes of my analysis in this final chapter: the derogatory names given to and the insulting meanings often attached to the names of the lowest castes and classes; and the abusive language used toward them (on occasion, even in letters to the press) when members of these long-subordinated castes and classes happen to mount a political challenge to the power of those providentially assigned to rule. In addition, as we know, evidence of prejudice is still to be found in routine attitudes and actions. The scarcely concealed gesture of hesitation and suspicion directed at Dalits and African Americans, the withdrawal and the caution, the sarcasm

> by which the Negro escapes from the masses into the middle class"; see E. Franklin Frazier, *The Negro Family in the United States* (1939; revised ed. Chicago: University of Chicago Press, 1966), 331.
>
> [3] M. S. S. Pandian, "Writing Ordinary Lives," in Pandey, *Subaltern Citizens and Their Histories*, 101 and passim.

The Persistence of Prejudice 197

and the patronizing insinuation of appropriate place and appropriate behavior, has hardly disappeared altogether – in spite of all the formal changes that have taken place over the last half century and more, and the declarations that continue of the need for further change. I shall have occasion to refer to such evidence again in these final pages.

Passing – into the Mainstream

Various surveys conducted toward the end of the twentieth century, using a variety of different indices, classified between 10% and 20% of the Dalit population in India as middle class. Around the same time, some 20% to 30% of the African American population was estimated to be of middle income, which is often taken as the crucial gauge of middle-class status in the United States, although, as I suggested in Chapter 1, income is by no means all there is to middle-classness. Significantly, there are strong suggestions of a fall in the number of African Americans who qualified as middle class in the 1990s, another indication of the fragile nature of a subaltern middle-class identity.[4]

Let us take these figures as broadly representative of a longer-term trend toward upward mobility in the ranks of the Dalits and African Americans over the latter half of the twentieth century. Even with these suggestions of the proportion of Dalits and African Americans who have "made it" into the ranks of the materially and socially more comfortable middle classes (plus a sizable number of blacks and a smaller number of Dalits who would qualify as belonging to the upper middle classes), the issues of appropriate belonging, of second-class citizenship, of being targeted as not quite right (not quite in the right place), continue to dog the Dalit and black populations across the board. Thus, as an uncle of the *New York Times* columnist Bob

---

[4] For Dalits, see Minna Saavala, "Low Caste but Middle Caste: Some Strategies for Middle Class Identification in Hyderabad," *Contributions to Indian Sociology*, 1, no. 35 (2001), 293–318; and D. L. Sheth, "Caste and Class: Social Reality and Political Representations," in *Contemporary India*, ed. V. A. Pai Panandiker and Ashis Nandy (New Delhi: Tata McGraw-Hill, 1999), 337–63. For African Americans, see William H. Frey, "Revival," *American Demographics*, October 2003 (Special Series: America's Money in the Middle), 27–31, http://www.frey-demographer .org/briefs/B-2003-5_Revival.pdf.; and A. J. Robinson, *The Two Nations of Black America, An Analysis: Percentage of Blacks and Income Group, 1970–1994*, http: //www.pbs.org/wgbh/pages/frontline/shows/race/economics/analysis.html.

198   *A History of Prejudice*

Herbert put it a generation ago, there is a continuing need for African Americans to "fight on all fronts, at home and abroad."[5] That need did not end in the 1970s.

Herbert sums up the present situation of the majority of African Americans as follows:

[A] third of black children live in poverty;... more than 70 percent are born to unwed mothers;... by the time they reach their mid-30s, a majority of black men without a high school diploma has spent time in prison.... No one has been able to stop this steady plunge of young black Americans into a socioeconomic abyss.[6]

It is not only, as some imagine, the dropouts and the incorrigibly poor among blacks who suffer the consequences of enhanced policing and surveillance but also the minority that have done exceptionally well. The number of well-to-do, respectable, and widely respected blacks who are pulled over for driving fancy (or indeed not-so-fancy) cars is legion. As an American Civil Liberties Union report of 1999 has it, "No person of color is safe from this treatment anywhere, regardless of their obedience to the law, their age, the type of car they drive, or their station in life. In short, skin color has become evidence of the propensity to commit crime, and police use this 'evidence' against minority drivers on the road all the time."[7] Nor, it seems, is a person of color, even the distinctly privileged, entirely safe trying to enter his or her own house in the event of losing the keys, if the house happens to be in a "non-black" neighborhood – judging by the arrest of Henry Louis Gates, Jr.

The renowned African American professor at Harvard, listed among *Time* magazine's 25 most influential Americans in 1997, was suspected of trying to break into his own house on his return from a trip to

---

[5] Bob Herbert, "This Raging Fire," *New York Times*, op-ed article, November 16, 2010.

[6] Ibid.

[7] David A. Harris, "Driving While Black: Racial Profiling on Our Nation's Highways," An ACLU Special Report, June 1999, http://www.aclu.org/racial-justice/driving-while-black-racial-profiling-our-nations-highways. The report notes that racial profiling is often justified by the police on the grounds that most drug offenses are commited by minorities, which is a self-fulfilling allegation because police look for drugs primarily among African Americans and Latinos and hence find them there more often than among other sections of the population.

The Persistence of Prejudice

China to the posh locality in Cambridge where he lives. A woman who worked down the street from Gates's home saw two black men, Professor Gates and his driver, trying to push his front door open, and rang the police about this suspicious activity. The fact that Gates is 60, bespectacled, walks with a cane, and was wearing a blue blazer, and that the hour was just after midday, made no difference. By the time the two men were inside the house and Gates got onto the phone to call someone about the door, a policeman had arrived to interrogate them about their *bona fides*. "A black man in a tony neighborhood simply seems out of place," as one commentator put it. "Any black person can stand in for any other, and be made to bear the burden of all," noted another,[8] an observation that the "crime" of "Driving While Black" demonstrates all too well.

The story of the ex-slave middle classes has thus diverged in some important respects from the modernist account of the emergence of an unmarked, privatized, and even invisible middle class; that is to say, one that does not parade itself as a collective or special interest group. We might set this history alongside the history of the mainstream middle classes in the Asian and African colonies. As they consolidated their position, the latter moved from the native town into the European enclaves, frequently advancing to take them over completely after the attainment of independence. The Dalit and the African American middle classes emerged at a later stage, without an equivalent exit route. With no sovereign state or territory of their own, they have continued to suffer from disguised as well as overt discrimination long after the formal establishment of independence and democracy. They remain tied as well to lower-class communities, cultures, and histories, and even to marked residential localities that other more invisible, yet once subaltern, groups have been able to escape more easily. Thus the Irish, the Jews, and the Italians in America were not identified by color. Perhaps more importantly, like Muslims or Christians in India, they have been seen as more differentiated internally, and not as naturally, necessarily, belonging to the lowest classes.

---

[8] Michael Eric Dyson, "Commentary: Professor Arrested for 'housing while black,'" July 22, 2009, http://articles.cnn.com/2009-07-22/living/dyson.police; and Brandon M. Terry, "A Stranger in Mine Own House: Henry Louis Gates, Jr. and the Police in 'Post-Racial' America," July 21, 2009, http://www.huffingtonpost.com/brandon-m-terry/a-stranger-in-mine-own-ho_b_242392.html.

A History of Prejudice

The situation of these late-arriving middle classes may be compared, in yet another significant aspect, with that of the modular European or even the North American white middle class. The latter are urged to build their culture and morality and peace of mind in the secluded home; the modern privileges privacy, individuality, and family as the site of improvement, of the individual and of society at large. By the mid-nineteenth century in upstate New York, as Mary Ryan notes, a good deal of popular literature was pushing the "responsible bread-winner, no less than... [the] loving mother, into a narrowing social universe, one even more solitary than privacy – the domain of the self, the individual, of 'manly independence.'"[9] The Dalit and African American middle classes are rarely allowed the luxury of such priva-tized retreat. "Among African Americans, marriage itself was polit-ical," writes Glenda Gilmore, "a testimony to capability as piercing white eyes peered through domesticity, searching for degeneracy."[10] If the subaltern middle classes celebrate individual achievement, pri-vacy, and the nuclear family, they must do so in the interests of the larger family, the "community" that nurtured them and gave them birth.

It is not only the establishment, the media, and a self-proclaimed popular common sense that calls on the successful individuals of once-enslaved communities to remember what *we* (the mainstream, upper-caste Hindus, upper-caste whites) have done for *you*. Members of the disadvantaged communities, too, urge the upwardly mobile – bureaucrats and teachers, doctors and lawyers, clergy and social workers – not to forget where they come from, to stay close to the community's experience, to foreground it and to work for the uplift of brothers and sisters left behind. The privileged position of black professional women workers in late nineteenth- and twentieth-century America did not relieve them of their "obligation to work in the public sphere," Stephanie Shaw notes, "Not to use their advantages for the advancement of the race was deemed selfish and even traitorous."[11]

[9] Mary Ryan, *Cradle of the Middle Class: The Family in Oneida County, New York, 1790–1865* (Cambridge: Cambridge University Press, 1981), 147, 238.

[10] Glenda Elizabeth Gilmore, *Gender and Jim Crow: Women and the Politics of White Supremacy in North Carolina, 1896–1920* (Chapel Hill: University of North Carolina Press, 1996), 18.

[11] Shaw, *What a Woman Ought to Be and to Do*, 119 and passim.

The Persistence of Prejudice

Henry Louis Gates, Jr., in his turn, writes of his "feelings of guilt and anxieties of having been false to our people, of having sinned against our innermost identity,"[12] although, as the preceding chapters should have shown, the category of "our people" as of "our innermost identity" is hardly so self-evident. In the African American and Dalit cases, as among other minoritized populations, not to say all sections of society in the world today, these continue to be politically produced.

It is in this context that we have to consider the nagging question, or temptation, to pass as white – for those African Americans who were light enough to do so – of "disappearing" into mainstream society and being forced to obfuscate, deny, and separate oneself from a significant part of one's background and roots. Once again, the examples are legion, although the anguish surrounding the question is far from being well recognized. Thus, at the very end of the nineteenth century, Anita Hill became the first black graduate of Vassar, an elite women's college in New York State. It was only a little before she graduated that her roommate and, through her, other members of the college learned of Hill's black background. The authorities felt betrayed but allowed her to graduate. The *New York World* reported the story as follows:

Society and educational circles...are profoundly shocked by the announcement...that one of the graduating class of Vassar College this year was a Negro girl, who concealed her race....She has been known as one of the most beautiful young women who ever attended the great institution of learning, and even now women who receive her in their homes as their equal do not deny her beauty....Her manners were those of a person of gentle birth, and her intelligence and ability were recognized alike by her classmates and professors.[13]

Over three-quarters of a century later, we have the now well-known story of Anatole Broyard. The protagonist of this tale was a prominent literary critic, regular book reviewer for the *New York Times* for two decades, and "one of literary America's foremost gate-keepers" in the 1970s and '80s.[14] In living his life and performing his editorial duties,

---

[12] Henry Louis Gates, Jr., *Thirteen Ways of Looking at a Black Man* (New York: Random House, 1997), 127.

[13] Randall Kennedy, "Racial Passing," *Ohio State Law Journal*, 62, no. 1145 (2001).

[14] Gates, *Thirteen Ways of Looking at a Black Man*, 180. The following account is based on Gates and on Bliss Broyard, *One Drop: My Father's Hidden Life – A Story of Race and Family Secrets* (New York: Little, Brown and Co., 2007).

202 *A History of Prejudice*

Broyard felt that he had to make a choice between being an aesthete and being a Negro. As he told close associates on more than one occasion, he wanted to be appreciated as a writer, not a black writer. Light enough to pass for white, he did so for most of the period during which he was an acknowledged and prominent literary figure. His own children did not find out that he was black until he was on his deathbed and they were in their late twenties, when his (Caucasian American) wife insisted on the need to tell them before he died. Others, even among some of his closest friends and associates, found out only at his funeral, which his sister and other relatives (many of them much darker than he was) attended.

As regards his willingness to live a lie all his life, Broyard appears to have put forward the following argument, to himself and to those friends who knew his background and with whom the question came up in his later years. "Why shouldn't I (and my children) pass for white if we can?" he asked, given the discrimination, disadvantage, and even humiliation that they would suffer simply for being black. Broyard's parents, light-skinned Creoles from New Orleans, "had to pass for white in order to get [certain kinds of] work in 1930s New York," and growing up in Brooklyn, New York, where the family moved when he was six, Anatole (the fairest of three siblings) was taunted by white and black kids alike, according to the account given to his son and daughter by their mother. Recalling their last meetings on his sickbed, his daughter, Bliss Broyard, writes of how his secret seemed even more painful than the advanced cancer he was suffering, and how hard her mother had to push him to reveal it. "He'd removed his legs from my lap and curled them into his body . . . he looked uncomfortable and cornered," she writes – as one would of a child, and perhaps a prisoner.[15]

Indeed, the issue of passing was frequently even more complicated than that, given the number of reverse propositions to which the question of being sufficiently black (or insufficiently so) regularly led. The distinguished philosopher Adrian Piper's experience as a graduate student and an academic illustrates the point all too well. Piper recalls being accosted, at the incoming graduate student reception in the prestigious graduate school that she attended in the 1970s, by the person who was the most famous member of the department, with

[15] Broyard, *One Drop*, 10, 11, 16, 17.

The Persistence of Prejudice

the words: "Miss Piper, you're about as black as I am." That is to say, she was just not as "black" as he expected. The implicit question here is the opposite of the one asked of Anatole Broyard: Why claim, or rather pretend, you're black?[16]

Earlier, as a light-skinned member of a light-skinned middle-class family in the predominantly black working-class neighborhood of Harlem, Adrian Piper had been taunted by black kids as a white and a paleface, not unlike Anatole Broyard's earlier experiences in Brooklyn or that of Viola Andrews's husband, George, and their "yaller" children over a rather more extended period in rural as well as urban Georgia. "I had always identified myself as black (or 'colored' as we said before 1967)," writes Piper, "But fully comprehending what it meant to be black took a longer time." Her parents had believed, "idealistically," that education and individual achievements would shield her from the effects of racism. They had even argued that she should refuse to name her racial classification in her application to graduate school to prove that she had been admitted on merit alone. The young woman refused because that seemed to her to be dishonest. However, she muses, "My choice not to pass for white in order to gain entry to the academy, originally made out of naiveté, [has] resulted in more punishment than I would have imagined possible."[17]

In large part the punishment has had to do with "an essentializing stereotype into which all blacks must fit" and the common expectation that as a black she must know how all blacks feel on questions of envy and resentment, broken families, drugs, the lot. "The individuals involved... make special efforts to situate me in their conceptual mapping of the world, not only by naming or indicating the niche in which they felt I belonged, but by seeking my verbal confirmation of it." In fact, as Piper notes, "no blacks... fit any such stereotype." The fault, as Bliss Broyard has it, lies in the question "What are you?" and in the expectation that Dalits, blacks, women, Native Americans, Australian Aborigines, and all other marked citizens may only answer once and in doing so provide one ("correct") answer.[18]

---

[16] Adrian Piper, "Passing for White, Passing for Black," in *Passing and the Fiction of Identity*, ed. Elaine K. Ginsberg (Durham, NC: Duke University Press, 1996), 234 and passim.

[17] Ibid., 238, 239, 241.

[18] Ibid., 238; Broyard, *One Drop*, 463.

204   *A History of Prejudice*

If Broyard's question "Why shouldn't we pass for white if we can?" captures one facet of the history of a stigmatized, subaltern middle class – gays and lesbians in the military ("don't ask, don't tell"), the promising schoolchild from a working-class background, the Jewish entrepreneur in 1930s and '40s Europe – an equally serious challenge appears in the question "Why should I pass for white, even if I can?" There are no correct answers.

Passing – by Other Names

There is to my knowledge no term for "passing" among the lower castes and classes in India, and given the practical indeterminacy of caste on the basis of skin color, the procedure for passing is very different from that found among Americans of African descent. Yet the question of whether a successfully mobile individual (or group) should try to pass, or refuse to do so – and the irresolvability of that question – is perhaps just as insistent. Among the various paths to this merging with a mainstream, as I have noted, has been the possibility of conversion out of the demeaning Hindu community with its institutionalized practices of untouchability.

The 1956 conversion to Buddhism initiated by Dr. Ambedkar has become part of the inspiring mythology of the modern Dalit struggle. It was an act that gave memory to a "memoryless" people, to invoke D. R. Nagaraj once more[19] – for the desire to look to the future alone must inevitably be a forlorn hope. It has instilled new pride among millions of downtrodden Dalits, and especially among the Dalit middle classes. And it is well known that the same sorts of claims to human dignity and self-respect were made through conversions to Christianity, Islam, and Sikhism in the recent as well as in the not so recent past.

That the call for conversion, for getting away from the shadow of Hinduism, has often been articulated in militant terms is scarcely surprising. As Ambedkar put it in his emotional address to the gathering at Nagpur on October 14, 1956, "This conversion has given me enormous satisfaction and pleasure unimaginable. I feel as if I have been liberated from hell."[20] Periyar, E. V. Ramaswamy Naicker,

---

[19] Nagaraj, *Flaming Feet*, 58, cited in chap. 2.
[20] D. C. Ahir, *Buddhism in India after Dr. Ambedkar (1956–2002)* (Delhi: Blumoon Books, 2003), 10.

The Persistence of Prejudice 205

another remarkable, and fiery, leader of the lower-caste struggle in the twentieth century, put it this way: "Our disease of being Shudras is a very big monstrous disease. This is like cancer.... There is only one medicine for it. And that is Islam.... To cure the disease, [and] stand up and walk as worthy humans, Islam is the only way."[21] And, in line with these thoughts, some Buddhist converts in Maharashtra have been heard to say, "We should have become Muslims first, then Buddhists when we had won equality."[22] Yet the break from the stigma of Untouchability has been far from easy or complete.

The experience of Bama, a Dalit woman schoolteacher from Tamilnadu who gave up her career to join a Catholic religious order and then gave up that order to continue the fight for the dignity of her fellow beings by other means, illustrates the point about the obstacles faced in the attempted break from the past. "If you look at our streets," Bama writes in her autobiography, "they are full of small children, their noses streaming, without even a scrap of clothing, rolling about and playing in the mud and mire, indistinguishable from puppies and piglets." In the churches, she tells us, "Dalits are the most, in numbers only. In everything else, they are the least. It is only the upper-caste Christians who enjoy the benefits and comforts of the Church." Of the convent she went into, she says: "[T]he Jesus they worshipped there was a wealthy Jesus.... There was no love for the poor and the humble." "You can sit on your chair inside a convent, and say whatever you like about the struggling masses, about justice and the law.... But in that place you can never experience another people's pain." And further: "[N]ow that I have left the order, I am angry when I see priests and nuns.... When I look at the Church today, it seems to be a Church made up of the priests and nuns and their kith and kin. And when you consider who they are, it is clear that they are all from upper-castes."[23]

Abdul Malik Mujahid, whom I cited in Chapter 3 on the matter of Dalit conversions to Islam, describes the same kind of outcome after

---

[21] *Periyarana*, 115–16, cited in Anand, *The Buddha: The Essence of Dhamma and Its Practice* (Mumbai: Samrudh Bharat Publication, 2002), 190.

[22] Eleanor Zelliot, "New Voices of the Buddhists of India," in Narain and Ahir, *Ambedkar, Buddhism and Social Change*, 201.

[23] Bama, *Karukku*, translated from Tamil by Lakshmi Holmstrom (Chennai: South Asia Books, 2000), 68, 69, 91–2, 93, and 102.

the conversions to Buddhism in western India, pointing to continued discrimination and humiliation of converted Dalits, accompanied by physical attacks, in Maharashtra, Gujarat, and elsewhere: "The term *neo-Buddhist* has become more or less synonymous with the terms *untouchable* or *Harijan*. . . . The Maharashtra riots of 1978 and a constant high rate of atrocities against them establish . . . the fact that the same stigmas are attached to this 'changed' identity as well."[24] There are indeed many striking illustrations of the discrimination that even well-to-do, relatively privileged, middle-class converts continue to suffer. Again, Dalit autobiographies and oral accounts, as well as more general journalistic and academic reports, provide innumerable examples. Perhaps one will suffice here.

This is the story recounted to me by a very successful member of the Indian Revenue Service of his experience as a government officer. The IRS is one of the most sought-after, "Class I," services of the government of India. Entry into it was a matter of pride for the middle classes, upper-caste and Dalit, until the era of globalization produced another, international, economic order that the most privileged among them could enter, with new "global" salaries and aspirations. A writer, a Buddhist preacher of some repute, a sophisticated and conscientious intellectual and professional who gained early recognition for his administrative abilities and was chosen for several challenging positions in consequence, the Dalit officer told me of a senior colleague, his boss, who treated him as a favorite junior, assigning him to numerous sensitive and difficult projects and showering him with uncommon praise. One day, however, he noticed an image of the Buddha in a corner of the younger man's office. Taken aback, the senior officer blurted out that he "could not have imagined that someone so brilliant was an SC [i.e., a member of the Scheduled Castes]." It was the kind of double-edged comment that students and independent professionals from Dalit, African American, and other "colonized" backgrounds – and, for a very long time, women – have had to face over and over again, and the outcome was also familiar. "His whole attitude and interaction with me changed after that," the young bureaucrat observed.[25]

---

[24] Mujahid, *Conversion to Islam*, 86 (emphasis original).
[25] Interview, Bombay, November 24, 2003. I have withheld the name of the interviewee at his request.

The Persistence of Prejudice

If individual or, more commonly, collective conversion was one way of seeking an escape from the humiliation of Untouchability, the adoption of new caste names and altered ritual, occupational, and social practices was another, and this appears as a closer parallel to the African American option of passing. Not surprisingly, there has long been debate over the use of inherited, and derogatory, caste names among the lower castes in India. The matter gained urgency with the inauguration of decennial census operations in the late nineteenth century, when, in a classic colonial move, colonial officials attempted to classify all castes and subcastes in India in a universally agreed hierarchy! Along with other low castes, many Dalit groups struggled to improve their "official" status and to gain better access to economic, social, and cultural resources through a claim to new names, new traditions, and new histories.[26] Today, in an ironic reversal, in a new stage of political struggle generated by growing lower-caste self-confidence and pride and by amplified state promises of affirmative action for historically disadvantaged groups, many lower-caste and lower-class groups are seeking recognition as Dalits (ex-Untouchables) or "backward castes." But the underlying unease about passing or not, of asserting citizenship by claiming the privileged, unmarked social origins of the mainstream, remains a daily choice – and conundrum.

The issue of how to name the collectivity, whether the larger assemblage of ex-Untouchables or Dalits or the smaller local caste group, has been one part of the struggle. Dalits from different walks of life continue to use inherited caste names – which can be deprecatory and humiliating in many contexts – in everyday descriptions of particular habitations and their populations, while describing themselves as Dalits or Buddhists or S.C.s in other situations. However, in line with the earlier struggle to upgrade themselves in the existing caste

---

[26] For just a few examples, see Owen Lynch, *The Politics of Untouchability: Social Mobility and Social Change in a City in India* (New York: Columbia University Press, 1969); Andre Beteille, "Caste and Political Group Formation in Tamilnad," in *Caste in Indian Politics*, ed. Rajni Kothari (New Delhi: Orient Longman, 1970); Juergensmeyer, *Religion as Social Vision*; Sekhar Bandyopadhyay, *Caste, Protest and Identity in Colonial India: The Namasudras of Bengal, 1872–1947* (Richmond: Curzon Press, 1997); Dube, *Untouchable Pasts*; Prashad, *Untouchable Freedom*; and Chinnaiah Jangam, "Contesting Hinduism: Emergence of Dalit Paradigms in Telugu Country, 1900–1950," PhD thesis, School of Oriental and African Studies, University of London, 2005.

208   *A History of Prejudice*

hierarchy, many Dalits argue that such caste names in fact derive from a history very different from that commonly associated with them. Thus, as a retired Dalit bureaucrat said to me, "Chamar [the most common north Indian name for groups associated with leather work and shoe-making] comes not from *chamra* [leather], but from Chinvar or Chanvar, names of lineages that once ruled this region."[27]

Among politically conscious Dalits, and middle-class Dalits more generally, there has been a corresponding contest in the matter of surnames. The question here is one of social and political identification, in the sense of "identifying with" particular populations or assemblages. Even today, family names are among the clearest indicators of caste background in this deeply caste-conscious society. The struggle over surnames has therefore been a central issue in the matter of passing, or being accepted in a class or collectivity that is not one's natal community or supposed social group.

The requirement of surnames is a fairly recent phenomenon in many parts of the world.[28] In India, surnames became mandatory in colonial times. They were needed for bureaucratic identification and classification, and for admission to schools and other civil and military institutions. Until recently – and in parts of small town and rural India, to this day – children and youths were known as the sons or daughters of so-and-so (the father), with the latter additionally being identified by caste, especially in the case of lower-caste people. The surnames subsequently adopted (or assigned by sundry authorities) often derived from caste names or what were thought of as the traditional occupations of particular castes, although some alluded to geographical origins, administrative or professional position, learning, and proficiency in various trades.[29]

In this context, upwardly mobile Dalit individuals and families, struggling against the discriminatory caste order, often assumed "neutral"

---

[27] Interview with Balwant Singh, Saharanpur, January 11, 2007. Such recasting of history was very much part of the nineteenth- and twentieth-century struggles for dignity and self-respect.

[28] Cf. James C. Scott, John Tehranian, and Jeremy Mathias, "The Production of Legal Identities Proper to States: The Case of the Permanent Family Surname," *Comparative Studies in Society and History*, 44, no. 1 (2002).

[29] Among certain groups, especially in southern India, the first name of the father came to be used as an individual's second name.

The Persistence of Prejudice   209

surnames, tied to places of origin or to unmarked administrative or social positions such as headman or soldier, which did not immediately reveal their caste background.[30] In other places, they adopted appellations hitherto used by higher castes or by people belonging to other religious traditions, such as Christians, Sikhs, or Buddhists. In many instances, they dropped surnames or titles altogether and lived with a single name. Sometimes this was supplemented by a middle name like Lal, Kumar, or Kumari (meaning "son or daughter of" or "junior" member), or Ram or Prasad (something like a "gift from the gods"), which could become a surname in its turn.

The following example from eastern Uttar Pradesh, in northern India, illustrates the point very well indeed. The oldest living male member of one Dalit family, who became a middle-rank district police officer in the 1960s, used the surname Ram throughout his career. Ram was the tag added to the names of men in the family in his father's generation, all of whom worked as farmers, craftsmen, and laborers in the village. By contrast, all the younger male members of the police officer's family, now educated and urban-dwellers, go by other surnames.

The police officer gave his younger brother, fifteen years his junior and now a prominent Dalit ideologue, the surname Prasad. His four sons use the surnames Chandra, Kumar, and in two cases Pracheta. The name Pracheta, first adopted by the older of these two sons when he went to college in Delhi, is particularly difficult to place in the existing social order because it has no established caste connotations. In this respect, it is a little different from Ram, Prasad, Chandra, and Kumar, which are commonly used by Dalits today without being exclusive to them. A cousin of the police officer has taken on the upper-caste surname Sahni, and like many other middle-class Dalits prefers to use the initials of his earlier name in place of a personal name: D. R., the "R" in this instance standing for Ram. He took the name Sahni after a young niece had adopted it on entering high school in a town near Delhi. Another cousin of the police officer continues to use the

---

[30] For the purposes of this exploration, I constructed over a hundred family trees, or more accurately (given the nature of the evidence) partial family trees, of Dalits in northern and western India. My information comes from interviews, supplemented by autobiographical writings and "fictional" accounts. I have kept footnotes to a minimum in order to protect the identities and confidentiality of my informants.

surname Ram, but his two daughters have adopted Chaudhri, traditionally meaning caste or village headman and now used by individuals and families belonging to several castes, high as well as low, in many parts of India. Among two generations of this one family, then, seven different surnames are in use – not counting those that come from marriage into other families.

In recent years, as the Dalit struggle has grown in strength and militancy, scores of Dalit activists have embraced once-derogatory caste names (Dusadh, Paswan, Jatav, Jadhav, Mahar, Chambhar, and the like) as their new surnames. But the urge, and the convenience, of adopting unidentifiable, not already marked, surnames remains strong. The double movement observable here says something about the predicaments of the subaltern middle classes. This may not be very far removed from the purificatory and modernizing quandaries observable among the mainstream middle classes in the past as they aspired to higher social position and respectability. But for particular historical reasons, which I have outlined, the questions appear to be more persistent in the case of the more recent, marked, ex-slave and ex-Untouchable middle classes. Where is it that they come from? How universal is their heritage? Whom can they speak for? I turn now to another aspect of this problem.

The Question of Community, or Appropriate Constituency

Early in 2001, a Dalit columnist began writing a weekly column entitled "*Samasyaen Daliton Ki*" (The Problems of the Dalits) in a major Hindi daily published from New Delhi. The following examination of the issue of appropriate political constituency or audience, or whom the lower-caste middle classes may speak for in India, is based on the public exchange that followed in the form of letters written to the columnist in 2001 and 2002.[31] To put the discussion in context, it needs to be said that this columnist's writings are marked by some aggression, and a polemical quality not unlike that found in many

---

[31] I am grateful to the columnist for his kindness in letting me read and copy the letters he received, and for his permission to let me use them. Translations from the Hindi in the quotations that follow are mine. After prolonged consideration, and consultation with the columnist, I have withheld his name and other particulars to prevent the personalization of the larger issues at stake here.

The Persistence of Prejudice 211

political interactions between Dalits and non-Dalits since at least the time of Ambedkar, the preeminent Dalit leader of the 1920s to the 1950s. This is hardly surprising, given the gross inequality and evident lack of respectful communication between the two parties over a very long period. Just as important, the aggression and polemic are hardly restricted to one side when it comes to open political argument.

Among the hundreds of letters written to the columnist, a large number come from Dalit youths asking advice or seeking help – to get a job or a loan, to find ways of continuing their education, to learn more about Ambedkar or Buddhism (the religion that Ambedkar and his followers embraced in the last year of Ambedkar's life, as we have seen, and that other Dalits have embraced since), and to express their own desire to contribute to the struggle to change society. There are numerous letters from Muslim readers, which is unsurprising given the contemporary ascendancy of an aggressive right-wing Hindu movement dominated by the upper castes. In the face of the latter, targeted and vulnerable communities like the Muslims have sought to build new political coalitions and found in the Dalits a potentially important political ally.

For these non-Dalit well-wishers as well as for Dalit readers, the columnist is more than just a writer. He is also, immediately, a leader – of the Dalits and other oppressed communities. Dalit correspondents condemn as traitors those Dalit intellectuals, officials, and other professionals who fail to represent the interests of the Dalits at large, and call on the columnist to continue to lead the struggle to raise Dalit consciousness and establish Dalit power. The stakes involved are indicated in the very forms of address: highly reverential in the case of letters from supporters and sympathizers, and often downright abusive in letters from opponents.

For some of his supporters or "followers," the columnist is no less than "today's Ambedkar": in one instance, he is called "more courageous than Ambedkar." For opponents, usually from higher castes (including some from the "backward castes," who have also suffered the indignities of lower-caste status but, having been classified technically as "clean" castes, do not see themselves as "Dalit"), he is anything from "Mr. Dalit," "Mr. Dalitji," "Dalit Maharaj" (or "Almighty Dalit"), "The all-knowing one," and "The pimp of the Dalits" to "Mr. Pig," "Mr. Shit," "Dog," "*Goonda, Suvar, Chamar, Dom*" (where

212   *A History of Prejudice*

the first two words translate as "hooligan," "pig," and the last two refer to two of the lowest ex-Untouchable castes), to provide a sample of the names used. More than a few of these letter-writers, from "respectable" backgrounds as they frequently aver, heap many kinds of sexual abuse on the female relatives of the Dalit columnist, freely using obscenities that they would normally be careful to keep out of their "middle-class" homes.

Some of the letters warn the columnist of anthrax attacks[32] if he does not stop abusing his upper-caste readers; that is, if he does not stop criticizing the Hindus and their religion, dividing the nation, forgetting the duties of Indian citizens, forgetting what *we* have done for *you*, and forgetting his – inherited – place. Some of the same letter-writers, while abusing and threatening the columnist and his relatives, also demand the publication of their letters and warn of untoward consequences if publication is refused. This exhibition of unashamed aggression on the part of the "respectable" must give us pause. The threat of open violence, accompanied by the use of lower-caste names such as Chamar and Dom as insulting epithets to humiliate the addressee, a usage that is now a cognizable offense under Indian law, speaks of the arrogance of power, of groups who believe they are above the law and other requirements of "civil" society, at least in their dealings with certain kinds of people, and of unshaken belief in the upper castes' right to rule.

Two letters make the point succinctly. One says: "*Upar vale ne tumhein banaya hai hamari seva karne ke liye*" ("The Almighty has made you [precisely] to serve us"). The second: "*Hamare joothe tukde khane vale, hamare bailon-bhaison ke gobar mein se dane nikal kar khane valon, hamare mare hue jaanvar khane vaalon, hamare saamne tumhari himmat kaise hoti hai hamare khilaf baat karne ki . . . ?*" ("You who eat the crumbs left over on our plates, who eat the grains you pick out of the shit of our cattle, who eat the remains of our domestic animals that have died, how dare you speak out against us, in our presence . . . ?")

I could multiply these examples of abuse and arrogant statement of inherited privilege. Instead, I will conclude by referring to a much

---

[32] Recall that many of these letters were written in the wake of the terrorist attacks of September 2001 in New York, Pennsylvania, and Washington, D.C.

The Persistence of Prejudice　　213

more polite intervention that nevertheless restates the dominant upper-caste and upper-class belief in the appropriate place of the Dalit, or any other minority voice, in the order of things and in the business of development. This particular letter comes from a Brahman male who lives in Delhi, on the eastern (less salubrious) side of the river Jamuna. Addressing the Dalit columnist in the most respectful traditional terms ("honorable Mr. ___," "respectful salutations"), he writes that he has been reading the column on "The problems of the Dalits" for some time and recognizes that "somewhere," in some important way, "what you say is true." However, he asks,

> Will you tell me whether you think of yourself first as a Dalit, [a member of] a so-called low caste, or as an Indian? If the answer is "Indian", then I plead with you not to divide this nation up further, physically or psychologically. In my view you are capable of lifting up the Dalit community of the entire country through education, thereby contributing to the progress of the nation. You must endeavor to lift them up out of the feeling of being Dalits or so-called low castes, and make them [conscious of being] Indians. Let them know that we are not Brahmans, Kshatriyas, Vaishyas, Shudras, we are nothing but Indians and will remain [nothing but] Indians.

The correspondent then expresses his judgment against affirmative action, or constitutional provisions for the reservation of a quota of educational and political positions for people from lower-caste back-grounds: "There are other ways of lifting up [the Dalits]." "Reservations," he declares, " . . . harm the nation."

This "sympathetic" reader believes in the necessity of the columnist playing the role of the leader, not of course of the country at large but of his community: "you are capable of lifting up the Dalit community" and thereby "contributing to the progress of the nation." Note the lack of self-consciousness in the inquiry "Are you an Indian first or a Dalit first?", a question periodically posed to Muslims and other minorities as well, but never to upper-caste/upper-class Hindus, for the latter are the nation, invisibly and axiomatically. In this framework, India (and "mainstream" Indians) are abstract and unmarked categories, while Dalits emerge as a local, vernacular grouping, with identifiable but manifestly local problems: minorities that must never forget that these are, in the end, sectional matters, minor in comparison with the universal concerns of mainstream India and mainstream humanity.

214   *A History of Prejudice*

A parallel invective, not entirely dissimilar from that heaped on the
Dalit columnist, is found in a very large number of right-wing commentaries on the current president of the United States. The canard
extends from claims about Barack Obama's supposed foreign birth,
suggesting that as someone who is not a native-born American he
is ineligible to be president of the country, to accusations that he
is a closet Muslim, a traitor, even a supporter of terrorists. Thus
Rush Limbaugh stated in August 2010: "I have not (called him)
Imam Hussein Obama. . . . Imam Barack Hoover Obama is the correct
nomenclature." However, says Limbaugh, the number of Americans
who believe he is Muslim is increasing: "Imam Obama is becoming
more well-known and the media can't protect him." He offers an
explanation: "[W]hy did I start calling him Imam Obama?" It was
"the natural thing to do when he came out in favor of the mosque
[a proposal to build a private Muslim community center in a building near Ground Zero in New York, which became notorious as the
"mosque" controversy]. It's no different than calling it the Hamasque,
because Hamasque [Hamas, the militant Palestinian party that cur-
rently forms the government in the Gaza strip] has come out in favor
of the mosque."

However much leftists, liberals, and other "'un-American" types
try to hide who they really are, Limbaugh goes on to say, "the truth
is eventually gonna surface." But "once you start telling lies and once
you start living a lie, you are doomed because you will not be able
to remember who you told what. You're gonna get found out, you're
gonna get caught at some point." Further: "[W]e are a great country
at risk in a dangerous world. We have threats external and internal.
And it is not a good sign. It is not something healthy for the American people to not know what religion their president is, . . . where he's
been and who he is, it's not healthy, it's not good."[33] The easy assumption of the position of proconsul, of the purveyor of the "good" and
the "healthy" and the defender of Americanness, is a mark of mainstream arrogance; more specifically, that of the white, Anglo-Saxon,
Protestant, heterosexual male. "It is inconceivable," as a *New York*

---

[33] Rush Limbaugh, "Imam Barack Hoover Obama and Fellow Democrats Are Living a Lie," August 19, 2010, http://www.rushlimbaugh.com/home/daily/site_081910/
content/01125110.guest.html.

Times editorial put it, "that this campaign to portray Mr. Obama as the insidious 'other' would have been conducted against a white president."[34]

Consider just one more example of this common-sense, modernist call to militarism and masculinism, with its singular reason and its singular understanding of the "natural" American and the healthy and good society. Dinesh D'Souza recently published an article in *Forbes* magazine previewing a longer statement in a book entitled *The Roots of Obama's Rage* – an article that drew praise from the former Speaker of the U.S. House of Representatives and candidate for the Republican nomination for president in 2012, Newt Gingrich. "Incredibly," writes D'Souza, "the U.S. is being ruled according to the dreams of a Luo tribesman of the 1950s [Luo being the Kenyan tribe Obama's father is said to have come from]. This philandering, inebriated African socialist, who raged against the world for denying him the realization of his anticolonial ambitions, is now setting the nation's agenda through the reincarnation of his dreams in his son." Thus, one can understand the president only "if (one) understands Kenyan, anticolonial behavior." And then we get to the clinching argument about "the Other." Barack Obama was raised "offshore": he spent "his formative years – the first 17 years of his life – off the American mainland, in Hawaii, Indonesia and Pakistan, with multiple subsequent journeys to Africa."[35] *Voilà*!

The call is this, in other words: "Imam Barack Hussein Obama, take yourself and your crazy, socialist ideas back to where you/they come from – Africa (or Indonesia, not to mention Pakistan)." Not quite on par with the extremist Hindu right wing's demand in India: "*Babar ki santan/Jaao Pakistan ya Kabristan*" ("Descendants of [the Mughal Emperor] Babar [i.e., Muslims of India], [take your choice]: go to Pakistan or to the grave"). There is no parallel foreign country to which people of African descent in the United States (or of Untouchable

---

34 "A Certificate of Embarrassment," *New York Times*, April 28, 2011, A22.
35 See Dinesh D'Souza, *The Roots of Obama's Rage* (Washington, DC: Regnery Publishing, 2010). I take the citations in this paragraph from Maureen Dowd, "Who's the Con Man?" *New York Times*, op-ed article, September 15, 2010, A25. For doubts about Obama's place of birth expressed by other leading Republicans, including another aspirant to the presidential nomination in 2012, Donald Trump, see Bill Carter and Brian Stelter, "If Trump Runs in '12, 'Apprentice' is in Limbo," *New York Times*, April 18, 2011, B4; and Kirk Johnson, "Despite the Evidence, 'Birther' Bills Advance," *New York Times*, April 22, 2011, A11.

216 *A History of Prejudice*

descent in India) may be banished, even ideologically. But the attack is not altogether different in its effect. It is a proposition that we have encountered many times over in the annals of American and Indian democracy and nationhood: don't forget how lucky you are; don't forget where you came from (and what you've attained); don't forget what *we* – the unmarked, natural citizens, the real Americans and Indians, the nation – have done for you.

It is instructive in this context to set the response elicited by the Delhi columnist and cited earlier – "Are you an Indian first or a Dalit first?" – alongside certain reactions to the popular 1980s American television series *The Cosby Show*, about an eminently normal African American family of successful professionals, reveling in loving parenthood, education, and affluence, and (to take a very different example) Zora Neale Hurston's *Their Eyes Were Watching God*, the story of a black girl's quest for a sense of self and independence in Florida in the early twentieth century.

Hurston's 1937 novel was panned in several quarters for turning black life into a minstrel show, in part because of her use of accents and vocabulary common among African Americans in the 1920s; the critics included leading intellectuals such as Richard Wright. At the same time, while it was applauded for its engagement with contemporary issues of gender and sexual politics, it was criticized for "its inability to speak to the local, particularized politics of its time" – that is to say, for not adequately addressing the specificity of the black experience in the post-Reconstruction South.[36] Decades later, the specificities of black experience were again an important part of the debate on Bill Cosby's television production, although in this instance the charge was more that the show was "not black enough." Several critics declared that the series "obscured the issues of class and race" and reinforced facile and unhistorical arguments about how African Americans, like anyone else, could make it in modern-day America if they had the will.[37]

There is a common thread here. What is posited is a choice of political/cultural/media constituency that is in fact a negation of choice.

---

[36] Carol Batker, "Love Me Like I Like to Be: The Sexual Politics of Hurston's 'Their Eyes Were Watching God,' the Classic Blues and the Black Women's Club Movement," *African American Review*, 32, no. 2 (1998), 199; and Mary Helen Washington, "Preface" in Hurston, *Their Eyes Were Watching God.*

[37] Sut Jhally and Justin Lewis, *Enlightened Racism: The Cosby Show, Audiences & the Myth of the American Dream* (Boulder, CO: Westview Press, 1992), 7. See also

The Vernacular and the Universal

Recall the appeal made to the Dalit columnist. What he must do, the suggestion goes, is to represent both Dalits and India. Yet, he can represent India only as a Dalit, acknowledging where he comes from, representing the community that is his from birth and recognizing its given – yet decidedly "improving" – place in the society.

A paradoxical, and inconsistent, demand is made of both the African American novelist and T.V. producer and the Dalit columnist. Each of these artists and professionals must write/create for everyone. They must entertain, inform, educate by universal – which is to say *our* – standards. At the same time, they must represent the Dalits or the African Americans first and foremost. In truth, they cannot represent anyone else. They must not imagine that they are, or might in some peculiar combination of circumstances be, the mainstream of society.

The Vernacular and the Universal

I have presented in broad brush strokes some of the conditions that make it necessary for important sections of the modern middle classes – in this instance, those who have emerged from ex-slave, ex-untouchable populations such as the Dalits and African Americans – to continue to struggle with the issue of quite where and how they belong in their modern, democratic societies. The fact is that the election of Barack Obama as the president of the United States, like the election of Indira Gandhi as India's prime minister or the election of a Dalit woman leader, Mayawati, three times over as the chief executive (chief minister) of India's most populous province, Uttar Pradesh, has not signaled a dramatic shift in the situation of middle-class women or Dalits or African Americans in general, to say nothing of those from poorer working or unemployed families. Even after large numbers of Dalits and African Americans have reached the point where they do not need to hide aspects of their caste or racial ancestry, and indeed many of them display it with increasing pride, the demand for conformity to "mainstream" norms continues to bedevil individual lives and careers – not excluding that of the U.S. president.

Let me conclude my reflections on this history of prejudice by drawing on an insight that has been foregrounded in many investigations

Leslie B. Inniss and Joe R. Feagin, "The Cosby Show: The View from the Black Middle Class," *Journal of Black Studies*, 25, no. 6 (July 1995), 692–711.

218 *A History of Prejudice*

of the history of rape and sexual violence. We know something now of the trauma frequently undergone by the victims of rape (or, more generally, sexual harassment) in the course of rape trials and investigations of sexual exploitation: the victim has too often become the accused in such moments. I want to suggest that the common sense of prejudice – vernacular and universal – functions through some of the same procedures of open attack and covert insinuation. It is not always in the form of physical torture or verbal abuse that practices of discrimination, objectification, and humiliation are perpetuated or that instigation to (renewed) violence occurs. The preceding pages should have provided enough examples of moments in which the paraphernalia of prejudice comes into view much more subtly.

Why can't you stop being Dalit or black, Dalits and blacks have long been asked, and simply be Americans or Indians? Sometimes Dalits or African Americans have asked the same question, and urged disadvantaged assemblages to stop pleading special circumstances: among them, on occasion, Bill Cosby and Barack Obama – not to mention Condoleezza Rice.[38] It is an argument with a long pedigree, extending back to the Jewish Question in nineteenth-century Europe, if not earlier. And the coercion persists in various forms: "As a practicing Jew [in the USA]," Hillel Levin wrote in 2006, "I am always aware of my minority status within the dominant secular and/or Christian culture, and at times I feel the pressure to cover." Again, John T. Molloy's popular self-help manual *New Dress for Success*, observing that the "model of success" in the country is "white, Anglo-Saxon and Protestant" (he doesn't even bother to mention "male" and "heterosexual," as these are so utterly taken for granted), still advises African Americans (men obviously) to avoid "Afro hairstyles" and to wear "conservative pinstripe suits, preferably with vests," and Latinos (Latinas are, once more, invisible) to avoid "pencil-line mustaches," "any hair tonic that ... give(s) a greasy or shiny look," and "any articles of clothing that have Hispanic associations."[39]

---

[38] On Condoleezza Rice's position that she, and her family, always stood and made it on their own, see Allen Tullos, *Alabama Getaway: The Political Imaginary and the Heart of Dixie* (Athens, GA: University of Georgia Press, 2011), 214–32.

[39] Hillel Levin, "Kenji Yoshino's 'Covering,'" January 23, 2006, http://prawfsblawg .blogs.com/prawfsblawg/2006/01/kenji_yoshinos_.html. John T. Molloy's *New Dress for Success* is cited by Kenji Yoshino, "The Pressure to Cover," *New York Times*,

The demands made by the mainstream – those in positions of power and privilege, masking the very marks of their privilege and their inheritance under the sign of the universal – can be much more vague and pernicious. Bear in mind the sympathetic upper-caste reader's appeal to the Dalit columnist: "Will you tell me whether you think of yourself first as a Dalit, [a member of] a so-called low caste, or as an Indian? . . . [W]e are not Brahmans, Kshatriyas, Vaishyas, Shudras, we are nothing but Indians and will remain [nothing but] Indians." The common sense of society, and reigning prejudices, affect the disenfranchised themselves in many surprising as well as unpredictable ways. Hence Baby Kamble's exclusion of her husband's physical abusiveness from the account of her life because it was "so common"; or Viola Andrews's refusal to contemplate a second marriage because it was "un-Christian"; or George Andrews's insistence that blacks should never try to get above themselves because they "should not."

With all that, once a formal citizenship, the abstract right to vote, and a putative equality of opportunity have been granted to the minority, mainstream demands change in ingenious ways. Recall the Indian parliamentarians' and the Indian Administrative Service bosses' statements to B. R. Ambedkar and Balwant Singh, respectively, that it was not the latter's actions, policies, or proposals that bothered their upper-caste colleagues but rather their attitude, their comportment and disposition. The prescription is now roughly as follows. Recently enfranchised (and naturalized) groups need to be less demanding, less sectional – less different and less emotional. They need, rather, to be more temperate, more reasoned: in a word, more like us. The follow-up in such matters is, however, a delicate affair – because the "us" and the "more" are eminently malleable.

That is what one might describe as the cunning of prejudice – also called reason: the beauty and subtlety of the language of modernity and of the self-generated, autonomous, unmarked subject of history.

January 15, 2006, http://www.nytimes.com/2006/01/15/magazine/15gays.html. Goffman and later Yoshino have called the practice of playing down "outsider identities" without denying them, "covering" – although the difference between covering and passing is not always so clear. See Erving Goffman, *Stigma: Notes on the Management of Spoiled Identity* (New York: Touchstone, 1963); and Kenji Yoshino, *Covering: The Hidden Assault on Our Civil Rights* (New York: Random House, 2006).

Consider once more the comment by Huntington that I quoted at the beginning of this chapter: "There is no Americano dream. There is *only the American dream* created by an Anglo-Protestant society. Mexican-Americans will share in that dream and in that society *only if they dream in English.*" If we needed proof of the demand for *one* language, *one* culture, *one* (disguised, white, male, "European") order, we could scarcely ask for a better example. Unsurprisingly, talk of multiculturism, the diversity and richness of human experience, the "United Nations," the social/historical construction of gender and nationality, minority rights and women's rights, minority histories and non-Western philosophy, all disappear.

The move brings us back to the issue we began with: of how mainstreams are established, of the differences that are suppressed to establish the *difference* (or outsider status) of some, of what goes into the making of the vernacular and the universal, the marked and the unmarked citizen. It brings us back to the question of political power for, to paraphrase the author of the Anglo-Protestant American dream, there is no unmarked modern and no unmarked citizen. It is only our dreaming, our historical privilege, and our current political clout that let us think it so.

Select Bibliography

African American and Dalit Autobiographies, Memoirs and other Writings

Ambedkar, B. R. *Dr. Babasaheb Ambedkar: Writings and Speeches*, vols. 1–22, ed. Vasant Moon. Mumbai: Education Dept. Government of Maharashtra Press, 1982–.

The Essential Writings of B. R. Ambedkar, ed. Valerian Rodrigues. Delhi: Oxford University Press, 2002.

The Untouchables: Who They Were and Why They Became Untouchables. Shravasti: Bharatiya Bauddha Shiksha Parishad, 1977 (originally published 1948).

What Congress and Gandhi Have Done to the Untouchables. Bombay: Thacker, 1945.

Dr. Babasaheb Ambedkar: Writings, Debates, Interviews, Handwriting, Photos, Voice, Video, CD compiled by Anand Teltumbde. Mumbai: Anand Teltumbde, 2004.

Anand. *The Buddha: The Essence of Dhamma and Its Practice*. Mumbai: Samrudh Bharat Publication, 2002.

Andrews, Raymond. *Rosiebelle Lee Wildcat Tennessee*. New York: Dial Press, 1980.

The Last Radio Baby: A Memoir. Atlanta: Peachtree Publishers, 1990.

Bama. *Karukku*, translated from Tamil by Lakshmi Holmstrom. Chennai: South Asia Books, 2000.

Sangati, translated from the Tamil by Lakshmi Holmstrom. New Delhi: Oxford University Press, 2005.

Borders, William Holmes. *Seven Minutes at the 'Mike' in the Deep South*. Atlanta: B. F. Logan Press, 1944.

Broyard, Bliss. *One Drop: My Father's Hidden Life – A Story of Race and Family Secrets*. New York: Little, Brown and Co., 2007.

Select Bibliography

Du Bois, W. E. B. *The Autobiography of W. E. B. Du Bois*. New York: International Publishers, 1968.

The Souls of Black Folk. New York: Signet Classic, 1969 (originally published 1901).

Halder, Baby. *A Life Less Ordinary*, translated from the Hindi by Urvashi Butalia. New Delhi: Zubaan, 2002.

Hughes, Langston and Faith Berry, eds. *Good Morning Revolution: Uncollected Writings of Langston Hughes*. New York: Carol Publishing Group, 1992.

Hughes, Langston and Christopher C. Santis, eds. *Langston Hughes and the Chicago Defender: Essays on Race, Politics, and Culture, 1942–62*. Chicago: University of Illinois Press, 1995.

Hurston, Zora Neale. *I Love Myself When I Am Laughing . . . and Then Again When I Am Looking Mean and Impressive*, ed. Alice Walker. New York: Feminist Press, 1979.

Their Eyes Were Watching God. New York: Harper and Row Publishers, 1990 (originally published 1937).

Ilaiah, Kancha. Interview by Yoginder Sikand, *Mukta Mona*, February 13, 2007.

Why I Am Not a Hindu: A Sudra Critique of Hindutva Philosophy, Culture and Political Economy. Calcutta: Samya, 1996.

Jadhav, Narendra. *Aamcha Baap aan Aamhi*. Second edition, Mumbai: Granthali, 1994; fifth edition, People's edition, Mumbai: Granthali, 2007 (originally published 1993).

Outcaste: A Memoir. Delhi: Viking, 2003.

Johnson, James Weldon. *Along This Way: The Autobiography of James Weldon Johnson*. New York: Viking Penguin, 1991 (originally published 1933).

Kamble, Baby, *Jina Amcha*. Third printing, Pune: Sugava Prakashan, 2008 (originally published 1986).

The Prisons We Broke, translated from the Marathi by Maya Pandit. Chennai: Orient Longman, 2008.

Kamble, Shantabai Krishnaji. *Mazhya Jalmachi Chittarkatha*. Third edition, Pune: Sugawa Prakashan, 1998.

Limbale, Sharankumar. *The Outcaste: Akkarmashi*, trans. Santosh Bhoomkar. Delhi: Oxford University Press, 2003.

Towards an Aesthetic of Dalit Literature, translated from the Marathi by Alok Mukherjee. New Delhi: Orient Longman, 2004.

Malagatti, Aravind. *Government Brahamana*. Chennai: Orient Longman, 2007.

Ottley, Roi. *New World a-Coming*. New York: Arno Press and the *New York Times*, 1968 (originally published 1943).

Pawar, Ishwar Das. *My Struggle in Life*. Chandigarh: I. D. Pawar, 1982; third edition 1993.

Pawar, Urmila. *Aaydaan*. Mumbai: Granthali, 2003.

Select Bibliography

The Weave of My Life: A Dalit Woman's Memoirs, translated from the Marathi by Maya Pandit. Calcutta: Stree, 2008.

Singh, Balwant. *An Untouchable in the I.A.S.* Saharanpur: Balwant Singh, n.d.

Valmiki, Omprakash. *Joothan: A Dalit's Life*, trans. Arun Prabha Mukherkjee. Calcutta: Samya, 2003.

Walker, Alice. *Anything We Love Can Be Saved: A Writer's Activism*. New York: Random House, 1997.

In Search of Our Mothers' Gardens. Orlando, FL: Harvest Books, 1983.

White, Walter. *A Man Called White: The Autobiography of Walter White*. New York: Viking Press, 1948.

Secondary Works

Agamben, Georgio. *Homo Sacer I: Sovereign Power and Bare Life*. Stanford, CA: Stanford University Press, 1998.

Ahir, D. C. *Buddhism in India after Dr. Ambedkar (1956–2002)*. Delhi: Blumoon Books, 2003.

Aloysius, G. *Nationalism without a Nation in India*. Delhi: Oxford University Press, 1997.

Anderson, Carol. *Eyes off the Prize: The United Nations and the African American Struggle for Human Rights, 1944–1955*. Cambridge: Cambridge University Press, 2003.

Apel, Dora. *Imagery of Lynching: Black Men, White Women and the Mob*. New Brunswick, NJ: Rutgers University Press, 2004.

Appy, Christian G. *Working-Class War: American Combat Soldiers and Vietnam*. Chapel Hill: University of North Carolina Press, 1993.

Arendt, Hannah. *The Jewish Writings*, ed. Jerome Kohn and Ron Feldman. New York: Schocken Books, 2007.

The Origins of Totalitarianism. New York: Houghton Mifflin Harcourt, 1994 (originally published 1951).

Asad, Talal. *Formations of the Secular: Christianity, Islam, Modernity*. Stanford, CA: Stanford University Press, 2003.

Bandhopadhyay, Sekhar. *Caste, Protest and Identity in Colonial India: The Namasudras of Bengal, 1872–1947*. Richmond: Curzon Press, 1997.

"Transfer of Power and the Crisis of Dalit Politics in India, 1945–47," *Modern Asian Studies*, 34, no. 4 (2000): 893–942.

Batker, Carol. "Love Me Like I Like to Be: The Sexual Politics of Hurston's 'Their Eyes Were Watching God,' the Classic Blues and the Black Women's Club Movement," *African American Review*, 32, no. 2 (1998), 199–213.

Benjamin, Walter. *Illuminations*. London: Fontana, 1973.

Berman, Marshall. *All That Is Solid Melts into Air: The Experience of Modernity*. New York: Penguin Books, 1982.

Beteille, Andre. "Caste and Political Group Formation in Tamilnad," in *Caste in Indian Politics*, ed. Rajni Kothari. New Delhi: Orient Longman, 1970.

Select Bibliography

Bhabha, Homi K. *The Location of Culture.* London: Routledge, 1994.

Bhatnagar, Rashmi. *World and Bhāsa Literatures: Revolutions in Philology* (forthcoming).

Bluestein, Greg. "Ex-governor Investigated in 1946 Lynchings," *Associated Press,* updated June 15, 2007, http://www.msnbc.com/id/19251476/.

Blum, Albert A. "Work or Fight: The Use of the Draft as a Manpower Sanction during the Second World War," *Industrial and Labor Relations Review,* 16, no. 3 (April 1963): 366–80.

Boyd, Valerie. *Wrapped in Rainbows: The Life of Zora Neale Hurston.* New York: Scribner, 2003.

Braxton, Joanne. *Black Women Writing Autobiography.* Philadelphia: Temple University Press, 1989.

Brooker, Peter. *Glossary of Cultural Theory.* London: Arnold, 2003.

Bunzl, Matti. *Symptoms of Modernity: Jews and Queers in Late-Twentieth-Century Vienna.* Berkeley: University of California Press, 1999.

Burkett, Randall K. *Black Redemption: Churchmen Speak for the Garvey Movement.* Philadelphia: Temple University Press, 1978.

Butalia, Urvashi. *The Other Side of Silence.* New Delhi: Viking Press, 1998.

Carson, Clayborne, et al., eds. *The Eyes on the Prize: Civil Rights Reader. Documents, Speeches, and Firsthand Accounts from the Black Freedom Struggle, 1954–1990.* New York: Penguin Books, 1991.

Chamberlain, Charles D. *Victory at Home: Manpower and Race in the American South during World War II.* Athens: University of Georgia Press, 2003.

Chatterjee, Partha. *The Nation and Its Fragments.* Princeton, NJ: Princeton University Press, 1993.

The Politics of the Governed: Reflections on Popular Politics in Most of the World. New York: Columbia University Press, 2004.

Chauhan, Brij Raj. "Scheduled Castes and Scheduled Tribes," *Economic and Political Weekly,* 4, no. 4 (January 25, 1969): 257–63.

Collins, Patricia Hill. *Black Feminist Thought: Knowledge, Consciousness, and the Politics of Empowerment.* New York: Routledge, 1991.

Crenshaw, Kimberlé. "Mapping the Margins: Intersectionality, Identity Politics, and Violence Against Women of Color," *Stanford Law Review* 43 (1991): 1241–99.

Dalfiume, Richard M. "The 'Forgotten Years' of the Negro Revolution," in Bernard Sternsher, ed., *The Negro in Depression and War: Prelude to Revolution, 1930–1945.* Chicago: Quadrangle Books, 1969.

Davis, Mike. *City of Quartz: Excavating the Future in Los Angeles.* London: Verso, 1990.

de Beauvoir, Simone. *The Second Sex.* London: Vintage, 1997 (originally published 1949).

Deliege, Robert. *The Untouchables of India.* Oxford: Berg Publishers, Oxford, 2001.

Dirks, N. B. *Castes of Mind: Colonialism and the Making of Modern India.* Princeton, NJ: Princeton University Press, 2001.

Select Bibliography

D'Souza, Dinesh. *The Roots of Obama's Rage*. Washington, D.C.: Regnery Publishing, 2010.

Dube, Saurabh. *Untouchable Pasts: Religion, Identity, and Power among a Central Indian Community, 1780–1950*. New Delhi: Vistaar Publications, 2001.

Dudley, J. Wayne. "'Hate' Organizations of the 1940s: The Columbians, Inc.," *Phylon*, 42, no. 3 (1981): 262–74.

Dyson, Michael Eric. "Commentary: Professor Arrested for 'Housing While Black,'" July 22, 2009. http://articles.cnn.com/2009-07-22/living/dyson .police.

Ellison, Ralph. *Shadow and Act*. New York: Quality Paperback Book Club, 1994.

Fanon, Frantz. *Black Skin, White Masks*, trans. Charles Lam Markmann. London: Pluto Press, 2008 (originally published 1952).

The Wretched of the Earth. New York: Grove Press, 1963.

Feimster, Crystal N. *Southern Horrors: Women and the Politics of Rape and Lynching*. Cambridge, MA: Harvard University Press, 2009.

Forbes, Jack D. *Africans and Native Americans: The Language of Race and the Evolution of Red-Black Peoples*. Urbana: University of Illinois Press, 1993.

Fox-Genovese, Elizabeth. "My Statue, My Self: Autobiographical Writings of Afro-American Women," in *The Private Self: Theory and Practice of Women's Autobiographical Writings*, ed. Shari Benstock. Chapel Hill: University of North Carolina, 1988.

Frazier, E. Franklin. *The Negro Family in the United States*. Revised edition. Chicago: University of Chicago Press, 1966 (originally published 1939).

Frederickson, Kari. "'The Slowest State' and the 'Most Backward Community': Racial Violence in South Carolina and Federal Civil-Rights Legislation, 1946–1948," *South Carolina Historical Magazine*, 98, no. 2 (April 1997): 177–202.

Frey, William H. "Revival," *American Demographics*, October 2003. (Special Series: America's Money in the Middle): 27–31. http://www.frey-demographer.org/briefs/B-2003-5_Revival.pdf.

Ganguly, Debjani. *Caste and Dalit Lifeworlds: Postcolonial Perspectives*. New Delhi: Orient Longman, 2005.

"Pain, Personhood and the Collective: Dalit Life Narratives," *Asian Studies Review*, 33, no. 4 (December 2009): 429–42.

Gates, Jr., Henry Louis. *Thirteen Ways of Looking at a Black Man*. New York: Random House, 1997.

Geetha, V. and S. V. Rajadurai. *Towards a Non-Brahmin Millennium: From Iyothee Thass to Periyar*. Calcutta: Samya, 1998.

Gerstle, Gary. *American Crucible: Race and Nation in the Twentieth Century*. Princeton, NJ: Princeton University Press, 2001.

Gilmore, Glenda Elizabeth. *Defying Dixie: The Radical Roots of Civil Rights, 1919–1950*. New York: W. W. Norton and Co., 2008.

Gender and Jim Crow: Women and the Politics of White Supremacy in North Carolina, 1896–1920. Chapel Hill: University of North Carolina Press, 1996.

Gilroy, Paul. *The Black Atlantic: Modernity and Double Consciousness*. Cambridge, MA: Harvard University Press, 1993.

Goffman, Erving. *Stigma: Notes on the Management of Spoiled Identity*. New York: Touchstone, 1963.

Goldstein, Eric L. *The Price of Whiteness: Jews, Race, and American Identity*. Princeton, NJ: Princeton University Press, 2006.

Goluboff, Risa L. "The Thirteenth Amendment and the Lost Origins of Civil Rights," *Duke Law Journal*, 50, no. 6 (April 2001): 1609–85.

Gopal, S., ed. *Selected Works of Jawaharlal Nehru*, vol. 7. New Delhi: Orient Longman, 1975.

Grant, Donald L. *The Way It Was in the South: The Black Experience in Georgia*. Athens: University of Georgia Press, 1993.

Grosz, Elizabeth. "Derrida, Irigaray, and Deconstruction," *Intervention: Revolutionary Marxist Journal*, 20 (1986): 70–81.

Gruber, J. Richard. *American Icons: From Madison to Manhattan, the Art of Benny Andrews, 1948–1997*. Augusta, GA: Morris Museum of Art, 1997.

The Dot Man: George Andrews of Madison, Georgia. Augusta, GA: Morris Museum of Art, 1994.

Guha, Ranajit. *Elementary Aspects of Peasant Insurgency in Colonial India*. Delhi: Oxford University Press, 1983.

"Subaltern Studies: Projects for Our Time and Their Convergence," in *The Latin American Subaltern Studies Reader*, ed. Ileana Rodriguez. Durham, NC: Duke University Press, 2001, 35–46.

ed., *Subaltern Studies: Studies in South Asian History and Society*, vol. II. Delhi: Oxford University Press, 1983.

Guru, Gopal. "Archaeology of Untouchability," *Economic and Political Weekly*, 44, no. 37 (September 12, 2009): 49–56.

"Power of Touch," *Frontline*, 23, no. 25 (December 16–29, 2006), http://www.frontlineonnet.com/fl2325/stories/20061229002903000.htm.

Guy-Sheftall, Beverly, ed. *Words of Fire: An Anthology of African-American Feminist Thought*. New York: The New Press, 1995.

Hall, Jacquelyn Dowd. "The Long Civil Rights Movement and the Political Uses of the Past," *Journal of American History*, 91 (March 2005): 1233–63.

Harris, David A. "Driving While Black: Racial Profiling on Our Nation's Highways," ACLU Special Report, June 1999, http://www.aclu.org/racial-justice/driving-while-black-racial-profiling-our-nations-highways.

Hemenway, Robert E. *Zora Neale Hurston: A Literary Biography*. Urbana: University of Illinois Press, 1980.

Hine, Darlene Clark. *Hine Sight: Black Women and the Re-construction of American History*. Brooklyn, NY: Carlson Publishing, 1994.

Select Bibliography

"Rape and the Inner Lives of Black Women in the Middle West: Preliminary Thoughts on the Culture of Dissemblance," *Signs: Journal of Women in Culture and Society*, 14, no. 4 (1989): 912–20.

Hochschild, Jennifer L. "Looking Ahead: Racial Trends in the United States," *Daedalus*, 134, no. 1 (Winter 2005): 70–81.

hooks, bell. *Ain't I a Woman: Black Women and Feminism*. Boston: South End Press, 1981.

Huntington, Samuel P. *Who Are We?* New York: Simon and Schuster, 2004.

Inniss, Leslie B. and Joe R. Feagin. "The Cosby Show: The View from the Black Middle Class," *Journal of Black Studies*, 25, no. 6 (July 1995): 692–711.

Jangam, Chinnaiah. "Contesting Hinduism: Emergence of Dalit Paradigms in Telugu Country, 1900–1950," PhD thesis, School of Oriental and African Studies, University of London, 2005.

Jelinek, Estelle C., ed. *Women's Autobiography: Essays in Criticism*. Bloomington: Indiana University Press, 1980.

Jhally, Sut and Justin Lewis. *Enlightened Racism: The Cosby Show, Audiences & the Myth of the American Dream*. Boulder, CO: Westview Press, 1992.

Jondhale, Surendra and Johannes Beltz, eds. *Reconstructing the World: B. R. Ambedkar and Buddhism in India*. Delhi: Oxford University Press, 2004.

Jones, Jacqueline. *Labor of Love, Labor of Sorrow: Black Women, Work and the Family, from Slavery to the Present*. New York: Vintage Books, 1985.

Juergensmeyer, Mark. *Religion as Social Vision: The Movement against Untouchability in 20th Century Punjab*. Berkeley: University of California Press, 1981.

Kaplan, Amy and Donald E. Pease, eds. *Cultures of United States Imperialism*. Durham, NC: Duke University Press, 1993.

Kaplan, Carla, ed. *Zora Neale Hurston: A Life in Letters*. New York: Doubleday, 2002.

Keer, Dhananjay. *Dr. Ambedkar: Life and Mission*. Mumbai: Popular Prakashan, 1990 (originally published 1954).

Kelley, Robin D. G. and Earl Lewis, eds. *To Make Our World Anew, Volume II: A History of African Americans from 1880*. New York: Oxford University Press, 2005.

Kennedy, Randall. "Racial Passing," *Ohio State Law Journal*, 62, no. 1145 (2001): 1145–94.

Khare, R. S. *The Untouchable as Himself: Ideology, Identity, and Pragmatism among the Lucknow Chamars*. Cambridge: Cambridge University Press, 1984.

Kruse, Kevin. *White Flight: Atlanta and the Making of Modern Conservatism*. Princeton, NJ: Princeton University Press, 2005.

Lal, Ruby. *Coming of Age in Nineteenth Century India: The Girl Child and the Art of Playfulness*. Cambridge: Cambridge University Press, forthcoming, 2013.

Lassiter, Matthew D. and Joseph Crespino, eds. *The Myth of Southern Exceptionalism*. New York: Oxford University Press, 2010.

228 *Select Bibliography*

Lester, Julius. "The Mark of Race," *The Civil Liberties Review*, 5, no. 4 (January–February 1979): 115–18.

Levin, Hillel. "Kenji Yoshino's 'Covering,' January 23, 2006, http://prawfsblawg.blogs.com/prawfsblawg/2006/01/kenji_yoshinos_.html.

Lewis, David Levering. *W. E. B. Du Bois: The Fight for Equality and the American Century, 1919–1963*. New York: Henry Holt and Co., 2000.

Limbaugh, Rush. "Imam Barack Hoover Obama and Fellow Democrats Are Living a Lie," August 19, 2010, http://www.rushlimbaugh.com/home/daily/site_081910/content/01125110.guest.html.

Lohr, Kathy. "FBI Re-examines 1946 Lynching Case," July 25, 2006, http://www.npr.org/templates/story/Id=5579862.

Lorde, Audre. *Sister Outsider*. Berkeley, CA: Crossing Press, 2007.

Lynch, Owen. *The Politics of Untouchability: Social Mobility and Social Change in a City in India*. New York: Columbia University Press, 1969.

Marable, Manning. *Race, Reform and Rebellion: The Second Reconstruction and Beyond in Black America, 1945–2006*. Jackson: University Press of Mississippi, 2007.

and Leith Mullings, eds. *Let Nobody Turn Us Around: Voices of Resistance, Reform, and Renewal*. Lanham, MD: Rowman and Littlefield Publishers, 2000.

Marx, Karl and Friedrich Engels. *On Colonialism*. Moscow: Foreign Languages Press, n.d.

McKinnon, Jesse. "The Black Population: 2000," *Census 2000 Brief*, C2KBR/01-5, accessed online at www.census.gov/prod/2001pubs/c2kbr01-5.pdf.

Mehta, Uday Singh. *Liberalism and Empire: A Study in Nineteenth-Century British Liberal Thought*. Chicago: University of Chicago Press, 1999.

Middleton, Townsend. "Beyond Recognition: Ethnology, Belonging, and the Refashioning of the Ethnic Subject in Darjeeling, India," PhD dissertation, Department of Anthropology, Cornell University, 2010.

Mufti, Aamir. *Enlightenment in the Colony: The Jewish Question and the Crisis of Postcolonial Culture*. Princeton, NJ: Princeton University Press, 2007.

Mujahid, Abdul Malik. *Conversion to Islam: Untouchables' Strategy for Protest in India*. Chambersburg, PA: Anima Books, 1989.

Myrdal, Gunnar. *An American Dilemma*, Volume 1: *The Negro in a White Nation*. New York: McGraw-Hill, 1964 (originally published 1944).

Asian Drama: An Inquiry into the Poverty of Nations, abridged by Seth S. King. New York: Pantheon Books, 1971.

Asian Drama: An Inquiry into the Poverty of Nations, Volume 2. New York: Twentieth Century Fund, 1968.

Nagaraj, D. R. *The Flaming Feet: A Study of the Dalit Movement in India*. Bangalore: South Forum Press, 1993.

Narain, A. K. and D. C. Ahir, eds. *Dr. Ambedkar, Buddhism and Social Change*. Delhi: Orient Longman, 1994.

Select Bibliography

Natrajan, Balmurli. "Place and Pathology in Caste," *Economic and Political Weekly*, 44, no. 51 (December 19, 2009): 79–82.

Nehru, Jawaharlal. *An Autobiography: With Musings on Recent Events in India*. London: John Lane The Bodley Head, 1936.

Nicholson, Linda, ed. *The Second Wave: A Reader in Feminist Theory*. New York: Routledge, 1997.

Norrell, Robert J. *The House I Live In: Race in the American Century*. New York: Oxford University Press, 2005.

Painter, Nell Irvin. *Southern History across the Color Line*. Chapel Hill: University of North Carolina Press, 2002.

The History of White People. New York: W. W. Norton and Co., 2010.

Pandey, Gyanendra. *Routine Violence: Nations, Fragments, Histories*. Stanford, CA: Stanford University Press, 2006.

ed. *Subaltern Citizens and Their Histories: Investigations from India and the USA*. London: Routledge, 2010.

The Construction of Communalism in Colonial North India. Delhi: Oxford University Press, 1990; second edition, 2006; Perennial edition, 2012.

Parvez, Atahar, ed. *Manto ke Numaindah Afsane*. Aligarh: Educational Book House, 1981.

Patillo-McCoy, Mary. *Black Picket Fences: Privilege and Peril among the Black Middle Class*. Chicago: University of Chicago Press, 1999.

Piper, Adrian. "Passing for White, Passing for Black," in *Passing and the Fiction of Identity*, ed. Elaine K. Ginsberg. Durham, NC: Duke University Press, 1996.

Poitevin, Guy. "Dalit Autobiographical Narratives: Figures of Subaltern Consciousness, Assertion and Identity," 13, http://aune.lpl.univ-aix.fr/-belbernard/misc/ccrss/dalitautobio.htm.

Prashad, Vijay. *Untouchable Freedom: A Social History of a Dalit Community*. New Delhi: Oxford University Press, 1999.

Rai, Lajpat. *A History of the Arya Samaj*. Reprint Bombay: Orient Longman, 1967 (originally published 1915).

Randhawa, M. S. *Out of the Ashes: An Account of the Rehabilitation of Refugees from West Pakistan in Rural Areas of East Punjab*. Chandigarh: Public Relations Department, Punjab, 1954.

Rao, Anupama. *The Caste Question: Dalits and the Politics of Modern India*. Berkeley: University of California Press, 2009.

Rege, Sharmila. *Writing Caste/Writing Gender: Reading Dalit Women's Testimonios*. New Delhi: Zubaan, 2006.

Robb, Peter, ed. *Dalit Movements and the Meaning of Labour in India*. Delhi: Oxford University Press, 1993.

Robinson, A. J. *The Two Nations of Black America, An Analysis: Percentage of Blacks and Income Group, 1970–1994*. http://www.pbs.org/wgbh/pages/frontline/shows/race/economics/analysis.html.

Rodrigues, Valerian. "Buddhism, Marxism and the Concept of Emancipation in Ambedkar," in *Dalit Movements and the Meaning of Labour in India*, ed. Peter Robb. Delhi: Oxford University Press, 1993, 299–338.

Select Bibliography

Ryan, Mary. *Cradle of the Middle Class: The Family in Oneida County, New York, 1790–1865*. Cambridge: Cambridge University Press, 1981.

Saavala, Minna. "Low Caste but Middle Caste: Some Strategies for Middle Class Identification in Hyderabad," *Contributions to Indian Sociology*, 1, no. 35 (2001): 293–318.

Sarukkai, Sundar. "Phenomenology of Untouchability," *Economic and Political Weekly*, 44, no. 37 (September 12, 2009): 39–48.

Saul, Scott. "Off Camera," *The Nation*, http://www.thenation.com/doc/20090622/saul.

Savarkar, V. D. *Six Glorious Epochs of Indian History*, trans. S. T. Godbole. New Delhi: Bal Savarkar Rajdhani Granthagar, 1971; reprint 1980.

Scott, Darryl Michael. *Contempt and Pity: Social Policy and the Image of the Damaged Black Psyche, 1880–1996*. Chapel Hill: University of North Carolina Press, 1997.

Scott, James C., John Tehranian, and Jeremy Mathias. "The Production of Legal Identities Proper to States: The Case of the Permanent Family Surname," *Comparative Studies in Society and History*, 44, no. 1 (2002): 4–44.

Scott, Joan W. "Deconstructing Equality-versus-Difference," *Feminist Studies*, 14, no. 1 (1988): 32–50.

Seigel, Micol. *Uneven Encounters: Making Race and Nation in Brazil and the United States*. Durham, NC: Duke University Press, 2009.

Shaw, Stephanie J. *What a Woman Ought to Be and to Do: Black Professional Women Workers during the Jim Crow Era*. Chicago: University of Chicago Press, 1996.

Sheth, D. L. "Caste and Class: Social Reality and Political Representations," in *Contemporary India*, ed. V. A. Pai Panandiker and Ashis Nandy. New Delhi: Tata McGraw-Hill, 1999, 337–63.

Singh, Kirpal. *The Partition of the Punjab*. Patiala: Punjab University, 1989.

Sitkoff, Harvard. "Racial Militancy and Interracial Violence in the Second World War," *Journal of American History*, 58, no. 3 (1971): 661–81.

Sosna, Morton. "More Important than the Civil War? The Impact of World War II on the South," in *Perspectives on the American South: An Annual Review of Society, Politics and Culture*, vol. 4, ed. James C. Cobb and Charles R. Wilson. New York: Gordon and Breach, 1987, 145–61.

Sternsher, Bernard. *The Negro in Depression and War: Prelude to Revolution, 1930–1945*. Chicago: Quadrangle Books, 1969.

Stover, Johnnie. *Rhetoric and Resistance in Black Women's Autobiography*. Gainesville: University of Florida, 2003.

Sugrue, Thomas J. *Sweet Land of Liberty: The Forgotten Struggle for Civil Rights in the North*. New York: Random House, 2008.

Suret-Canale, Jean. *French Colonialism in Tropical Africa, 1900–1945*, English trans. Till Gottheiner. New York: Pica Press, 1971.

Takaki, Ronald. *Double Victory: A Multicultural History of America in World War II*. Boston: Little Brown and Co., 2000.

Select Bibliography

Tan, Tai Yong and Gyanesh Kudaisya. *The Aftermath of Partition in South Asia*. London: Routledge, 2000.

Tendulkar, D. G. *Mahatma: Life of Mohandas Karamchand Gandhi*, vol. 4. New Delhi: Publications Division, Ministry of Information and Broadcasting, Government of India, 1960.

Terry, Brandon M. "A Stranger in Mine Own House: Henry Louis Gates, Jr. and the Police in 'Post-Racial' America," July 21, 2009, http://www.huffingtonpost.com/brandon-m-terry/a-stranger-in-mine-own-ho b 242392.html.

Tribhuvan, Shailesh, ed. *Aamcha Baap aan Aamhi: Svarup ani Sameeksha*. Mumbai: Granthali, 2008.

Tullos, Allen. *Alabama Getaway. The Political Imaginary and the Heart of Dixie*. Athens: University of Georgia Press, 2011.

Vaknin, Sam. "Russia's Middle Class," http://samvak.tripod.com/brief-middleclass01.html.

Vishwanathan, Gauri. *Outside the Fold: Conversion, Modernity, and Belief*. Princeton, NJ: Princeton University Press, 1998.

Visweswaran, Kamala. *Un/common Cultures: Racism and the Rearticulation of Cultural Difference*. Durham, NC: Duke University Press, 2010.

Ward, Jason M. *Defending White Democracy: The Making of a Segregationist Movement and the Remaking of Racial Politics, 1936–1965*. Chapel Hill: University of North Carolina Press, 2011.

Webster, John C. B. *Religion and Dalit Liberation: An Examination of Perspectives*. Delhi: Manohar Publications, 1999.

Wexler, Laura. *Fire in a Canebrake: The Last Mass Lynching in America*. New York: Scribner, 2003.

Williams, Raymond. *Keywords: A Vocabulary of Culture and Society*. Oxford: Oxford University Press, 1976.

Yoshino, Kenji. *Covering: The Hidden Assault on Our Civil Rights*. New York: Random House, 2006.

Zelliot, Eleanor. *From Untouchable to Dalit: Essays on the Ambedkar Movement*. Delhi: Manohar Publications, 1996.

Index

Aalo Andhari, 168–169
Aamcha Baap aan Aamhi, 90, 163, 170, 172, 181–189, 191–193
Aaydaan (The Weave of My Life), 44–45, 163, 170
adivasi, 12, 20, 57. *See also* indigenous populations; Scheduled Tribes
affirmative action, 13, 22, 64, 163, 207, 213. *See also* reservations
Africa, 4, 15, 47, 51, 69, 70, 98, 116, 148, 151, 153, 215
    colonial, 20, 51, 99, 110, 111, 112, 199, 215
    postcolonial, 29
    students from, 10
    See also South Africa
African American
    church, 54–55, 107, 110, 116, 121–122, 123, 124, 125, 127, 141, 142–143, 147, 152, 153, 158
    conversion, 97, 150
    criminalization, 22, 105, 148, 198–199
    elites, 17, 196
    history, 1, 6, 10–12, 16–18, 23, 46–47, 49–51, 97, 100–102, 131, 134, 137, 159, 194
    identity, 32, 46–47, 57, 60, 126, 137, 153, 160, 161, 200
    labor, 48, 102–111, 114, 134
    leadership, 16, 102, 103, 104, 107, 113, 124, 125, 150

living conditions, 15–16, 18, 50, 54, 113, 138–139, 198
middle class, 21, 113, 195–204, 216
militancy, 7, 97
military service, 100, 101–105, 108–109, 113, 116, 121, 126, 128–129, 142, 150, 161
nationalism, 98
struggle, 6–7, 23, 27, 97–98, 106, 138, 149–150
violence against, 16, 21, 103, 109, 113–126, 128, 161
See also Negro; people of color
agency, 23–24, 25, 168, 169, 191
Alabama, 105, 108, 109, 110, 115, 129
Ambedkar, B.R., 11, 26, 32, 211, 219
    and conversion, 43–46, 51–52, 64, 67–68, 83–94, 204, 211
    on Dalits as a minority, 41, 66–67
    on history, 42–43, 67, 94
    on the Hindu Code, 67–69, 78–81, 179
    movement led by, 58, 163–164, 171–181, 187–189, 190, 207
    on untouchability, 6, 82–83, 89, 94
American Civil Liberties Union, 198
An American Dilemma, 22–24
An Untouchable in the I.A.S., 69–71
Andrews, Benny, 137, 138, 141, 143–144, 145, 146, 148, 150, 153–156, 161

233

234 Index

Andrews, Raymond, 137, 140, 141, 143, 146, 148, 150, 155, 156
Andrews, Viola, 54–55, 131–161, 166, 167, 168, 175, 196, 203, 219
anti-colonial struggles, 3, 7, 40, 132, 215. *See also* colonialism; postcolony
apartheid, 4, 70
Apel, Dora, 126, 128, 161
archive, 131, 165
  body as, 170, 177
  of prejudice, 2, 30–31, 196–197
  See also history; unarchived histories
Arnall, Ellis, 103, 104, 120
Arya Samaj, 64
Asad, Talal, 4
Ashraf-un-nisa Begum, 166
Asia, 22, 115, 151
  Asian Americans, 11, 15, 152
  colonial, 20, 51, 99, 111, 112, 199
  postcolonial, 24, 29
Asian Drama, 24–25
assimilation, 63, 195. *See also* difference; sameness
Atlanta, 10, 16, 103–104, 110, 115, 116, 117–120, 124–127, 137, 138, 142–145, 148, 150, 151, 153–156, 157–158. *See also* Georgia
Atlanta Constitution, 118, 123, 124
Australian Aboriginals, 34, 203
autobiography
  African American, 16, 49, 103, 112, 131–161
  bourgeois, 132, 133, 165
  and community, 131–133, 168, 170
  Dalit, 44–46, 69–71, 78, 94, 162–193
  as history, 31, 131
  production of the self, 165, 167, 191
  as protest literature, 162, 163
  subaltern, 131–133, 164, 165, 167–168
  translations of, 163, 170, 182–189, 192
  and women, 44–46, 49, 112, 131–161, 165–170, 172–181, 190, 191–192, 205

Baluta, 162, 164
Bama, 205
Baraka, Amiri, 98

Bhabha, Homi, 56
Bhargava, Gopichand, 76
Bhatnagar, Rashmi, 164
Bible, 54–55, 97, 135, 143, 152, 155, 159, 161
bigotry. *See* prejudice
Bilbo, Theodore G., 115
Black Panthers, 7
Black Power, 98, 129
blacks. *See* African American
body
  of African Americans, 53–54, 126, 128, 161
  of Dalits, 7, 162, 177–179, 188, 189–193
  question of dress, 89–92, 173, 177, 184, 218
  rescripting of, 53, 89–90, 161, 172, 177–178, 188, 189–193
  subaltern, 53, 55, 161, 170, 172, 177–179
  of women, 7, 147, 149, 151, 160, 161, 178–179
Bombay. *See* Mumbai
Brady, Thomas P., 99–100
Brahmanism, 27, 42–43, 67, 88, 95. *See also* caste; Hinduism
Brahmans, 27, 42, 60, 68, 80, 94, 95, 167, 213, 219
  Dalit Brahmans, 27, 195
Brooker, Peter, 3
Broyard, Anatole, 201–204
Buddha and his Dhamma, 84
Buddhism
  conversion to, 44–46, 51, 61, 64, 68, 83, 84–95, 163, 178, 204, 205–207, 211
  history of, 42–43, 67–68, 95
Burke, Emory, 115

capitalism, 3, 4, 13, 17, 18, 99, 122. *See also* development; industrialization; modernity
caste
  as class, 43
  forced labor, 88, 175, 176
  hierarchy, 13–14, 17, 44, 46, 59, 65, 74, 94, 207–208
  history of, 10–12, 42–43, 55, 67–68, 72, 94, 134, 162

Index

identity, 57, 59–60, 66, 95, 188, 207–210
logic of, 2, 9, 16, 24, 65, 192
names, 7, 40, 57, 66, 80, 196, 207–210, 212
as slavery, 6
census
American, 14–15
Indian, 13, 41, 65–66, 86, 207
Cesaire, Aime, 176
Chamar, 14, 83, 94, 208, 211, 212. *See also* Dalit; Harijan; Scheduled Castes; untouchability
Chandala, 80–81. *See also* Dalit; Harijan; untouchability
charitra (as genre), 164, 168. *See also* autobiography
Chicago, 98, 107, 114, 123, 124, 125, 145
Chicago Defender, 106
Christianity, 61, 64, 68, 85, 97, 204
and caste, 205
as faith, 54, 136, 143, 144, 146–147, 149, 161, 219
as modern, 4
and race, 55, 152
as values, 23, 55, 110, 121, 122, 124, 127, 151, 218
Christians, 29, 36, 209
Dalit, 27, 64
as a minority, 13, 41, 60, 64, 199
missionaries, 64, 161
citizenship
conversion to, 30, 61–62, 89, 92, 95, 97
global, 172, 192, 193, 206
military service and, 99–101, 103–105, 107, 126, 161, 195, 204
second-class, 19, 27, 37, 99, 105, 197, 219
struggle for, 12, 17–18, 29, 60, 72, 74, 75, 77, 79, 86, 92, 99, 101, 103, 104, 124, 127, 128, 133, 207
subaltern, 27, 29, 37, 57, 81, 92, 136, 195, 212
unmarked, 3, 27, 30, 33, 35, 36, 196, 203, 213–216, 220
See also franchise; nation; rights

Civil Rights Movement, 25, 29–30, 50, 60, 98–108, 127–129, 131, 138, 150, 151, 161
Civil War (USA), 50, 101–102
class, 2, 9, 19, 25, 26, 70, 190, 193
and caste, 94
consciousness, 42
hierarchy, 50, 135, 159
inequality, 46, 49, 50, 68
laboring poor, 37, 72, 179, 183
lower class, 7, 21, 193, 196, 199, 207
ruling, 8, 24, 29, 105
struggle, 10, 23, 42, 94
upper class, 18, 20, 82, 133, 165, 167, 191, 196, 213
working class, 19, 20, 48, 50, 98, 172, 183, 193, 203, 204. *See also* middle class; social mobility
colonialism, 17, 34, 63, 99, 112, 199
anti-colonialism, 3, 7, 40, 132, 215
British, 5, 6, 13, 19, 25, 27, 29, 40, 64, 65, 69, 163, 172
colonial knowledge, 25, 91, 207, 208
decolonization, 62, 90
and race, 111–112
See also imperialism; internal colonialism; postcolony
color line, 10, 50, 122, 149. *See also* race
colored. *See* African American; people of color; Negro
Columbians (fascist organization), 115. *See also* conservatism (America); Ku Klux Klan; right-wing; white supremacy
Communal Award (1932), 66–67. *See also* reservations (under Indian constitution)
communalism, 9, 70, 91
community
belonging, 13, 15, 19, 36, 193, 194–195, 197, 217
communal rights, 17
identity, 64
and the individual, 131–133, 169, 170, 181, 185, 189, 190
internal differentiation, 40, 57, 94, 165, 199
obligation to, 200, 211
political, 51, 190

Index

conservatism (in American politics), 99,
119, 122, 135, 151. *See also* right
wing (in USA)
constitution, 28, 55
American, 97, 102, 120, 124, 129,
190
Indian, 1, 13, 29, 40, 61, 68–69,
78–80, 92, 213
conversion, 51, 52, 57, 84, 92
African American, 97, 150
of the community, 84, 92
Dalit, 30, 43–46, 51–52, 57, 61–96,
97, 99, 163, 204–207
to modernity, 61
See also liberation
Cosby, Bill, 216, 218
cotton farming, 54, 119, 156, 157
Criminal Tribes, 20, 76–78

D'Souza, Dinesh, 215
Dalit
citizenship, 37, 61–62, 67, 72, 74–75,
81, 86, 89, 92–93, 95
community, 40, 46, 55, 165
conversion, 43–46, 51–52, 61–96, 97,
99, 163, 204–207
criminalization, 76–78, 81
history, 1, 6, 10–11, 12, 16, 41, 42–43,
57, 62, 63, 66, 72, 91, 94, 95–96,
163, 164, 171, 189, 194, 196, 208
identity, 7, 55, 57, 59–60, 64, 66, 95,
188, 192, 208–210, 213
labor, 7, 13, 41, 60, 72, 83, 88, 91,
162, 169, 172, 175, 176, 177, 178,
179, 181, 182, 192–193, 209
leadership, 40, 57, 63, 66, 89, 91, 95,
163, 211, 213, 217
living conditions, 14, 18, 162,
172–180, 187–188
middle class, 167, 195, 197, 199–200,
204–213, 217
militancy, 6, 26, 57, 163, 204, 210
minority status, 40–42, 63–67
patriarchy, 58, 95, 170, 171–172,
178–180
struggle, 6–7, 28, 46, 55, 61–63, 72,
83, 86, 162, 163, 171, 175,
179–181, 187, 204, 210
violence against, 21, 85, 91, 187, 206,
212

See also caste; Harijan; Scheduled
Castes; untouchability
Dalit Panthers, 7, 57, 88, 163
Debi, Rassundari, 166, 167
democracy
concept of, 3, 4, 8, 12, 22, 25, 30, 98,
190
limits of, 13, 18, 22, 30, 31, 63, 91,
112, 114, 121, 122, 135, 163, 199,
216
struggle for, 7, 17, 18, 40, 77, 79, 81,
92, 96, 97–130
Depressed Castes, 7, 12, 40, 78. *See also*
Dalit; Scheduled Castes
Detroit, 109, 110, 111
development, 4, 18, 22, 24, 26, 42, 69,
213. *See also* capitalism;
industrialization; modernity
dhamma. See Buddhism
dharmaantar. See conversion
difference
and the body, 53, 161
as empowering, 38, 39, 41, 46, 51, 56
insider/outsider, 36, 41
and power, 32–40, 46, 56, 57
proclamation of, 29, 31, 35, 37, 40,
52, 53, 56, 220
See also discrimination; sameness
discrimination, 1, 16, 39, 57, 60, 199,
218
against women, 48, 95
caste, 1, 9, 29, 41, 57, 69–70, 78, 82,
94, 162–163, 165, 172, 187,
205–206
racial, 9, 15, 16, 48, 98, 106–109,
202
See also prejudice
disenfranchisement, 5, 12, 30, 136, 169,
171, 194, 219. *See also*
enfranchisement; franchise;
marginalization
Dixon, Frank M., 108, 115
Dorsey, George, 116, 118, 120–121, 126
Dorsey, Mae Murray, 116
"Double Victory" Campaign, 30,
99–108, 115, 126, 127–129, 151
Douglass, Frederick, 6, 101
Du Bois, W.E.B., 6, 10, 46–47, 50–54,
60, 122, 149
Dust Tracks on a Road, 112

Index

237

education
  against social evils, 11, 123
  exclusion from, 48, 60, 72, 127, 166,
    176, 177, 179, 180
  and gender, 48, 166
  and race, 153–155, 159, 203
  reservations for, 61, 64, 85, 213
  uplift through, 19, 89–90, 143, 144,
    150, 151, 174, 176, 178, 181, 195,
    213
  value of, 46, 55, 83, 89, 90, 92, 94, 95,
    157, 167, 178
  and women, 11, 48, 143, 166
Ellison, Ralph, 23–24, 106
emancipation, 34, 35, 38, 50, 102, 129,
    172
  Emancipation Proclamation (USA),
    102
  legal, 50, 102, 129
  political, 35
  See also liberation; slavery
enfranchisement, 30, 219. See citizenship;
    disenfranchisement; franchise; rights
Enlightenment, 31, 34
  human subject of, 133, 191, 193
  See also modernity
equality, 4, 8, 19, 25, 38–39, 44, 67–70,
    79, 83, 86, 104, 105, 122, 174, 205,
    219
  equal opportunity, 4, 7, 12, 26, 27,
    98–99, 122, 219
  See also inequality; sameness
Ethridge, Mark F., 110, 115
exclusion, 9, 19–20, 49, 98, 99,
    108–109, 162. See also
    discrimination; disenfranchisement
Executive Order 8802, 106, 108, 129.
    See also Fair Employment Practices
    Committee; labor
exploitation, 16, 41, 55, 57, 95, 101, 178
  economic, 50
  sexual, 2, 14, 15, 169, 218

Fair Employment Practices Committee,
    106, 110. See also discrimination;
    Executive Order 8802; labor
family, 17, 19, 48, 135, 136, 149, 176
  and autobiography, 138, 151, 171,
    172, 181–183, 190, 191
  domesticity, 20, 200

honor, 174
  marriage, 58, 68, 79, 87, 144–146,
    148, 157, 161, 174, 180, 186, 187,
    188, 200, 219
  middle class, 19, 193, 195, 200, 203,
    216
  surnames, 208–210
Fanon, Frantz, 53, 90
Federal Bureau of Investigation, 118, 119
feminism, 7, 39, 71, 137
  black feminism, 47–49
  See also gender; women
Fitzgerald, Timothy, 62, 92
franchise, 25, 29, 61, 90, 116, 120, 219
  poll tax, 119–120
  voter registration, 119, 120
  women's suffrage, 129
  See also citizenship;
    disenfranchisement;
    enfranchisement; rights
Frederickson, Kari, 116

Gandhi, Indira, 217
Gandhi, Mohandas K., 75, 90–92, 166
  and anti-colonialism, 6, 25, 112
  and untouchability, 7, 26, 41, 51, 57,
    66–67, 73, 82–83, 174
Gates, Jr., Henry Louis, 198–199, 201
gay, 1, 30, 36, 57, 204. See also
    heterosexual; lesbian; LGBTQ;
    sexuality
gender, 2, 33, 34, 39, 46, 49, 95, 134,
    135, 161, 190, 193, 216, 220
  and caste, 172
  equality, 188
  inequality, 34, 50, 68, 94, 95, 127,
    180
  intersectionality, 49, 50
  and race, 47–49
  sexism, 47
  See also gay; heterosexual; femininity;
    lesbian; LGBTQ; masculinity;
    patriarchy; sexuality; women
Georgia, 16, 54, 103, 104, 110, 111,
    113–114, 123–129, 131, 137–156,
    158–159, 203. See also Atlanta;
    Madison, Ga.; Monroe, Ga.
Ghulamgiri, 6. See also caste; slavery
Gilmore, Glenda, 200
Gilroy, Paul, 21

238 *Index*

Goldstein, Eric, 59
Guha, Ranajit, 84
Gujarat, 85, 192, 206

Halder, Baby, 168–169
Hamas, 214
Harijan, 7, 40, 57, 73–76, 82–83, 174, 206. *See also* Dalit; Scheduled Castes; untouchability
Harlem (NY), 59, 102, 103, 109, 113, 165, 203. *See also* New York
Hartsfield, William, 126, 127
Hayes, Roland, 113
heterosexual, 29, 34, 214, 218. *See also* gay; lesbian; LGBTQ; sexuality
Hill, Anita, 201
Hindu Code Bill, 42, 67–69, 78–81, 179
Hinduism
    community, 41–42, 63–67, 79–82
    Dalit rejection of, 42–44, 51, 83–84, 88, 204
    Hindu leadership, 64
    Hindu Right, 194, 211, 215
    militancy, 64, 85
    reform of, 42, 51, 64–65, 67–69, 78–81
Hine, Darlene Clark, 49–50, 135
Hispanics. *See* Latina/Latino
history, 1–12, 30–31, 34, 131, 134, 193, 196, 219
    African American, 1, 6, 10–12, 16–18, 23, 46–47, 49–51, 97, 100–102, 131, 134, 137, 159, 194
    autobiography as, 131
    comparative, 8–9, 16
    Dalit, 1, 6, 10–12, 16, 41–43, 57, 62, 63, 66, 72, 94–96, 163–164, 171, 189, 194, 196, 207–208
    discipline of, 31, 131
    of the nation, 4–5, 10–12, 16–18, 30, 42–43, 47, 51, 98–101, 102, 104, 189, 194, 199, 219
    struggle over, 5, 7, 10–12, 42–43, 49–51, 55, 57, 62, 63, 66, 71, 80, 159, 171, 179, 207, 208.
    of subaltern groups, 7–12, 17–18, 27–31, 37, 39, 55, 56, 57, 63, 71, 99, 132, 170, 196, 204
    See also archive; unarchived histories
hooks, bell, 47–48, 49

Hughes, Langston, 15, 106, 114, 122, 137, 165
humiliation, 10, 57, 71, 91, 129, 132, 162, 193, 196, 202, 206, 207, 212, 218. *See also* untouchability; stigmatization
Huntington, Samuel, 194, 220
Hurston, Zora Neale, 111–113, 134, 137, 138, 150, 161, 216

identity
    African American, 32, 46–47, 57, 60, 126, 137, 153, 160, 161, 200
    Dalit, 7, 55, 57, 59–60, 64, 66, 95, 192, 208–210, 213
    question of, 9, 39, 40, 46–47, 51–60, 63, 64, 158, 197, 201, 202–203, 206
    representation of, 66, 81, 217
    See also difference
Ilaiah, Kancha, 2, 59–60
immigrants, 1, 11, 15, 17, 20, 38, 97, 194
imperialism, 3, 4, 6, 8, 20, 47, 51, 70, 99
Indian Administrative Service, 69–71, 219
Indian National Congress, 105
indigenous populations, 1, 12, 13, 20, 32, 34, 37, 38, 57. *See also* adivasi; Native Americans; Scheduled Tribes
individual
    individualism, 17, 132, 133, 181, 185, 186, 191, 192, 193, 200
    individuality, 35, 38, 137, 165, 186, 193, 200
    rights, 17, 61
    subjectivity, 168, 169
industrialization, 3, 20, 76, 102, 107. *See* capitalism; development; modernity
inequality, 17, 24, 43, 67, 68, 85, 91, 193, 211. *See also* equality
inner life, 134–135, 136, 157, 158, 165, 167, 168. *See also* autobiography; individual
interiority. *See* inner life
internal colonialism, 12, 13, 20, 29, 53, 62–63. *See also* colonialism; postcolony
Irish, 20, 37, 199
Italians, 20, 37, 199

Index

Jadhav, Damodar, 167, 182–191
Jadhav, Narendra, 90, 163, 168, 170–172, 181–184, 188–193
Jews, 1, 20, 29, 35–36, 37, 41, 53, 56, 59, 113, 115, 194, 195, 199, 204, 218
  Jewish Question, 35–36, 194, 218
Jim Crow laws (USA), 15, 111–113, 119, 120, 122, 134, 136. *See also* discrimination; inequality; race; segregation
Jina Amcha (The Prisons We Broke), 170, 171–181. *See also* Kamble, Baby
Johnson, James Weldon, 103, 122
Jones, Jacqueline, 48
Joothan, 162, 163

Kamble, Baby Kondiba, 46, 55, 58, 89, 167, 168–181, 189–191, 193, 196, 219
Kamble, Shantabai Krishnaji, 46, 87–88
Kenya, 215
Khare, R.S., 83
King, Martin Luther, Jr., 6, 129, 150
Kruse, Kevin M., 119
Kshatriyas, 42, 213, 219
Ku Klux Klan, 109, 116, 120. *See also* conservatism (in America); Columbians; right-wing; white supremacy
Kumar, Meera, 71

labor, 7, 19, 20, 24, 37, 38, 41, 55, 60, 76, 92, 102–111, 134, 172, 177–179, 181–183, 192, 193, 209
  organized, 108, 114, 116, 124
  struggle, 98
  of women, 48, 106, 134, 160, 169
  See also class
Latina/Latino, 27, 37, 195, 196, 198, 218, 220
lesbian, 57, 204. *See also* gay; heterosexual; LGBTQ; sexuality
Lester, Julius, 134
Levin, Hillel, 218
LGBTQ, 57. *See also* gay; heterosexual; lesbian; sexuality
liberalism, 3, 4, 8, 16, 20, 23, 32, 35, 37, 79, 110, 122, 165, 186, 191, 195, 214

liberation
  black, 151, 159
  Dalit, 10, 30, 62, 176, 179, 187
  history of, 30
  liberated castes, 78
  as a motif, 144, 145, 157, 158, 161
  from slavery, 149
  of women, 144, 179
  See also conversion; emancipation
Limbale, Sharankumar, 87, 169–170
Limbaugh, Rush, 214
literacy, 25, 92, 156, 166, 167, 169
  illiteracy, 5, 89, 94
  See also education
Lorde, Audre, 32–33, 39, 48–49
lynching, 114, 116–118, 121–126, 150, 161
  of women, 117, 128

Madison, Ga., 137, 142, 147, 148, 154–156. *See also* Georgia; Monroe, Ga.
Mahar, 44, 58, 82, 86, 94, 164, 171–180, 182, 187, 191, 210. *See also* Dalit; untouchability
Maharashtra, 85, 86, 94, 163, 164, 170–175, 205, 206. *See also* Mumbai; Nagpur; Ozer; Pune; Satara
Malagatti, Aravind, 166
Malcolm, Dorothy, 116–118, 121
Malcolm, Roger, 116–118, 120–121
Mandela, Nelson, 69
Manto, Saadat Hasan, 28–29
marginalization, 2, 5, 7, 12, 17, 30, 35–40, 56–57, 63, 65, 163, 194, 195. *See also* difference; disenfranchisement; subalternity
Marx, Karl, 35
Marxism, 3, 51
masculinity, 4, 19, 127, 141, 178, 185
  masculinism, 28, 95, 99, 100, 101, 128–129, 215
  See also femininity; gender; patriarchy
Mayawati, 217
Mazhya Jalmachi Chittarkatha, 87–88
Meenakshipuram (Tamilnadu), 85
Mehta, Uday, 32
memoirs. *See* autobiography

240   *Index*

middle class, 10–11, 18–21, 27, 33, 69, 92, 113, 167, 169, 191, 193, 195–212, 217. *See also* class; social mobility
minorities
  insiders/outsiders, 36, 213
  minoritization, 9, 27, 35–38, 41, 201
  rights, 55, 63, 64, 219, 220
  and the state, 22, 36, 53, 63, 108, 198
  See also difference; stigmatization; subalternity
Mississippi, 99, 105, 115, 124, 129
modernity, 3–5, 12, 27, 31, 86, 184, 190
  colonial, 17
  discourse of, 4, 219
  middle class, 20, 217
  modernization, 4
  philosophy of, 2, 3, 4, 31, 34
  and religion, 4, 25, 44
  self-made individual, 4, 19, 61, 84, 92, 133, 185, 219
  See also capitalism; industrialization; liberalism
Molloy, John T., 218
Monroe, Ga., 117, 121, 123–126, 128
Moore's Ford lynching, 120, 121, 123–126. *See also* lynching; violence
Mufti, Aamir, 37
Mujahid, Abdul Malik, 85, 205–206
Mumbai, 45, 52, 90, 167, 172, 173, 177, 181, 182, 183, 186, 187–189
Muslim League, 42
Muslims
  in India, 10, 13, 26–27, 34, 43, 60, 62–66, 72, 73, 74, 79, 199, 205, 211, 213, 215
  as a minority, 35, 36, 40–41, 53, 56, 63, 66, 194–196, 211
  prejudice against, 1, 27, 29, 34, 79, 194–196, 213–215
Myrdal, Gunnar, 10, 22–25, 122

Nagaraj, D.R., 43, 82, 90, 91, 204
Nagpur, 84, 85, 90, 204
naming
  and caste background, 7, 40, 80–81, 196, 207–210
  and political struggle, 7, 27, 57, 66, 207–210
  See also identity; passing

nation
  nationalism, 3, 25, 38, 50, 82, 98, 100
  nationhood, 5, 12, 26, 35, 38, 53, 55, 103, 216
  nation-state, 4, 35, 36, 99
National Association for the Advancement of Colored People, 16, 103, 105–108, 111, 119–120, 123, 124, 127
Native Americans, 12, 15, 20, 22, 27, 47, 63, 98–99, 100, 153, 203. *See also* indigenous populations
Negro, 16, 22–24, 46, 47, 51, 53, 57, 100, 102–107, 111–114, 137, 202. *See also* African American; people of color
Nehru, Jawaharlal, 10, 25–26, 80, 163
Nehru, Rameshwari, 75, 77–78
New York, 48, 59, 82, 102, 103, 106, 123–125, 143, 144, 148, 200, 201, 202, 212, 214
non-violence, 6. *See also* violence

Obama, Barack, 214–215, 217, 218
othering, 1, 34, 36, 37, 53, 56–59, 160, 162, 214–216. *See also* difference
Ozer (Maharashtra), 182, 185, 187

Painter, Nell Irvin, 135, 158
Pakistan, 10, 72, 77, 215
Pandit, Maya, 45, 88, 170, 171, 173, 181, 182
Partition, 72–78, 79
  Dalit refugees, 72–78
  resettlement, 72–76
passing, 197, 204, 208, 218, 219
  as upper caste, 204, 208
  as white, 158, 201–204, 207
  See also identity; naming
patriarchy, 1, 17, 19, 28, 58, 95, 129, 135–137, 144, 159, 170–172, 178, 190. *See also* gender; masculinity
Pawar, Daya, 86–87, 164
Pawar, Ishwar Dass, 76, 78
Pawar, Urmila, 44–45, 163, 170
people of color, 48, 57, 106, 138, 139, 150, 151–152, 155, 198. *See also* African American; Negro
Periyar. *See* Ramaswamy E.V. Naicker
Phaltan, Satara District, 174, 175, 180, 191

Index

Philadelphia, 123, 125
Phule, Jyotirao, 6, 88
Piper, Adrian, 202–203
Pittsbugh Courier, 124
Poor Laws, 50
postcolony, 5, 13, 17, 21, 29, 65
  postcolonial scholarship, 7, 35, 37
  postcolonial struggles, 40
  See also colonialism; imperialism
poverty, 15–19, 24–26, 48, 50, 52, 162,
  175–177, 190, 198. *See also* class
prejudice
  caste, 60, 70–71, 78–82, 94–95, 134,
    162, 172, 218–219
  as common sense, 2–3, 11, 22–23, 33,
    193, 196, 218–219
  historicization of, 1–2, 11, 29, 30–32,
    131, 196, 217
  politics of, 1–2, 18, 29, 34, 38–39, 53,
    81, 136
  racial, 1, 9–11, 21, 47–48, 99, 101,
    104, 108, 111, 119, 121, 131, 134,
    137, 155, 159, 203
  vernacular and universal, 1–2, 5, 11,
    27, 31, 32, 162, 194, 218
  See also discrimination
Presidential Committee on Civil Rights
  (1946), 127, 128
Pune, 172, 175
Punjab, 72–77, 83

race
  as caste, 6
  and class, 98, 216
  concept of, 2, 9, 14, 46, 50
  hierarchy, 50, 110, 116, 135, 159
  history of, 10–12, 134
  identity, 32–33, 46–47, 51, 60, 137,
    141, 153, 192, 201
  integration, 98, 109
  and power, 9, 21, 34, 55, 100, 119,
    131, 151, 155, 159
  racism, 1, 9–11, 21, 47–48, 99, 101,
    111, 119, 122, 137, 159, 203
  relations, 47, 97–130, 136, 138, 150,
    151, 159, 160
  See also passing
Rai, Lala Lajpat, 64–65
Ramaswamy Naicker, E.V., 26–27,
  204
Randolph, Asa Philip, 104, 107

Rankin, John E., 115
rape, 21, 50, 170, 218. *See also*
  exploitation (sexual); violence
reform, 11, 19, 42, 51, 64–65, 68, 74,
  79
Rege, Sharmila, 132
reservations (under Indian constitution),
  61, 64, 66, 85, 213. *See also*
  affirmative action
Rice, Condoleezza, 218
right wing (in India), 194, 211, 215
right wing (in USA), 214. *See also*
  conservatism
rights
  civil, 29, 36, 82, 99, 101, 107–108,
    110, 123, 124, 127–129, 150
  discourse of, 55, 133
  human, 3–4, 55
  individual, 17, 61
  minority, 27, 38, 55–56, 63–64, 66,
    219, 220
  political, 19, 29, 32, 39, 61, 64, 74, 76,
    97, 99, 102, 172, 196
  state, 123
  women's, 38, 49, 79, 151, 188, 220
  See also citizenship
Roosevelt, Franklin D., 104, 106, 107,
  108, 112, 129
rural life, 119, 143. *See also* village life
Ryan, Mary, 200

sameness, 34, 37, 38, 39, 51, 57, 61, 92,
  98, 127
Scheduled Castes, 1, 7, 13, 40, 41, 57,
  70, 80, 85, 206. *See also* Dalit;
  Harijan; untouchability
Scheduled Tribes, 12, 13, 32. *See also*
  adivasi; indigenous populations
secularism, 4, 8, 12, 86, 122, 218
segregation, 4, 6, 15–16, 21–22, 28, 60,
  78, 99, 101, 105, 110, 113, 128,
  138, 149, 151, 155, 159–160. *See
  also* discrimination; Jim Crow laws
Self-Respect Movement, 26
sexuality, 34, 47, 49, 147, 216
  control of, 50, 135, 160
  sexual identity, 158
  sexual minorities, 38
  sexual mores, 115, 147–149, 169
  See also gay; gender; heterosexual;
    lesbian; LGBTQ

sharecropping, 117, 131, 140, 141
Shaw, Stephanie, 200
shuddhi campaign, 64–65
Sikhs, 13, 41, 64, 72, 73, 74, 85, 204, 209
Singh, Balwant, 69–71, 219
Sitkoff, Harvard, 109
slavery, 5, 6, 11, 13, 15, 21, 46, 101, 132, 135, 138
    abolition of, 15, 29, 108, 136
    abolitionism, 6, 8, 48, 99, 102
    and caste, 6
    as a motif, 48, 58, 142, 157, 158, 159, 161, 178, 180
social justice, 12, 40, 44, 75
social mobility, 94, 163, 181, 182, 193, 195, 196, 197, 200, 204, 208. See also class; middle class
Souls of Black Folk, 52
South Africa, 4, 69, 70
South Asia, 5, 10–11, 24, 43
South Carolina, 115, 116, 122, 123, 124, 129
South India, 26, 83, 85, 166, 207, 208. See also Tamilnadu
Southern U.S.A. See U.S. South
stigmatization, 1, 10, 11, 12, 16, 18, 42, 61, 63, 69, 101, 162, 204, 205, 206. See also marginalization; minoritization
Stover, Johnnie M., 132
Subaltern Studies, 43
subalternity
    and the body, 53, 55, 161, 170, 172, 177–179
    and citizenship, 27, 29, 37, 57, 81, 92, 136, 195
    and difference, 32–33, 34–35, 37–41, 51, 53, 63, 95, 167, 219
    of middle classes, 19, 21, 195–196, 197, 200, 204, 210
    subaltern militancy, 59
    subaltern movements, 8, 17, 27, 55, 57, 59, 92
    and subjectivity, 168, 170, 181
    of women, 7, 172
    See also difference; disenfranchisement; marginalization; minorities
Sudras, 41, 43, 68, 79, 205, 213, 219. See also caste; Dalit; Scheduled Castes

Talmadge, Eugene, 113, 115, 119–121, 127
Tamilnadu, 85, 205. See also South India
Their Eyes Were Watching God, 161, 216
Thurmond, J. Strom, 122–123
trauma, 158, 218
Trump, Donald, 215
Truth, Sojourner, 48, 109, 129

U.S. South, 15–16, 17, 38, 54, 102–105, 108–111, 114, 115–116, 122–123, 124–125, 129, 134–137, 138–140, 143–145, 149, 151, 155, 159, 160–161, 216
unarchived histories, 1–2, 29, 71–72, 95, 135, 161, 177, 178, 196. See also archive; history
untouchability
    abolition of, 16, 29, 51, 61, 67, 80
    concept of, 2, 5, 13–14, 17, 28, 82–83, 94
    history of, 10, 11, 13, 43, 94, 132
    and minority status, 36, 40–41, 63–64, 65–67, 82
    routine violence of, 2, 14, 21, 70, 81, 167–168, 196, 204
    as slavery, 6
    as stigma, 10, 42, 89, 163, 205
Untouchable. See Dalit
Untouchables, The, 43
upper castes, 11, 27, 64, 78–82, 91, 94, 95, 162, 168, 169, 211–213
    distancing of, 14, 21–22, 59–60
    privilege of, 13, 18, 71, 83, 88–89, 95, 176–177, 200, 205
    See also Brahmans; caste
urbanization, 3, 66

Vaishyas, 213, 219
Valmiki, Om Prakash, 94, 163, 165–166, 196
village life, 72–74, 82, 91–92, 175. See also rural life
violence, 2, 4, 18, 21, 28
    against women, 49–50, 58, 95, 141, 144, 156, 180, 188, 219
    colonial, 29, 111–112
    in language, 2, 28, 81, 113, 152, 196, 211–212, 218

Index

intercaste, 21, 85, 91, 187, 206, 212
interracial, 16, 21, 103, 109, 111–126, 128, 161
police, 21, 77, 85, 113, 116, 120
routine, 2, 28, 71, 196
sexual, 15, 21, 50, 129, 170, 218
See also lynching; non-violence; rape
Vishwanathan, Gauri, 84

Walker, Alice, 32, 33, 60, 134, 137, 138, 139, 148
Washington D.C., 105, 107, 109, 114, 123, 125, 212
Washington, Booker T., 153
Wells, Ida B., 129
white supremacy, 109, 115, 120. *See also* conservatism (in America); Columbians; Ku Klux Klan; right-wing
White, Walter, 16, 113, 124
whites, 15, 18, 48, 55, 59, 102, 107, 109–115, 119–122, 127, 150–156, 159, 200
Why I Am Not a Hindu, 59–60
Williams, Raymond, 3

women
and autobiography, 44–46, 49, 112, 131–161, 167–170, 172–181, 190, 191–192, 205
and child-bearing, 146–149, 168, 179
and citizenship, 5, 19–20, 37–40, 79, 99, 128
and the community, 179
domestic duties, 58, 135, 146, 168, 174, 175, 178
and labor, 48, 106, 134, 160, 169
and race, 47–50
rights of, 38, 49, 79, 151, 188, 220
subordination of, 7, 14–15, 34–35, 37, 55, 58, 95, 135–136, 141, 172, 178–180
violence against, 49–50, 58, 95, 141, 144, 156, 180, 188, 219
and the vote, 129
women's movement, 20, 40, 49, 53, 56
Woodard, Isaac, 116, 124
World War I, 101, 102, 103–104, 108, 114–115
World War II, 99–115